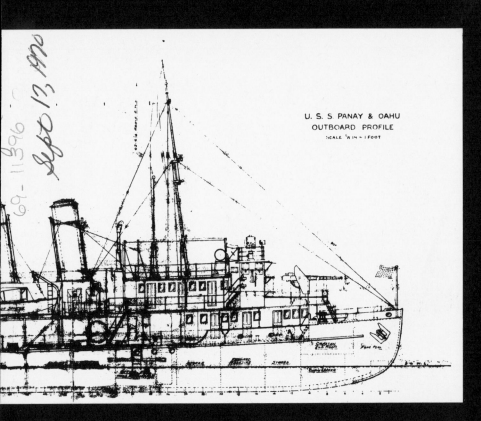

U. S. S. PANAY & OAHU
OUTBOARD PROFILE
SCALE ⅛ IN = 1 FOOT

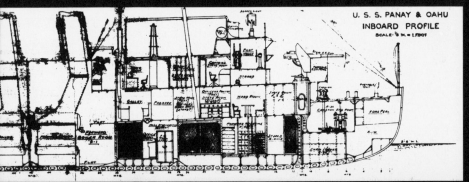

U. S. S. PANAY & OAHU
INBOARD PROFILE
SCALE: ⅛ IN. = 1 FOOT

The Panay Incident

THE *Panay* INCIDENT

PRELUDE TO
Pearl Harbor

★ ★
★

Hamilton Darby Perry

INTRODUCTION BY *Luigi Barzini*

THE MACMILLAN COMPANY

Acknowledgment is gratefully made to the following copyright holders, publishers, and proprietors for permission to reprint the following:

General Frank Roberts, U.S.A. (Ret.), for excerpts from his previously unpublished account of the sinking of the USS *Panay;* *Corriere della Sera* and Luigi Barzini for excerpts from accounts of incident, published in December 18, 19, 1937, issues © Corriere della Sera; Estate of Hallett Abend for excerpts from *My Life in China* © Estate of Hallett Abend; Estate of Hallett Abend for excerpts from article of December 18, 1937, in *The New York Times* © 1937 by The New York Times Company, reprinted by permission; excerpts and illustrations reprinted from *I Witness* by Norman Alley, by permission of the publishers, Funk & Wagnalls, New York.

For photographs: Wide World Photos for photograph of Colonel Kingoro Hashimoto; General Frank Roberts, U.S.A. (Ret.), for photograph of himself; U.S. Navy for photographs of USS *Panay*, blueprints of USS *Panay* (endpapers), USS *Oahu*, HMS *Bee*, HMS *Ladybird*, and USS *Augusta*; Norman Alley for photographs of attack and sinking of USS *Panay* and return of survivors and Peter Klumpers for photograph of Browning, Klumpers, and Mahlmann.

Library of Congress Catalog Card Number: 69-11396

THIRD PRINTING 1969

The Macmillan Company
Collier-Macmillan Canada Ltd., Toronto, Ontario

Printed in the United States of America

Dedicated to
two small and resolute groups of American sailors
and civilians who, in peacetime and in distant
waters, were victims of surprise attacks that resulted
in the loss in action of their ships

USS PANAY

Bombed and sunk, December 12, 1937

USS PUEBLO

Boarded and captured, January 22, 1968

Acknowledgments

THIS BOOK REALLY begins, I suppose, in the balcony of the old Palace Theater in Jacksonville, Florida, one gray Saturday afternoon in January 1938.

I hadn't come to see the newsreel of the bombing of the *Panay*. Whatever the feature was (and the name has long since faded from my mind) seemed much more important at the time. I can remember being annoyed at the crowd that had lined up outside to see the newsreel; that meant a long wait getting into the theater.

As it turned out, I sat through the news film twice. And then I realized why there had been so much talk around my house about the threat of war. For the first time, a war seemed real—not just something you read about for a dime in *G-8 and His Battle Aces* down at Lane's Drugstore.

The subject of the *Panay* faded fast in the press of news that winter. But I fancied myself something of an expert and thought I remembered the details vividly. A few years ago, trying to explain the incident to a friend, I realized I knew very little about it. Several libraries were of no help. Outside of a few accounts written at the time in papers and news magazines, I could find almost nothing on the *Panay*. That was a challenge to dig further.

Encouragement to turn the research into a story came first from Oliver Jensen, editor of *American Heritage*. And in April 1967 the magazine ran a short account I had written of the attack. In the process of preparing that article, however, I had come across enough tantalizing material to make me want to know more.

Like all good history, this story comes mostly from the minds and the experiences of all the people who lived the adventure. Captain John Geist spent all one long, hot Labor Day laying out before me for the first time the way the attack looked to the men on *Panay*. Commander Tex Anders was a patient and faithful correspondent, interviewee, and checker-of-facts on dozens of points in the story. Often, when trying to recollect a point, I could remember the living room of his San Diego home with newspaper clippings, photos, and maps spread across the floor as he straightened me out on various false leads and suggested good ones. His wife, Muriel, supplied a colorful description of life in China before the war—the part of the book that was hardest of all to research. Tex Anders' son Bill, crewman on the historic Apollo 8 moon shot, provided a scholarly Naval Academy thesis on the *Panay* sinking that offered a son's insight into a father's experience. As a one-time fighter pilot, Major Bill Anders can never believe the attack was a case of mistaken identity; most of the *Panay* men still agree with him.

Norman Alley came up with almost a hundred fine photographs from which most of the final illustrations in the book were selected. He also gave over several days of a fishing vacation to recall for me the details of those final days in Nanking and on the gunboat. His own account of the incident in his book *I Witness*, written a few years after the event, supplied me with authentic background—particularly on the activities of the newsmen and the other civilians involved in the incident. I am particularly indebted to Mr. Alley for making available the missing frames of attacking Japanese aircraft that were cut from his newsreel film at the request of President Roosevelt. These have never been published before.

In Washington, I found stories of red tape highly exaggerated—certainly among the men who staff the Navy's various history facilities. Dean Allard at the Naval History Division gave me much valuable assistance during one long week of concentrated work in the official reports of the incident. Lieutenant S. B. Smith promptly fielded all requests for pictures—even back to the first Spanish gunboat that bore the name *Panay*. Captain J. Henson and Captain Kent Loomis, cutting lots of red tape themselves, I expect, provided detailed information about the decorations and combat records of every member of the *Panay* crew. Their help enabled me to contact seventeen old *Panay* sailors who contributed to the book. Speed Adams, Frank Fisher, John Hennessy, Fon Huffman, Karl Johnson, Bill Lander, John Lang, William Mc-Cabe, Thomas Spindle, Homar Truax, Marcus Williamson, and Stanley McEowen patiently filled out long questionnaires, wrote personal accounts, answered numerous questions, and supplied pictures and mementos.

Bob Hebard lent me his personal sketchbook, still water-stained from the abandoned ship and containing a series of drawings that conveyed the atmosphere of life on the Patrol in prewar China. Peter Klumpers came up with a group of touching snapshots of the Chinese urchins who lived along the waterfront and ran errands or did odd jobs for the gunboat sailors. Andy Wisler, now a commercial radioman in Hawaii, wrote for me on several long night watches a superb account of life aboard the *Panay* and of the sinking. Wisler's fine eye for detail was the next best thing to having been aboard myself.

Radioman James Murphy drafted for me a careful catalogue

of events on that last radio watch. His report helped clear up the mystery of the SOS the Japanese claimed to have heard—but which Murphy is sure *Panay* never sent. Commander Denis Biwerse sent on valuable information about communications security measures taken in the Patrol.

Ernest Mahlmann, tall, straight, and salty as ever, came up with perhaps the finest collection of *Panay* information of all, including a fascinating and perceptive diary that covered his whole career in the Navy. His descriptions of life along the river, the Chinese river cities, and the trip up through the Yangtze gorges should be a book.

I am particularly grateful to Major General Frank Roberts for letting me quote extensively from his moving and never-published personal narrative of the sinking. General Roberts wrote it in Canton in the first week of January 1938—about three weeks after the sinking—after sweating out another Japanese bombing attack. Roberts wrote to steady his nerves and get the *Panay* episode out of his mind. It is a powerful and precise recollection. Added to this contribution by Roberts were half a dozen letters, packed with information, and an afternoon given up to conversation in the hospitality of his Claremont, California, home.

Mrs. David Reilly, daughter of Commander Hughes, was gracious enough to offer me all of her father's material that was in her possession. She supplied several letters and documents that clarified the commander's private opinions of the incident.

Commander Robert Brewer, editor of *Naval Institute Proceedings*, turned up several valuable early articles about the Yangtze Patrol and was helpful in suggesting various authorities on the period. Miss Doris Maguire, reference librarian at the Naval Academy, dug through yearbooks and undergraduate records of the *Panay* officers. Walter Van Buren and Walter Lord were frequent suppliers of magazine and newspaper clips that offered good leads on finding old crewmen and checking hard-to-check facts.

Any reader wishing to check the facts for himself or go further into the repercussions caused by the incident is urged to consult these sources first: *The Panay Incident: Prelude to War* by Manny T. Koginos, Purdue University Studies, 1967; *Year of the Tiger* by Alvin D. Coox, Orient/West Incorporated, Philadelphia, 1964. Two excellent magazine articles pertaining to the incident have appeared in *Naval Institute Proceedings*: "How the Panay Was Sunk," by Masatake Okumiya and Roger Pineau, June 1953, and "The Panay Incident: Prelude to Pearl Harbor," by Harlan J. Swanson, December 1967.*

Yuzuru Sanematsu probably should be listed as co-author of several of the chapters you'll read here. This retired Japanese naval officer handled all of the arduous legwork and interviews in Japan. He not only did an efficient job but an imaginative one, taking a few sparse leads and turning them into a dozen fruitful interviews. In addition, because he had been on duty in sensitive naval posts in Tokyo at the time of the *Panay* crisis, he was able to supply accurate personal recollections of reactions in the Navy Ministry. And he was able to lay to rest the rumor that the Japanese Navy was involved enough in the plot to have secret war plans ready to open in the event the United States declared war. Commander Sanematsu uncovered the unpublished memorandum from Admiral Mitsunami, the scapegoat of the *Panay* incident, which appears for the first time in this book.

My thanks go also to General Masatake Okumiya whose letters gave me early encouragement to proceed with the

* Note: The title for this book, *The Panay Incident, Prelude to Pearl Harbor*, was selected when the author first started working on the book in the early months of 1967. Regrettably, the article mentioned above was unknown to us.—EDITOR

story, and who suggested the names of others in Japan who might be helpful.

Three ladies who didn't know a Lewis gun from a drain pipe—but who learned—helped me fit all the pieces together over a period of several years. Patricia d'Abbraccio and Mary Hull fought the battle of the Yangtze at various stages through old newspaper clippings, photostats of plans, copies of muster lists, questionnaires and letters and the various persistent negotiations that sometimes ensue when doing business with even the most cooperative government archive and picture agencies. Mrs. Audre Proctor, in preparing the manuscript, made any number of contributions to the logic and good sense of the whole with a sharp seaman's eye for accuracy and a layman's quest for clarity. The three weren't "gunboat sailors" when they started, but they certainly qualify now.

Last of all, I am grateful to James O. Wade, one-time destroyer man and full-time editor, for his enthusiasm and encouragement. And to Luigi Barzini, war correspondent, best-selling author, and gentleman, who in the midst of his own high-priority writing chores took time out at several points to help this book along the way with information, corrections, suggestions, a review of the whole manuscript, and, finally the moving introduction which opens the book.

Signore Barzini, I know, made some warm friends in his few short days aboard *Panay*. It's easy to see why.

H. D. P.

Contents

Introduction

THERE IS A little street in Milan, about two or three hundred feet long, with a row of small trees, one newspaper kiosk, and a stand selling gelati in summer and roasted chestnuts in winter. It is called Via Sandro Sandri. Every time I pass it I shudder a little. There, of course, but for the grace of God, could be my name, nicely engraved on a Carrara marble tablet; it could now appear on many colored envelopes, illustrated post cards and urgent telegrams; it could be shouted to taxi-drivers by travelers in a hurry who never bothered to find out who I had been.

For Sandro Sandri and I were both on board the USS *Panay* when she was bombed and sunk by Japanese planes on the Yang Tse Kiang in December 1937. He died. I am alive. It was one of the most sensational and frightening international incidents of the time; it foreshadowed what was to come a few years later (as distant lightning foreshadows the coming storm) and it gave the American public the uneasy sensation that war was not something that happened to other people but could also happen to them, anytime, without warning.

Why two Italians played such a central role in an event which had little to do with them and their country can only be explained as one of the many examples of History's erratic casting. We two were far from wanting to attract attention. We were not courting death and immortality, particularly journalistic immortality, that is, the kind that lasts a few weeks. In fact we were being cautious when we asked to be taken aboard. Sandri did not want us to stay behind in Nanking, which would be conquered by the Japanese in a matter of hours, and risk embarrassing the Japanese by getting killed by one of their stray bullets. The USS *Panay*, we thought, meant obscurity and safety.

A *posteriori* I can say that the whole thing was probably my fault. I had been the instrument of Fate. Sandri and I had decided to go from Shanghai (which was already in Japanese hands) to Nanking (which was preparing to defend itself, or so we thought). To avoid the Yang Tse Kiang and to cross the fighting line we traveled over the network of little canals which crisscrossed the flat and muddy plains between the two cities. We chartered a motor sampan with a sailor-interpreter. The trip was wonderful, though cold. We saw little Chinese villages, slept in Chinese inns, ate Chinese food, and discovered that two Italians from the Po valley could find themselves curiously at home in such surroundings. The good humor, patience, and realism of the people were familiar and we could eat *tagliatelle in brodo di cappone* or *anatra arrosto* at any meal, dishes whose corresponding Chinese names I have forgotten.

Once outside Shanghai, of course, Sandri was in my power. He was older than I (he had fought in the First World War) a swashbuckling soldier who resembled Floyd Gibbons. He wrote, someone said, like Giuseppe Garibaldi, which meant enthusiastically but not well. His political ideas were embryonal and inarticulate, and this saved me from prolonged discussions, he being a Fascist and I being definitely skeptical about the tragic carnival being staged in my country. (Three years later I was imprisoned by Mussolini as an enemy of the regime.) Sandri spoke not a word of English, little French, and rough soldiery Italian, mostly cusswords. He could only communicate to the outside world through me. I spoke English and English was the most common second language in China. I had graduated seven years before from the School of Journalism at Columbia University and was practically bilingual.

My natural penchant was to consort with Americans. When we arrived in Nanking I immediately looked for the American correspondents (as I had done in Shanghai before and in other parts of the world). They usually were better informed about what went on, knew good bars and restaurants, had picked up a retinue of local aides, secretaries, interpreters, informers, mistresses, and pimps, each of whom could be useful in his or her particular way. They also were better supplied with everything one could have needed—tobacco, paper, whisky, maps, binoculars, razor blades.

In Nanking I went every day to the American Embassy for informal briefings but especially to exchange what little news we had picked up. The American journalists were almost all the guests of the American Embassy and when it closed and threw them all out on the sidewalk with their personal belongings, I felt very proud to open the doors of the Italian Embassy to them, which was next door. We lived together for days as members of a club, and when they moved to the *Panay*, it was only natural that I move with them. Sandri had to follow me meekly.

How he was killed and what happened to the rest of us the reader will find out from the following pages. The author has collected more authentic facts, correct names, exact chronologies, background explanations, and general information about the incident than any one of us possessed at the time or even later. I can point to only one small detail he forgot, or perhaps it was too unimportant to mention. I was awarded a small decoration by the U.S. Navy, four years after the incident; it reached me, through various vicissitudes, only ten years after. The medal arrived at the American Embassy in Rome just before war broke out between the United States and Italy. It was tossed in a dusty cupboard and forgotten. In 1947 Paul Bonner, the writer and diplomat, who was stationed in Rome, rang me up and asked: "Luigi, have you ever been in China?" I admitted I had. "Were you on the *Panay?*" Of course I was. "Well," he declared, "there seems to be a medal here waiting for you . . ."

A few hours later the American naval attaché pinned it on my chest. It is called the Navy Expeditionary Medal, has an elegant silk ribbon, striped yellow and blue, shows a soldier, a sailor, and a marine pulling a lifeboat ashore, on one side, and, on the other, the American eagle sitting with folded wings on an anchor from which olive branches are sprouting. The letter which accompanied it was signed by a Secretary of the Navy who had died long before, Frank Knox. It said, in part, that the medal was conferred upon me "in commemoration of the services rendered . . . to the survivors of the U.S. Ship *Panay*." I am naturally attached to it. It reminds me of one of the biggest stories I ever wrote, of Sandro Sandri, who thought his death was "a stupid death," and of my first glimpse of Americans at war, their resourcefulness, courage, and instinctive comradeship.

It also reminds me of the fact that, through my life, whether I want to or not, I get entangled with Americans, usually with good results. There must be a natural affinity between me and them.

LUIGI BARZINI

Rome
July 13, 1968

The Panay Incident

1

"The Soap Dish Navy"

THE POLISHED BRONZE plaque in the tiny wardroom said simply:

USS PANAY

Mission

For the protection of American life and property in the Yangtze River Valley and its tributaries, and the furtherance of American good will in China.

But the ship hardly looked capable of doing either job. The assignments were so big. And she was so little. Fat. Stubby. Top-heavy in appearance. Decks seeming to be nearly awash. High, sedate superstructures crowded with an array of funnels, ventilators, rigging wires, floodlights, and a thoroughly unmilitary "grape arbor" of awning frames and awnings to keep off a persistent Asiatic sun. Yet she was superbly designed for the work. And to her officers and crew and to hundreds of Americans deep inside China in 1937, USS *Panay* could be a beautiful sight indeed, slicing through the coffee-colored current of the Yangtze River at a surprising 15 knots, guns trained outboard, and United States ensign standing straight out in the breeze from the gaff of her after mast.

She was one of a proud little squadron. There were eight of them in all. Odd-looking ships, each one. But rugged and efficient. And they were helping to keep the peace on the lower Yangtze River 30 years ago. If their silhouettes might now appear strange to an American familiar with today's sleek frigates and guided-missile destroyers, the names of the Yangtze ships would sound even stranger to an ear tuned to the modern Navy's roster of ships that have been christened to commemorate men and battles familiar to generations of American schoolboys: USS *Bennington, Enterprise, Coral Sea, John Paul Jones, Bainbridge, Decatur . . .*

The Yangtze squadron had a style of its own. Both the look of the ships and the lettering on their nameboards gave a clue to history, to the interests of the day, and to United States involvement in the Far East in the decade before World War II.

In the late 1920s and early 1930s six of the gunboats that were operating in the Yangtze in 1937 had been specially designed, had been constructed in Asiatic shipyards, and had entered the Patrol. Their christening list could have been made up by Teddy Roosevelt after a "bully" cruise through the western Pacific with the Great White Fleet: USS *Luzon, Guam, Tutuila, Mindanao, Oahu,* and *Panay.* The six joined USS *Isabel,* then flagship of the Patrol, and USS *Monocacy,* a squared-off and sedate older craft that had also been built for river duty.

Monocacy was comfortable and cool—but slow. She looked a bit like a latter-day Mississippi River steamer, with an imposing boxlike pilothouse on her hurricane deck and three shielded machine guns peeping out through steel-shuttered sets of windows on the deck below the pilothouse. The sight of the guns reminded one old Yangtze hand of a trio of spinsters leveling shotguns out of second-story windows at small boys raiding the watermelon patch.

Isabel looked like a yacht. And her name was distinctly un-Navy. A yacht was what she had been built to be. Constructed by the Bath Iron Works in Maine to embody considerable luxury, *Isabel* had been taken over by the Navy for submarine patrol duty in World War I. Her spacious and palatial deck cabins and salons had been wiped clean and replaced by the bridge structure of a destroyer. Two tall destroyer funnels were added. On her flush deck, 3-inch guns and torpedo tubes were mounted fore and aft, presenting a fairly businesslike appearance. She had tasted the world and had never gone back to Marblehead Race Week.

In 1921 *Isabel* was brought out to China and assigned to the Patrol. She offered a fairly dashing picture charging up and down the river at flank speed, boiling out a substantial wake astern—enough wake on one occasion to send a triple line of swells rolling toward each riverbank with sufficient force to up-end grazing water buffalo, capsize sampans, and bring a sobering set of attendant damage claims from irate Chinese farmers and boatmen. In addition to her speed and style, *Isabel* also held several other distinctions among the crews of the Patrol ships and among the American colony in China. She was noted for the succulence of her Boston baked beans—pots of which were sent ashore from time to time as handsome bread-and-butter presents, in return for some hospitality to her officers and crew. But duty on board was not always as good as it appeared to be. With her small portholes and below-decks arrangements having been designed for pleasant New England summers rather than the heat of the Orient, *Isabel* was unbearably hot during much of the year.

Isabel had been flagship for her first dozen years on the Patrol. As such she had a standard of performance and beauty to uphold. When first brought out to China, she had replaced the old gunboat *Helena*, known as the "Swan of the Yangtze" because of her peculiar and distinctive long-necked funnel and her ability to slide over the shallows and sandbars with ease. The need for more such shallow-draft vessels had dictated the more functional design of all the new gunboats that followed. With functionality—and more efficiency and comfort—had come a certain loss of dash to the look of the gunboats, a look that appalled some of the old shellbacks in the Bureau of Ships.

Put out of service by the arrival of the new boats was a mixed bag of older vessels, including two converted minesweepers and a pair of former Spanish gunboats—both Spanish-American War prizes, one of which had been at the bottom of Manila Bay for more than a year before being salvaged and eventually sent to China for the Patrol.

USS *Panay* was representative of the new gunboats. She was named after one of the larger islands in the Philippines. An earlier gunboat in the Philippines had also carried that name. Aboard her, duty was among some of the best. *Panay* and a sister ship, *Oahu*, had been built in 1927 from identical plans and specifications at Kiangnan Dock & Engineering Works in Shanghai. Chinese shipyard workers had predicted a bad time for *Panay* because she had experienced a fire during construction and had stuck on the ways at launching. But once afloat, all seemed to go well. Both ships were specially designed for the Yangtze and were little fit for any other service, even coastal patrol. Their hulls were low to the water and their drafts were shallow—about five and a half feet forward and aft. Their bottoms were completely flat, without a trace of a keel running beneath the hullplates. They could ground on a Yangtze sandbar as harmlessly as a soap dish and could be dragged or floated off equally easily. Seen at a distance running at flank speed in the river, one of the gunboats might appear to be a sinking ship, with deck apparently at water level and a captain intent on driving her under in one last, grand gesture. But resting at anchor, all gleaming white paint and glistening mahogany, *Panay* and the others looked commodious and even stylish. And when "dressed" with flags from bow to stern for a national holiday, she could cut a knobby enough figure to have run with the brokers' yachts at a Harvard-Yale boat race.

Panay was lightly armed for a ship of war. But gunboats as a class were spawned by a certain damned-if-I-care-if-the-natives-are-restless approach to imperialism; they were only intended to fight against an enemy seriously outgunned from the start. On a platform forward and slightly below the bridge, and again on the open upper deck above the stern, *Panay* carried 3-inch guns. The guns were mounted behind steel splinter shields thick enough to deflect rifle fire even at close range; sniping from ashore by bandits was a common danger. Both guns, however, were capable of elevating to a vertical position for defense against aircraft.

Panay's upper deck was a spacious tropical veranda that her crew called the Palm Gardens. It ran nearly the length of the ship one level above the hull and provided a roof for most of the main-deck cabins. On each side of the upper deck about midship were placed .30-caliber Lewis antiaircraft machine guns, eight in all. These were also behind heavy, oblong splinter shields that looked a bit like upended water troughs. Each gun mounted a simple ring sight of World War I vintage. But a good gunner had to have a skeet shooter's instinct for a wing shot if he were to score a hit on anything moving much faster than a river pirate's junk.

Panay was built for 4 officers, 49 enlisted men, and a native crew of about a dozen. The commanding officer had a compact but well-appointed two-room suite behind the bridge that served all functions of bedroom, sitting room, dining room, and office. In these quarters he received and entertained the rather steady flow of Oriental and Occidental visitors that tradition and circumstance brought aboard. Sharing the forward part of the upper deck with the captain's suite was a single officer's stateroom. The radio room, with transmitters for contact with other ships of the Patrol and with the flag-ship of the Asiatic Fleet at Shanghai, was just aft of the captain's quarters, too.

The chief petty officers lived in comparable pleasant circumstances on the upper deck astern. A tiny two-bed sick bay adjoined the chiefs' quarters and opened out onto the platform that held the aft 3-inch gun.

On the main deck below were arranged, from bow to stern, single cabins for the other officers, a compact wardroom that could seat ten for dinner jammed elbow to elbow, a galley that turned out the meals for all hands, and finally quarters for the enlisted men other than chiefs. Big shore-type windows in glistening mahogany frames let in light and air. No port-holes, forced ventilation, or rancid atmosphere. No overheating like *Isabel*.

Two-thirds of the ship was engine room. The powerful twin engines could push *Panay* at 15 knots through the racing spring flood currents that ran like a millrace down from the Yangtze gorges. The machinery was tended by an engine-room gang of 15 sailors and by several Chinese who wore Navy dungarees, worked like the coolies they were, and lived in the "coolie flat" crammed in under the after deck on the port side (starboard was reserved for potatoes). Coolie quarters and pay were not much, but compared to the average coolie's life ashore, *Panay* provided such luxury that no one worried unduly.

A gunboat could carry just about as many Chinese supernumeraries as the crew could arrange to pay off at the end of the month. According to an officer serving aboard at the time, *Panay* boasted a respectable complement of Chinese. They were styled as "boatmen" but held no real rank or official status. They washed, dried, ironed, swept out, scrubbed up, waited tables, scoured dishes, polished engines, pitched in on all heavy work, fetched supplies, ran a boat service to shore, and generally made life quite gentlemanly for both officers and men. They lived aboard as long as the *Panay* stayed in one area. But if the ship had to move any distance, it was considered easier to recruit and train a whole new batch of boatmen at the next station than to take them along. The Chinese provided another more subtle advantage for all hands. The ship's commissary officer was granted a per diem allowance to feed each Chinese boatman, comparable to the allowance provided for other crew members. Because the Chinese wanted little more than rice and vegetables, 90 percent of their commissary money went to fatten the general mess fund. All dined well.

Good as the food was on board, for the officers there was even more sumptuous dining ashore. The invitations were frequent, the social life heavy. The drinking demands that could be put onto the shoulders of a young ensign or lieutenant dedicated to holding up the honor of his country could be staggering. But there was riding, shooting, and tennis to sweat it all out the next day. *Panay* was well able to handle all departments. An officer had only to make the casual remark at noon around the wardroom table that the afternoon was good for tennis, and he would return to his cabin to find his tennis whites and his racket laid out in expectation by one of the Chinese.

In 1937 duty on the Yangtze was probably the best available, outside of assignment to the dwindling White House flotilla. The treaty right to patrol Chinese rivers and territorial waters had been won by the United States, France, Britain, and Russia after subduing the terrorist mandarin Yeh in 1858. Yeh was captured at Canton after pursuit by a punitive expedition mounted by the four nations. The United States had sent USS *Minnesota*, whose draft was too deep to let her be of much service in the rivers. But *Minnesota*'s big guns glowered, and a United States commissioner was on hand to sign a Sino-American treaty guaranteeing that our presence in China from then on was legal.

The Patrol had done its job over the years with diligence—

and, at times, with cost. It was, however, a job that had its rewards. A rather pukka life was one of them.

On the gunboats of the Patrol discipline was no less demanding, drills no less frequent, and spit-and-polish no less admired or required than in the big-ship Navy. But there were extenuating circumstances to ease the pain of Navy routine. The quarters, with few exceptions, were light, airy, and unusually comfortable, with bunks for all hands instead of hammocks. Beards were allowed (no other ships or stations tolerated anything bushier than a pencil-line mustache). Moreover gunboat cooks took great pride in their tables. The menus were varied and even exotic.

When even a second-class seaman could live so handsomely attended by an almond-eyed gentleman's gentleman, it is not surprising that the good word had gotten around the Fleet. A transfer to the Yangtze Patrol—rather than being regarded as an assignment to Siberia—was largely sought after, hard to come by, not easily chucked away.

A sailor's wages, though low by today's standards, went a long way in China. Patrol sailors were rarely rocked by any sea larger than the wake of a river steamer. But they got full sea pay. There were not too many places to spend it. The entertainments that did exist tended to be cheap—as almost everything in China was. And dirty—as almost everything in China was. But sailors have never been known to grouse about the "dirt, sin, and iniquity" that can be found in most of the world's notorious liberty ports: Marseilles, Hamburg, Rio . . . And if there was serious reluctance to go ashore into the sin of Hong Kong or Shanghai with a pocketful of pay and a big thirst, those complaints have not been adequately recorded in the history of the Yangtze Patrol.

2

"The situation is pregnant with crisis"

LIEUTENANT COMMANDER JAMES Joseph Hughes of Washington, D.C., knew as well as anyone the advantages of duty on the Yangtze. He certainly knew better than anyone on board *Panay* the extreme responsibilities of being a commanding officer on the river.

Hughes had come aboard the gunboat as captain on October 23, 1936. Since then the officers who had served under her old commander had been relieved in the normal course of events, until in December 1937 Hughes had a completely new staff. He seemed pleased with them all. And with his crew. Hughes ran a "taut ship," which some of the more easy-going crewmen didn't particularly regard as a "happy ship." But the Yangtze was no place for slack discipline. Hughes trained his crew hard. Kept largely to himself, as commanding officers—of small ships, particularly—are advised to do. To some, he had the reputation of being a hard man, and an intense one. And his habit of repeatedly checking the readiness of his ship and crew had earned him the nickname of Jittery Jim among some of the men. But if he was respected by his crew more than he was "loved," it may well have been because all his schooling for command had told him that leadership need not necessarily mean "palship."

The skipper was just 39. He had celebrated his birthday on November 23. And he had been in the Navy for 22 of those 39 years.

Hughes was a native of New York City. He had entered the Naval Academy during the summer of 1915 as the war in Europe was about to go into its second year. Isolationist sentiment—even pro-German sentiment—was still strong in the United States in 1915. It would be almost two more years before America worked itself up enough to enter the war. Hughes' attraction to the service was clearly not wartime patriotism but came from a long and well-considered determination to be a career naval officer.

At the Academy he earned a reputation for being quiet, serious, a good student, and particularly apt at seamanship. For a man who was not large of frame, he had a surprisingly deep voice, but was reserved in conversation. He walked with an unusual sleuthlike walk his classmates found entertaining. Hughes' naval education would be modeled along the pattern that John Paul Jones had specified when he first suggested the need for a naval academy:

None other than a Gentleman, as well as a Seaman both in Theory and Practice, is qualified to support the Character of a Commission Officer in the Navy, nor is any Man fit to Command a Ship of War, who is not capable of communicating his Ideas on Paper in Language that becomes his Rank.

For almost 13 of his 22 years in the Navy, Hughes had served at sea. And in the periods of shore duty in between his ships, he had pushed himself through a number of the widely assorted courses that a professional naval officer would need for advancement and a Yangtze Patrol officer might need for survival when operating independently and with almost unlimited authority deep inside China.

On two separate occasions Commander Hughes had completed the stiff junior and advanced courses at the Naval War College. And while at sea he had plowed through Naval War College correspondence courses in strategy and tactics and later international law. The latter would be handy background material on the Yangtze with American, British, French, Italian, German, Japanese, and Chinese naval craft elbowing each other up and down the river, as edgy as a pack of bird dogs. Under conditions like that, it would be easy enough for international disputes to start inadvertently. And there would always be a foreign captain or two who, on the instruction of his government or because of his own egotism or cussedness, might choose to play some sort of maritime game of "chicken" to establish his own superiority or that of his navy.

In addition, Commander Hughes had trained briefly in submarines and had qualified for a steamboat master's license. The latter qualification would be particularly useful on the Yangtze, where a whole new series of ship-handling techniques applied when operating a vessel in the tremendous currents through the tricky and constantly changing channels.

With service in the Yangtze Patrol considered a choice berth, neither morale nor discipline was a great problem. A constant troublemaker in the crew could not have lasted long. He would have been pulled up before a captain's mast and sent back to the Fleet. Most of the men who had tasted the advantages of the Yangtze duty wanted to hang on to them. But commanding half a hundred men kept together in a small vessel halfway around the world from home had its problems under the best morale and discipline. Hughes' tactic was never to give trouble the laxity it needed to start.

Most of the captain's daily contact with the crew and with the running of the ship came through his executive officer,

Lieutenant Arthur F. Anders of Weimar, Texas. "Tex" Anders was also a Naval Academy graduate, Class of 1927. At the Academy he had gained a reputation for pulling good marks without seeming to study. Classmates grew used to finding him "caulked off" asleep when all the rest of the midshipmen were grinding hard at their books. Tex Anders claimed his marks came from luck—not brains. He was always ready to plop down on a bunk for a bull session or to talk on the grandeurs of Weimar. The arrival of the weekly paper from Texas and Anders' reading from it was something many classmates remembered at the end of the Academy years.

Even in naval uniform, Anders looked like a Texan—tall, lean, sinuous. His voice was soft. But he spoke with a quiet authority, even without the epaulets of his command. Hughes and Anders worked well as a team. Each morning the executive officer would confer briefly with his captain to get the orders of the day, the schedule of work to be done, drills to be conducted, and other ship's business to be attended to. There was not much small talk between them. The captain never gave an order twice. With Anders, he never had to.

Shortly before coming to the Yangtze, Anders had put in a tour of duty on battleships. The strictness of the routine there was good training for the somewhat formal relationship he and Hughes would have to maintain. Then after the battleship there had been a shore post. When it came time to go back to sea, Anders was asked what sort of duty he would like next. Without too much thought, the young Texan had put down several requests, including service in China. He had heard the duty was good and that a naval officer's pay, not overly generous in the mid-1930s, would go a lot further in the Orient. In addition, Anders had married an American girl who had been born in the Philippines. She had had experience in running a household in the Far East. The prospect seemed appealing, rather than formidable. But the whole thing was a long shot. Anders put in for China, then pretty much forgot about it.

A short time later the Navy informed him that there were numerous requests for the first two choices of duty he had opted for but that they were short of China volunteers. Would he still like to go? He would.

Navy budgets were tight in the 1930s. The annual fuel allowance for the Fleet had to be husbanded for full-scale maneuvers each year. And ammunition had to be conserved for the rare chances at target practice. Navy transport ships were practically nonexistent; officers and their families heading for duty with the Asiatic Fleet traveled out from San Francisco not aboard Navy vessels but on the old Dollar Line steamers. Anders had boarded the ship with sealed orders, as had the other naval passengers. Once they crossed the international dateline, the officers were then under the jurisdiction of the commander in chief of the Asiatic Fleet, and they could open their orders to see exactly where they were headed. When Anders slit open the big brown manila envelope and found that he was slated for the Yangtze Patrol, he immediately received several offers to swap orders with others. That was a good sign, he figured. No swap. He would stick with it. The decision would almost cost him his life, would eventually cause him to accept premature retirement from the service, but would win him the second highest naval decoration his country could award.

Three other officers would make up the final crew that Anders would help command on *Panay*. Lieutenant Junior Grade John Willard Geist of Altoona, Pennsylvania, the engineering officer, also doubled in brass at several other jobs —disbursing officer, commissary officer, and procurer of motion pictures for the crew's entertainment. Ensign Denis Harry Biwerse of Sheboygan, Wisconsin, would be communications officer, navigator, educational officer, intelligence officer, and commander of *Panay*'s landing force, whenever one was put ashore. Lieutenant Clark Gilson Grazier, Medical Corps, of Ingomar, Pennsylvania, ship's doctor, was also in charge of the ships service store and was the organizer of various athletics and recreational activities to keep a crew in shape physically as well as mentally.

Biwerse, the junior in rank, was senior in the time he had been on board. He had reported to *Panay* in April 1937. Biwerse had graduated from the Academy in 1934. A quiet disposition had let him in for considerable "running" from upperclassmen during his plebe year. And he was often the target for practical jokes. But as his yearbook noted, he invariably "came up smiling." Denny Biwerse was a likable midshipman, often ready to stand a weekend watch for a classmate who had a date coming down to Annapolis. He made a mark for himself in Academy wrestling and boxing. And in his final year he began to get interested in radio. Aboard *Panay* he would take special interest in the efficiency of the radio gang.

If some of Biwerse's classmates had trouble recalling that rather quiet midshipman a few years later, almost everyone in the Class of 1934 remembered John "Gunner" Geist. He left the Academy an All-American soccer player, having excelled in the sport in each of his four years and captained the team when he was a senior. Geist could sew a Navy "N" and two stars on his Academy bathrobe. He was known as "Gigolo" for his way with his classmates' girlfriends. Academics were not his strong point. Practical knowledge was; he seemed to have the instinct for always knowing in advance the next rumor that was coming around the bend. It was a valuable instinct for a Navy man.

Anders had joined the ship on April 24, four days after Ensign Biwerse. Dr. Grazier had come aboard in July. Geist has joined in August.

Although the officers were relatively new on board, most of the crew were old, experienced Yangtze hands. Their leading petty officer, Chief Boatswains Mate Ernest R. Mahlmann of Astoria, Long Island, was a Navy man of twenty years' service who saw to it personally that everything ran smoothly.

The year 1937 was not a bad time to be a career Navy man on duty in the relative luxury of China service. And most of *Panay*'s crew knew it. The year had seemed to begin auspiciously enough. As the New Year came in, radio announcers across the country had reported the local celebrations in New York, Chicago, Denver, Los Angeles with enough enthusiasm to make it sound as if there had never been a New Year's Eve before. And in a round-up story headlined "Wild Throngs Greet 1937 in the Old Champagne Way" *The New York Times* reported that Times Square was jammed early in spite of rain, that the theaters were all sold out, and that the customers were three deep at the midtown bars. It was, the *Times* noted, the best-dressed crowd since 1929, with "high hats and ermine in unusual abundance."

But the easy atmosphere reported by the *Times* story may not have extended much further back than the third row in those same Manhattan bars. At Flint, Michigan, that New Year's Eve several hundred workers had taken over most of the General Motors plants in the area in a surprise "raid." Then they announced that production would come to a complete halt. Within two days 33,400 workers were idle and the $350,000 that General Motors payrolls had poured into the Flint area every day dried up. A judge, who turned out to own $200,000 in General Motors stock, slapped an injunction on the workers to vacate the property and stop picketing. They wouldn't. The siege was on. After two weeks of deadlock, the peaceful proceedings erupted into a riot. Some 24 were hurt and the National Guard was called. When a truce was finally reached, the strikers marched out of the besieged plant victorious and singing:

> The boss is shaking at the knees,
>   Parlez-vous.
> The boss is shaking at the knees,
>   Parlez-vous.
> The boss is shaking at the knees,

He's shaking in his BVDs,
Hinky-dinky parlez-vous.

The strike had served notice on industry. The nation's biggest industrial giant had been forced to sit down to bargain collectively with labor. In the next six months the "sit-downs" would hit other automotive plants, rubberworks, steel mills, textile plants, shipyards, refineries. More than a quarter of a million workers took part in strikes or stayed away in sympathy. They did not all end so peacefully. In the late spring at the gates of the Republic Steel Corporation plant in South Chicago, workers and police clashed in a bloody Memorial Day massacre that left 5 killed and 90 hospitalized. It wasn't a bad time at all to be in China. The pay wasn't up to union scale. But nobody was cracking your head either.

Abroad, the Spanish Civil War was erupting with new fury and threatening to spread. In February naval vessels of Great Britain, France, Italy, and Germany had set up a neutrality patrol along the Spanish coasts. The fighting on land was dividing more than Spaniards; the debate about who was right went hot and heavy in United States living rooms and college campuses. Some Americans were already beginning to back their sympathy with action and enlistments. And in Germany, Hitler announced to the Reichstag that Germany formally repudiated the admission in the Versailles Treaty that she was responsible for starting World War I; as far as the Führer was concerned, the German railways and the German Reichsbank were now free from any obligations to the Allies imposed by the treaty.

Closer to "home" for the *Panay* men, the Japanese had started the year with ominous talk. But then ominous talk had always been plentiful in the Orient. There was going to be a navy build-up: "Termination of the Washington and London treaties liberates us from unjust restrictions," Admiral Osami Nagano, the Navy Minister, had said at the start of the new year. "With free hands, we can confidently proceed to replenishment of the national defense on principles of nonaggresion and nonmenace." The last six words seemed to have been thrown in as an afterthought. Then Nagano gave a hint of the future by referring to Japanese Manchuria, the Chinese province Tokyo had bitten off for itself in 1931 after manufacturing an incident to justify invasion: "Japan has many difficulties to overcome in protecting Manchuko's independence, and to meet those difficulties the Japanese people must act as one man." Nagano's words were hardly encouraging. "The international situation is pregnant with crisis." On July 29 Japanese planes bombed Tientsin. On August 11 Japanese marines landed in Shanghai. Another incident had served its purpose. The undeclared war was on.

To those aboard *Panay*, it had the appearance of just another crisis. The living was easy and the routine was much as it had been. There were, as always, warships of half a dozen nations in the Yangtze. But except for the demands of naval protocol—and the unpleasant upstaging that always took place between senior officers when protocol wasn't observed exactly—all the nations seemed to get along reasonably well. On assorted days *Panay*'s log carried such colorful entries as:

0800 Full-dressed ship in honor of the Japanese Emperor.
0800 Dressed-ship honor of Coronation King George VI.
1235 H.I.J.M.S. *Ataka* fired 13-gun salute to Commander Yangtze Patrol; salute returned gun for gun by USS *Luzon*.
1010 Republic of France Ship *Savorgnan de Brazza* passed standing down river, and fired 13-gun salute to Commander Yangtze Patrol. Salute answered gun for gun by USS *Luzon*
1005 German Republic Ship *Emden* stood in from down river. [21-gun salute to Chinese government. 13-gun

salute to flag of the Chinese admiral and 13-gun salute to flag of Commander Yangtze Patrol. All returned gun for gun.]

It could have been the Battle of Jutland.

But to the men, the more exciting log entries were likely to be the stories behind such cryptic items as:

0830 Held quarters for inspection. Cheatham, W.; Coxswain, AWOL Hebard, R. R.; Fireman First Class, AWOL.

That usually meant a particularly good party ashore. Later in the day, a seedy-looking sampan water taxi might be seen putting out from shore with the somewhat worse-for-wear liberty men in the seats. There would probably be a tear here and there in their dress blue uniforms, some scratches around the jaws, and several sets of red eyes, the kind that did not come from poring over the stateside newspapers in the YMCA. Up over the side they'd come, somewhat gingerly, under the stern eye of the officer of the deck. The following Saturday morning at captain's mast, the splitting heads would be gone. The uniforms would be cleaned and brushed. The three creases down the flap collars would be razor sharp. And the stories of what happened would likely out-Munchausen Munchausen in their color and sheer audacity. Though the excuses offered up often entertained in the wardroom and were repeated with relish in the crew's space, they rarely worked. The punishments were laid out. And accepted, usually as small-enough payment for a hell of a good night of liberty; it was the sort of caper that cleansed the soul from time to time. Apparently it didn't permanently harm the character either; both Cheatham and Hebard would receive Navy Crosses for their conduct during the sinking of *Panay*.

Cheatham, Hebard, and the others could look back on "some wild ones." There had been the time in Chungking when Tom Spindle, a quartermaster third class from Denver, and a bunch of the deck petty officers had spent almost a day and a night getting a Chinese general drunk so his coolie troops could be persuaded to wire-brush, chip, prime, and paint *Panay*'s two anchor chains. But if they worked the Chinese men hard, they romanced the women with equal enthusiasm. And with plenty of money to spend—at least in Chinese terms—the American sailors were favorites with the women, especially the ones in business. One *Panay* veteran still remembers the crew lining the rails in Hong Kong as USS *Guam* sailed, escorted by three motorboats loaded with fallen ladies of Ship Street, who alternately cheered, cried, and blew off strings of firecrackers in a farewell salute. It was a moving sight.

By the same token, such close affection could lead to problems, of hygiene, if not morale. One gunboat skipper who firmly believed that "plenty of lovin' kept his crew from being wound up too tight" decided he would establish the gunboat's own private pleasure palace in a large junk moored offshore at Chungking. The ship's doctor could inspect all the girls regularly. If the outsiders were kept out of the junk and any of his own VD men restricted to the ship until cured, then the skipper figured all the enlisted men could be "unwound" regularly in fine, sanitary Navy style.

But that particular skipper reckoned without considering the impact of China's New Life Movement, which Madame Chiang and the local version of the Red Guards were pushing at the time. Floating whorehouses were not part of the movement's program—no matter how well run, inspected, or subsidized. Local officials clamped down, the girls went back to their respective farm teams, and the sailors resumed their occasional and somewhat risky trips to a Chungking cultural center known as the Dutchman's Hotel.

The sailors represented a true cross section of the nation. Not all saw the inside of the Dutchman's Hotel. But not all were first on deck for church call, either. They came from 25 states. From the big cities—Washington, Philadelphia, Los Angeles, Chicago, St. Louis, Des Moines, Denver. And from tiny towns—Milaca, Wisconsin; Lisbon, Louisiana; Siluria, Alabama; Baxter, Iowa; Mishawaka, Indiana; Bouckville, New York; Vallejo, California. And four of them, though enlisted in the American Navy, would soon be fighting for their lives on their native soil: Ducey Ting, Far Ze Wong, and King Fong Sung of Hankow and Yuan Te Erh of Shanghai were all mess attendants first class aboard *Panay*. Sung would receive the Bronze Star after *Panay* went down. Ducey would win a Purple Heart in World War II but would be lost at sea and presumed dead before the war's end. Wong would also win a Purple Heart and would be missing in action when the USS *Houston* went down early in World War II.

In the fall of 1937, however, what talk there was on *Panay* about action in the Far East usually was restricted to the old salts on the Patrol. With minimum prompting, they would sit around the mess tables after the evening meal and spin sea stories for the benefit of the "boot" sailors who had only been in China a year or two. It made quite a yarn to tell "how it really was" in China service back in the turbulent era from 1916 to 1926, when the warlords were ranging up and down the Yangtze. And when the warlords had the situation disrupted ashore, that made it easy for the river bandits to flourish afloat.

In 1925 there had been student riots at Canton and Shanghai. The Navy had been forced to land shore parties to protect United States lives and property. In the following year new troubles had broken out that had taxed the diplomacy and the prestige of all the foreign governments with interests in China. A Nationalist army under Chiang Kai-shek had marched north from Canton in a punitive expedition against the northern warlords. Spread through the units were cadres of Soviet-trained propagandists and *agents provocateurs*. The Nationalist Army easily captured Changsha, Wuchang, then Hankow. Hankow was the center of the whole industrially advanced central China area. It was a railroad center and the head of navigation for deep-water shipping. Its foreign concessions were busy, wealthy—and vulnerable. The communists among the Nationalist occupying troops went into action with a campaign of harassment and persecution. This brought business activity to a standstill. Most of the campaign was aimed at the British, who, with the largest imperial interests, were the chief targets of the communists. British women and children were evacuated to steamers and gunboats anchored in the river off Hankow. British men holed up in the Asiatic Petroleum Company's office building at the edge of the river. The few British troops available and a British Volunteer Corps, which had been formed to protect the concession, were pressed into service around the area. The French and American concessions took similar measures; sailors and civilians went on guard on shore, and gunboats in the river were ready to lay down a protective barrage if necessary. The "foreigners and their running dogs," as the communists called any Chinese who were friendly with Westerners or served them, seemed well enough able to defend themselves. But then the word began to come back from the interior. There were hundreds of other unprotected missionaries and businessmen spread all through the area under Nationalist control, most of them in spots too remote to get any help from the British, French, or American military. British versus Chinese clashes at Hankow would bring Chinese retaliation against the isolated and defenseless British missionaries in the interior. There was nothing for the British to do but cave in. The British Volunteer Corps was disarmed and the exclusive British business and residential area was taken over by the Chinese. Britain's first imperial retreat in China had begun.

A year later it was the United States' turn to suffer. Moving east in 1927, the Chinese Nationalist Army overran Nanking.

A great collection of Western refugees gathered in the Nan-king consulate under the formidable protection of 11 marines! It eventually took an artillery barrage laid down by naval units in the river to enable the Americans to escape to vessels brought up to receive them. "The white man's burden" was taking on some real weight.

But those were the old days. And old-timers always told any story better than it should have been, anyway. Time had mellowed most of the Nationalist and warlord hotheads. The Japanese invasion of Manchuria in 1932 had convinced Chinese of many persuasions that they might really need Western friends in the future. The Japanese invasion in 1937 proved it.

Aboard *Panay* in 1937 the Chinese were indeed friends. They also made things work a lot better, too. The four mess attendants, of course, were in a class set apart. They were real Navy men, enlisted for specific terms like the rest of the crew. They had all the benefits of any other crewman —except citizenship. And although their work as mess attendants was hard and the hours were longer than those of most other ratings, they did have some advantages their opposite numbers in the Fleet did not enjoy; there was an almost unlimited supply of Chinese boatmen to call on for the hardest, dirtiest jobs.

The boatmen were hired and paid through their own coolie "boss," who was paid for his gang at the rate of $1 (Mexican) per man per day. How much the boss took off the top was his own business. There was never any fuss about it—or at least in the hearing of the Americans. That was another one of the conveniences of the system. Most Chinese had lived all their lives under a colossal system of graft. Though they may not have liked it, they accepted it. The boss got his graft. They got their jobs.

Even among the Americans, Chinese graft eventually became a sort of sport. Supplies were usually bought through large and long-established English, American, French, and German grocery companies ashore that had gained a reputation over the years for excellent groceries, meats, and vegetables, as well as for a reasonable amount of honesty. But occasionally when the gunboats were cruising far from the cities, the commissary officer would be offered particularly fresh and tempting items from a farmer or a small merchant who did business right out of his sampan. Vegetables, potatoes, and any small fruit grown in the earth were viewed with suspicion; the Chinese had probably grown them with an ancient fertilizer that would bring up a bumper crop on even the meanest farm: human excrement. No earth-grown food could be served without the most rigorous inspection by the medical officer—and then a thorough cooking. But tree fruits were not suspect. There were delicious honey oranges to be had in the Yangtze Valley and fine persimmons, huge and without the mouth-puckering flavor usually associated with that fruit. Eggs were incredibly cheap. They were fresh and good, too. An American half-dollar would buy more than a hundred eggs. Wild fowl and game were plentiful in the rural markets particularly. And domestic chicken and duck were a favorite purchase of ships' cooks from farmers along the river. Here the Chinese practiced an Oriental variation of the grocer's thumb on the scale: A crate of birds would be force-fed water while they were being rowed out to the ship. With speed, a little luck, and the proper timing, the farmer might be able to spot his mark among the gunboat cooks, weigh the birds, close the sale, and be well on the way to shore before the true nature of the fattening process became evident. The word would pass up and down the Patrol to keep an eye out for that particular flimflam. Then both sides would sit back to scheme the next attack and defense. Enough money changed hands to make it interesting. Not enough was won or lost to take the sporting nature out of the exchange. It was something of a game.

And the Chinese usually won. But even when their watery purchases were deflated, the Americans invariably ended up with a far better bargain and far more tender birds than they could have acquired back home. The food aboard was far better than could be obtained anywhere on shore in China. Nevertheless, both officers and men spent much of their time thinking about the last shore leave, planning the next one, and figuring out ways in which they might spend more time ashore than they would normally get.

Enlisted men could not entertain aboard the ships except on certain special occasions when an open house was being held on some national holiday. And although the officers frequently arranged dinners in the tiny, spotless wardrooms, there was the traditional U.S. Navy ban on alcohol that was something of a social dampener in the area where the British had made Scotch-and-soda and gin-and-bitters social rituals that were almost necessities.

Ashore, the Americans could match anyone drink for drink. In the big cities there were plenty of good bars catering to all ranks. For the officers and their wives there were foreign clubs that were centers of all sorts of social activity, from tennis and golf to drinking, card playing, dancing, dramatics, and whatever minor philandering could be conducted within a fairly tight community watched over by a large number of self-appointed guardians-of-the-morals and gossiping servants.

In Shanghai, the glitter of the club life was brightest. In the downtown area the Shanghai Club and the American Club were notable citadels of Western sociability. The local businessmen and officials began to gather in the lounges and bars in the early afternoon. In the days before the "business lunch," the first drink of the afternoon was the high point of many an expatriate's day. Nobody even pretended he had to go back to work afterward. As a result, the drinking could go on with considerable enthusiasm and always with an easy conscience. A few conservatives stopped for tea. A few played their tennis first. But the cocktails and the highballs were the reward for it all. Whiskey and gin were cheap and plentiful. The service was good. The amount of credit extended to a man who was a reasonable risk was staggering. And after all, didn't the British maintain that a generous ingestion of alcohol was a reliable tropical-disease preventative? And shouldn't the British know? They had been at it longer than anyone else. "Another round for all hands and put it on my chit."

The Navy people might have to join the afternoon gatherings a little bit late. The routine aboard ship and in the embassies and consulates was more formal than the business world. But the ship's day started decently early, and work was usually secured in the early afternoon. Then perhaps one-half or one-quarter of the crew were free to head for shore. Officers and their wives were welcome additions to almost any gathering. They brought the fresh air, new styles, and current talk of the States with them. Those things were missed. Sooner or later—no matter how the old China hands rambled about the glories of the East—the conversation got around rather nostalgically to "home." There was a certain amount of homesickness under even the toughest skin. The Scotch and gin eventually made passable memories of home tender ones, and fond memories almost unbearable.

As evening came around, the tennis courts at the Country Club on Bubbling Well Road and at the Cercle Sportif Français in the French concession began to empty. The athletes showered, shaved, dressed, and sallied forth to the terrace cocktail tables or bellied up to the men's bars with a terrible thirst. The regulars felt it a point of honor to stay with the new arrivals drink for drink.

Finally it was time to change for dinner. The courses were likely to be numerous. And drawn out. They had to be. There would be nothing much to do afterward. If the cocktail hour had been decently prolonged and if there were enough courses served, timing after dinner might allow for cigars and brandy, one Scotch and soda with the ladies, and then it would be a decent hour for a guest to excuse himself for bed without the impression of rudeness. A civilized ritual.

For any who stayed too long, the after-dinner conversation was not what it should have been—rarely the witty, brittle repartee of a Somerset Maugham best-seller, rarely the sort of incisive observation an outsider might expect from the principals and the subordinates who were on the scene and behind the scenes in a part of the world where intrigues were rife, politics wild, and the whole pot about to boil over. Most of the old-timers had been together in China too long, had covered the same ground over and over again already. It was old boring stuff by now, like a long-run play in which every actor knows everyone else's lines almost by heart.

When it was too hot to drink and talk in Shanghai the dancing was good in the roof garden of the French Club. Sometimes there were amateur dramatics. And occasionally a good touring company took the boards at Shanghai's Adelphi Theatre.

Upriver in Nanking or Hankow the pattern of life was much the same. But the facilities for it were neither so well equipped nor so plentiful. For *Panay*'s crew there was the Navy Club at Nanking, not very big or very elaborate, but the beer was kept the coldest of any in town, American style. For the officers, the embassy personnel, the military attachés, and a few American businessmen, there was the American Club. The name was far grander than the establishment. But it was reasonably clean and comfortable, was equipped with some presentable second-hand furniture, and was a good place to meet friends or exchange books and magazines from home.

Of the *Panay*'s officers, Commander Hughes and Lieutenant Anders had brought their wives to China. The two women followed the gunboat up and down the river as she changed station. Moving all the time was something of a problem. Closing up one house. Finding, renting, and staffing another. But the abundance of inexpensive help made these chores easier in China than they might have been elsewhere. Mrs. Anders had no trouble hiring an adequate staff for $15 a month. There was a Number 1 Boy and an assistant, whose duties were unclear, though his chief job seemed to be opening the door for the lieutenant every morning, then handing him his cane and helmet as he departed for duty. The ritual was reversed every night. Tex Anders never could figure out how the door-opening fellow knew just when he was coming home, unless he stood beside the door all day long peeking out. Of course, that was a possibility. It would have been a tremendous waste of time but not entirely un-Chinese.

Then there were two cooks and a "makie-learn" cook, a boy who carried water, three sedan-chair bearers (two varsity men and a spare), one amah for the baby, and a night watchman. The latter was a critical employee. Anders' home was in a large compound behind high walls and a locked gate. The foreigners seemed terribly rich to those outside, who were, in turn, terribly poor. The Chinese figured that anything that could be stolen was fair game. To some extent, the same thing held true for the staff. Petty theft was thought to be a fringe benefit. A certain amount of it was expected. At one point, when it got too bad, Mrs. Anders fired the Number 1 Boy, whom she suspected was responsible for it all. He then retaliated by taking the whole crew off the job—including the night watchman—and a certain amount of household plunder besides.

Upriver, the social life was largely centered in the homes rather than clubs. Invitations would be delivered by a runner coming around to each compound and announcing the date, time, and nature of the occasion. The guests were almost always Westerners. Because the naval families were so often on the move, there were few chances to make friends among the Chinese. There'd be a handful of Navy people, a few

English and Americans working for the big tobacco and oil companies, the embassy men and their wives, perhaps.

The more the Westerners stuck together, the more distant the Chinese seemed: They were simply people who *did* things. People to manage around a house. People to run errands. "You had to watch them, too. They stole." And they were often hard to manage and hard to understand. In short, the Chinese were regarded as suspicious, childish, and petulant. Unpredictable. Superstitious. There was a river ferry that capsized one day just off the bank at Chungking in front of a stretch where there were half a dozen Western compounds. The current was swift. The boat went down almost immediately. There was no debris to cling to. Most of the Chinese passengers drowned. Because it had happened in front of the foreign compounds, there were dark mutterings that the Westerners were responsible. There were glares in the street and sullen looks from some of the servants. But it passed. In China with so many lives available and with life so cheap, the accident was soon forgotten as people struggled to live through the next crisis.

3

"Fist in a pot of glue"

SUNDAY, DECEMBER 12, 1937, was fair and cold along most of the Eastern Seaboard. The country was cranking up for an uneasy Christmas. The weather, certainly, had been doing its part. Buffalo, New York, with the aid of National Guard trucks mounted with plows, was digging out from one of the worst snowstorms in its history. In Pennsylvania 14 were dead after heavy snows and a cold wave there. In Glenn, Michigan, 160 motorists were marooned by the same elements. The town's one restaurant had a captive clientele; ordinarily that would be a bonanza, but now the chef was down to a menu of pancakes only. Gales and rain lashed the West Coast from Mexico to Alaska. In Riverside Church on Manhattan's upper West Side, Dr. Harry Emerson Fosdick was preparing to preach "This Is a Miraculous World."

Indeed it was. And filled with inconsistencies. The League of Nations listed armament expenditures for the year at a whopping $11,857,000,000. But small amounts would go a long way toward more light-hearted pursuits. French champagne was selling for $1.89 a 26-ounce bottle. An eight-day

Caribbean cruise cost $105; a new convertible coupe $960—and that included Federal taxes, spare tires, safety glass, the works.

But if the price of living was low, there were some unseen carrying charges building up around the world. The papers on December 12 carried stories of wars and rumors of wars. A column by military expert Hanson Baldwin discussed a report that the Japanese were building three new battleships armed with 16-inch guns. Baldwin reported that 63 other new Japanese men-of-war were projected.

There was kindred uneasiness and trouble in other corners of the world. In Rome that December weekend, from the balcony of the Palazzo Venezia, Benito Mussolini had just told a large crowd that stood below in a driving rain that Italy was leaving the League of Nations. The Duce, pounding his fist repeatedly for emphasis, condemned the League as a "tottering temple where they are not working for peace but are paving the way for war." The applause was lukewarm. Correspondents, huddling in the downpour and trying to keep their notes dry, agreed the Duce was not in his best form. His voice was hoarse and he had to stop repeatedly to clear his throat. The move out of the League of Nations was really not much of a surprise. And Mussolini's "support of peace" sounded to some very much like a hint of more war, more shortages, more restrictions and sacrifices.

But even the most suspected statements can sometimes take on the guise of truth if shouted loud enough and often enough. Stalin was trying it too. The first Soviet election campaign was over and Stalin had announced to the foreign press corps that the voting had proved to be the "freest and most democratic election in the history of the world." Pencils scratched paper—with something less than complete conviction.

But the headlines that most disturbed many a good American breakfast came from the Far East or concerned that part of the world. It was in turmoil. There were big, important stories and little niggling ones. The Japanese military machine was pushing hard through China. Nanking was under siege but seemed to be holding. *The New York Times* reported the fight in a story headlined:

INVADERS CHECKED
BY MANY DEFENSES
IN NANKING'S WALL

Shells Pour Into City

PLANES AID LAND FORCES
BUT NAVAL ATTACK FROM
YANGTZE HAS NOT YET BEGUN

Other stories, relayed usually from Shanghai, dealt with the situation inside Nanking. Speculation was grim about the slaughter and rape that might take place when the city was eventually captured.

The "China War" had started in July. A manufactured incident in a garrison town not far from Peking in North China eventually gave the Japanese the excuse under the old Boxer Rebellion protocol to "reinforce" their troops in Peking and Tientsin. The reinforcement soon amounted to a full-fledged invasion, with fighting breaking out in a dozen places between Japanese and Chinese forces.

By early August 1937 it was clear that the Japanese intended to extend the war to Shanghai and South China. Japanese transports and warships were observed off the southern coast. Japanese marines and bluejackets were landed in Shanghai and soon clashed with Chinese troops at various points in and around the city. The foreign powers, with the hope that they could remain uninvolved by sticking their heads in the sand inside their own enclaves, tried to wall out the trouble and hope for the best.

With both Chinese and Japanese aircraft soon in action over the densely crowded city, there was almost one incident a day. Two Chinese bombs falling inside the French Concession on one occasion killed 2,000 refugees!

The bloody, confused, and senseless fighting went on in, around, and over Shanghai for a total of 92 days. When a truce was finally signed on November 12, the Japanese estimated 92,000 Chinese combatants had been killed, and there had been some 300,000 casualties in all.

With Shanghai subdued, the Japanese quickly pushed west and inland along the south bank of the Yangtze, pressing to capture Nanking, the capital. Another Japanese column paralleled the Nanking attacking force—this one headed for the river city of Wuhu, about the same distance inland as Nanking but, because of the twisting of the river, further upstream. By December 8 the first Japanese units were in sight of Nanking's massive and historic walls.

In addition to its political importance, Nanking was a tempting target on several counts. The coast of China curves from Port Arthur in the north to Hong Kong in the south like some giant, lazy, pin-headed "S." The tiny top loop of the "S" circles around the Yellow Sea. Shanghai perches near the coast about halfway down the "S." The city sits near the south shore of the vast Yangtze estuary, comfortably fronting on the sheltered Whangpoo River, which opens into the Yangtze. Shanghai is an ideal port, with room off the city or in the roads for several hundred ships.

A vessel heading up the Yangtze from Shanghai follows a gentle, arching westward curve of more than 200 miles from Shanghai to Nanking. At Nanking the river takes a sharp left turn. And that same ship would find itself sailing almost due south for 50 miles before reaching the town of Wuhu, where the river takes a gradual, dipping 330-mile swing back to a westward direction through the beautiful lake regions and into the city of Hankow. The territory on both sides of the lower Yangtze is relatively low, pleasant farming land, with plenty of water at hand.

For thousands of years, the Yangtze has been the principal artery for southern China. It is navigable by steamer all the way to Chungking—some 1,325 river miles from Shanghai. Japanese control of the lower Yangtze could effectively cut China in half. It would also put the invaders astride the major "highway" by which every sort of material originating from hundreds of miles on either side of the river is moved out of the interior. And in the process of controlling the river, the Japanese would naturally capture half a dozen of China's most productive cities along the way.

As the Japanese advanced along first one side of the river and then the other, Chinese forces were forced to withdraw deeper and deeper inland. With the lower reaches of the Yangtze blocked by the Japanese or by sunken Chinese boom ships, safety for foreigners also tended to be upriver. To skirt the battle area and reach the coast by road or rail was difficult. And always thinking the war "could not last much longer," hundreds of Westerners had made the long trip inland with the retreating Chinese.

A winning war is likely to be a popular war. And the Japanese were turning all the screws. Japanese ships carrying mail to Shanghai were quietly crossing out the word "China" on every envelope. And in Tokyo the people were prematurely celebrating the capture of Nanking with parades and lanterns. A group of grateful civilians went on record with their enthusiasm for the anticipated feat of arms by presenting the War Office and the Navy Office, respectively, with two barrels of saki and two 25-pound sea bass.

Elsewhere the optimists of Chinese persuasion were still optimistic. A national magazine in the United States carried an article speculating authoritatively that after taking Nanking, the Japanese would rest on their positions and seek peace. T. V. Soong, head of the Bank of China and brother of

Mme. Chiang Kai-shek, predicted Japanese bankruptcy and revolution against the invaders within three months—if the Chinese could only hold out. He was certain they could.

In New York, 500 people, mostly women, had paraded 27 blocks up Lexington Avenue wearing cotton lisle or rayon stockings and carrying signs informing the somewhat bewildered strollers that the whole thing was an "antisilk parade" aimed at urging a boycott of Japanese silk for stockings. Thereupon a noted Japanese-American artist tried to improve the Nipponese public image by donating one of his drawings to an auction being run by the Chinese Women's War Relief Association. "It is my way," he told the press, "of showing the world that not all Japanese are militaristic." The value of the drawing was not discussed but the wire service pick-up clearly made it all worthwhile.

Anti-Japanese feeling was running high. A parade of planes was being organized to fly from Long Island's Floyd Bennett field over the Temple of Peace in Flushing Meadows and then to buzz New York's City Hall "to protest against the use of planes as destructive war machines, especially in the bombing of civilian populations in the Far East." Jacqualine Cochran had just set the New York–Miami speed record with a dash of 4 hours and 12 minutes at an average speed of 280 mph, and the backers of the peace flight thought it would be great if she could come back and lead their parade. She declined.

In the Far East, the Japanese were busy on the one hand horrifying the world with their brutality and on the other giving the apologists reason to tut-tut that Japanese were "not so bad after all."

Newsreels had come out of China showing refugees machine-gunned in the back as they tried to cross into relative safety in the international settlements. Americans were furious. But then came word that 200 stranded passengers—presumably Americans—had been bravely rescued by

a Japanese cruiser from the *President Hoover*, the Dollar
Line's $8-million-dollar flagship that had gone aground and
was breaking up on an island off the east coast of Formosa.
Two other Japanese cruisers were standing by, awaiting the
arrival of three American destroyers and the Canadian Pacific
liner *Empress of Asia*, all coming hard to the rescue. The 200
people taken off were all first-class passengers. Some 300
Chinese in steerage and a crew of 400 stayed with the ship.
If the Japanese aimed at influencing the "opinion makers,"
they rescued the right crowd.

Early in the fall as the invading Japanese Army began to
push inland from Shanghai, Chiang Kai-shek had evacuated
the Chinese government from Nanking up the river to
Hankow, "the Chicago of China." Most of the foreigners in
Nanking had followed. This move to Hankow touched the
life of the *Panay* men, too. The gunboat had been far up
the Yangtze at Chungking when things began to get tense
along the river. Kay Hughes, the captain's wife; Edith Ford,
the wife of a recently detached *Panay* officer; and Tex Anders'
wife, Muriel, and his infant son, Bill, had been in Chungking.
Now they headed downriver by steamer to follow the gunboat
to Hankow.

Hankow was jammed with Chinese businessmen and petty
officials, who were practically submerged by wives, children,
servants, and relatives. The American women moved into the
Lutheran Mission, a somewhat spartan and formidable set
of quarters that had been designed for salvation work among
the Chinese rather than for family living. Food, especially
for Anders' infant son, was already getting hard to come by.
The Chinese stores had been well picked over by the time
they arrived.

Kay Hughes and Muriel Anders used all their ingenuity
to come up with a working supply that would last for a few
days at a time. From Chungking they had brought along in
trunks and boxes whatever canned and nonperishable food

they could carry. Then they set about "scrounging," as they described it, through the local canteens and the scruffy little foreign "clubs" to see what else they could find. There wasn't much. What was left was meager and already becoming high priced. It wouldn't last long. But it didn't have to. Soon all dependents were evacuated by train to Canton to safety and relative luxury. It was a long, hot roundabout ride. But there were a lot of Chinese who wished they could have taken it.

Aboard ship, headed for Nanking, the officers and crew tried to maintain the same routine as they had in the more relaxed days of the Patrol. It was hard to believe that the whole Chinese war was anything more than a temporary inconvenience. The inevitable drills continued: fire, rescue, general quarters for air attack, landing force over the side, collision, man overboard. The last drill was carried on with some realism and concern. Earlier in the year in Hankow, two members of the crew had drowned. There was a suspicion that one of them, a seaman who was something of a loner among the crew, had jumped overboard to commit suicide. The other, a machinist mate, had fallen off a pontoon to which the ship was moored a short distance off the riverbank. He had been coming back from liberty and apparently was steering an erratic course. Even going overboard in the Yangtze cold sober was serious business. The current was too swift in most places to swim against. So if you were not spotted immediately and a boat put out to pick you up, you were pretty much of a goner. Added to that, if you swallowed any of the foul, brown Yangtze water, which was draining thousands of miles of China, the results were usually fatal. There were numerous cases where a man had been saved from drowning but had died from some brutal fever within 24 hours.

So the drills went on. Giving many of them new meaning over the same routine a year ago was the echo of Chinese and Japanese guns in the distance, always coming closer.

Liberty ashore had been somewhat curtailed since the fighting moved nearer Nanking. By early December only a handful of civilian Americans remained in the city. Ambassador Nelson T. Johnson had moved the main staff of the embassy to Hankow, following the Chinese government. Left in charge of the embassy at Nanking and the Americans who remained in the city was George Atcheson, second secretary, a native of Berkeley, California, and an old China veteran. After a stint in Ontario, Atcheson had come to Tientsin in 1927 as vice-consul. Then he had been promoted to full consul at Shanghai. Tense times were not completely new to Atcheson. Three years before, in 1934, he had been sent from Shanghai up the river to Wuhu when an outbreak of banditry in the Anhwei Province threatened the safety of Americans there. With the instincts of an old bird dog, Atcheson, using authority, reason, and cajolery, had shepherded all the Americans to safety in Wuhu until the bandits were captured or driven away. The job caught the eye of his superiors.

Watching out for his fellow Americans was a demanding and, to some extent, a thankless task, Atcheson knew. Most of his countrymen were the sort of individualists who wouldn't have been in China in the first place if they didn't have that characteristic ruggedness. Short of feeling the cold metal of an enemy gun pressed to the temple, most United States nationals in the Far East lived in the happy state of assurance that no Oriental would dare touch an American. And then no matter how bad the situation might get before they were taken in hand by the embassy, as soon as things quieted down, the average American seemed to feel that the gravity of affairs had probably been ballyhooed out of all proportion just to inconvenience him personally and to set back United States business and prestige generally.

The missionaries didn't fall into this category. Most of them felt they stood nothing to fear—not because of the threat of

United States reprisals but because the Chinese loved them and God was watching out.

Both groups were difficult to handle. And now with the Japanese approaching Nanking, Atcheson was faced with a similar evacuation situation again.

His second in command was J. Hall Paxton, a tall, thin, dark-haired career State Department man from Danville, Virginia. Paxton had plenty of China experience, too. In the spring of 1927 he had been vice-consul at Nanking when the Nationalist armies, with the cadres of Russian-trained political advisers and agitators among them, overran the city and started their harassment pogrom against all Westerners. The Nanking consulate had been practically under a state of siege then. When a gunboat artillery barrage and an armed landing party of sailors rescued them all, Paxton had acquitted himself well. He had been publicly commended by President Coolidge for his "courageous, loyal, and efficient devotion to duty during the trying and dangerous crisis." A grateful government had then delivered him a promotion in grade and a pay raise from $2,500 a year to the staggering sum of $3,000 per annum. Even in China, where United States dollars went far, it was not the sort of money to send a man on a wild spree through the fleshpots, gin mills, and gambling parlors. The title "career diplomat" obviously carried a measure of devotion.

Remaining with Atcheson and Paxton in Nanking for the clean-up work was a single embassy clerk, Emile Gassie, a great figure of a man from Louisiana who would be interned by the Japanese at Peking at the start of World War II. Except for a skeleton Chinese staff, the only other American in the embassy was Captain Frank N. Roberts, a tall, ramrod-straight West Pointer from Oskaloosa, Kansas. Roberts was an assistant military attaché who had had considerable experience observing the Japanese Army in Manchuria. He had a newspaperman's instinct for observation, a reporter's habit of taking careful, detailed notes about everything he saw and did, and an English instructor's appreciation for good writing style, clarity, and a perceptive turn of phrase. His reports would be well circulated and annotated in the tiny Army pre-World War II "G-2" back in Washington.

Roberts had seen the Japanese Army move into Chinese cities in several relatively peaceful occupations. In such a situation, its tactic was to break down any bit of Chinese morale and strength of character that remained by flooding the civilian population with heroin, opium, and lesser drugs, made cheap and easy for all. "You could smell opium all through the streets. It hangs in the air, not overpowering but always there." Roberts had also seen the Japanese Army on the rampage. He and the others knew what the capture of Nanking could be like. The heavy fighting coming up the Yangtze Valley would not have put the conquerors in a conciliatory mood. When the Chinese war had first started in the summer, the Western powers—as well as the Japanese —had expected Chinese resistance to cave in quickly. But the resistance had been surprisingly stiff and stubborn. One Western newsman likened the Japanese Army to a fist striking into the heart of China. But the fist did not meet another fist. Instead it seemed to stab into a pot of glue. It was pushing in, all right. But the farther it went in, the more effectively it was surrounded by the glue.

Admiring Western comment on the effectiveness of Chinese resistance and the slow Japanese progress seemed to infuriate the invaders. They reacted by showing new ruthlessness and savagery whenever they took a stoutly defended objective.

In Nanking there seemed to be no plan by the Chinese to evacuate the city and spare it from this savagery. During November the gates in the North, East, and South Walls had been slowly sealed up with massive stone and mortar works. The West Gate, the one nearest the river, remained open for the last-minute evacuees. The walls themselves, 45 feet

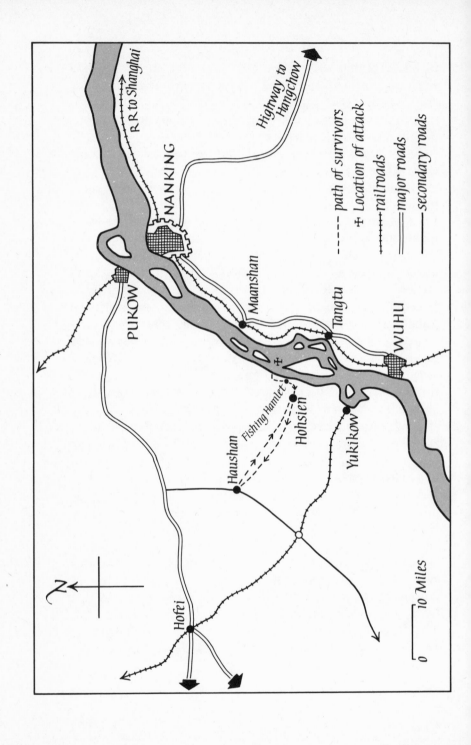

high and about 25 to 30 feet thick in most places, were dotted with newly constructed pillboxes, bombproofs for the defending troops, and gun emplacements. The Chinese general left in charge was drilling his defenders for a last-ditch, suicide defense of the city. Everyone knew this defense had to fail. Roberts had seen in other Chinese battles the pattern of what would take place next. As the attackers closed in, some of those "suicide troops," sworn to die in that last-ditch defense, would change their minds, shuck their uniforms for the flapping jackets and trousers of coolies, and melt away into the night. Often a fair share of their officers, particularly the senior ones, would already be on the road ahead of them. Once the city was stripped of defending troops, with the Japanese nearing the walls, and with the knowledge that a terrible bloodbath was likely to come, the fatalistic Chinese mind would start to work. The reasoning went like this: Those remaining would figure that in 48 hours they might all be dead anyway. And yet all around them was left some of the wealth that they could never have. The rich and powerful merchants and government officials had taken what they could take, closed up their houses and stores, and fled. Inside those houses and stores were things to eat, things to take, things simply to smash and soil in anger and defeat. The mob would take over. There would be no one to stop them. There would be looting, rape, drunkenness—until the Japanese broke through. Then it would begin again when the enemy started after what little was left, infuriated, more than likely, because the Chinese had beat them to it.

In any event, it would be a difficult and dangerous week or ten days. Atcheson had orders, as soon as it was certain that the Japanese were pressing their attack into Nanking, to round up all Americans who would go, close down the embassy, and take refuge aboard *Panay*.

By December the air raids occurred almost daily. All precautions were being taken. *Panay* now carried two large

American flags painted on the awnings that covered the spacious fore and aft "palm gardens." Under way or at anchor she flew her "Sunday flag," the largest ensign in her flag locker. At night all those flags were lighted so they could be seen from ashore or aloft. The myth of protective neutrality still hung on from courtlier days of warfare. And *Panay*, well marked and lighted, was considered a safe refuge—so much so that Chinese shipping tended to squeeze menacingly close to the gunboat when raid alarms sounded. An ungainly black Chinese river ferry had the annoying habit of steaming up and dropping anchor alongside *Panay* whenever the Japanese Air Force appeared overhead; the Americans were less afraid of the bombs hitting them than they were of being rammed. Soon the Japanese aim would get much better.

4

"One suitcase, one bedding roll"

On DECEMBER 2, Atcheson had sent around coolie messengers with a circular to all Americans in Nanking whose whereabouts he knew:

THE EMBASSY HAS ISSUED REPEATED WARNINGS TO AMERICANS OF THE INCREASING DANGER TO THOSE WHO REMAIN IN NANKING. UNDER TELEGRAPHIC INSTRUCTIONS FROM THE DEPARTMENT OF STATE, THIS CIRCULAR IS ISSUED AS A FULL WARNING TO ALL AMERICANS THAT THEY SHOULD WITHDRAW FROM NANKING AS SOON AS POSSIBLE AND PROCEED UP THE RIVER TO A PLACE OF GREATER SAFETY.

THE EMBASSY WOULD BE GRATEFUL IF EACH AMERICAN IN NANKING WOULD INDICATE ON THE ACCOMPANYING SHEET WHETHER HE IS PLANNING TO LEAVE THE CITY BY ARRANGEMENT INDEPENDENT OF THE EMBASSY, OR WHETHER HE DESIRES TO TAKE REFUGE ON THE "U.S.S. PANAY" WHEN ADVISED TO DO SO BY THE EMBASSY, PROBABLY WITHIN THE NEXT FEW DAYS.

IT SHOULD BE NOTED THAT IN AN EMERGENCY IT MAY BE NECESSARY FOR THE NAVAL VESSEL TO MOVE OUT OF RANGE OF ARTILLERY IN ORDER TO PROTECT THOSE TAKING REFUGE ON BOARD AND THAT ACCORDINGLY THOSE WHO DO NOT EMBARK WITH THE MAIN BODY OF AMERICANS MAY LATER FIND DIFFI-

CULTY IN REACHING THE VESSEL. IT SHOULD ALSO BE BORNE IN
MIND THAT IF FIGHTING OCCURS NEAR NANKING EGRESS FROM
THE CITY GATES WILL PROBABLY BE IMPOSSIBLE.

FOR THE AMBASSADOR
(SIGNED) GEORGE ATCHESON, JR.
SECOND SECRETARY OF EMBASSY

The Americans who were left to receive Atcheson's circular
were a small, hardy group: some Standard Oil personnel who
managed ships and facilities in the area, a few ruggedly inde-
pendent businessmen who had stayed behind to try to protect investments that could not be easily shipped out of the
way of the war, and a handful of correspondents and photographers. They had quartered themselves out around the town
in areas where they felt they might be relatively safe from
Japanese bombs. But whereas in Shanghai the Japanese had
appeared to be making a decided effort to restrict their air
attacks to legitimate military targets, the results of Japanese
carelessness—or designed harassment—were beginning to show
in Nanking. The bombing seemed suddenly erratic. The
places that promised relative safety were becoming fewer and
fewer. On the night of December 1, the Hotel Metropolitan,
the city's best, owned and managed by a German syndicate,
had been badly hit. Almost 50 people were killed. As a result
of the increasing danger and to help avoid an embarrassing
incident, the Italian embassy was ordered to close on instruction of the Duce himself.

On December 4 there was a particularly heavy raid on
Nanking's Pukow railroad yards just across the river to the
northwest of the city. Norman Alley, a Universal newsreel
cameraman, was one of the correspondents who headed for the
scene. Alley had covered murders, gang wars, world wars,
disasters. But he was sickened by what he saw. He described
it later in his book *I Witness:*

We ferried across the river on a sampan putt-putt and wormed our way, adroitly, into the walled enclosure of this great Chinese railroad terminal, where we saw coolie, merchant, and mandarin rubbing common shoulders as they groped aimlessly about like bees on a hive in honeytime.

I lensed here, there, and here again, piecing together a neutral's-eye view of this mad exodus, this broken retreat from hell. With Joe [his Chinese driver] at my elbow, I wandered a half mile down the tracks, what was left of them, making pictures as I went. It was here that I made a picture of a scene that I shall never forget to my dying day. A coolie widow, with an infant clutched to her breast, is squatted and wailing away beside her dead husband, while her young son of seven years or so, realizing the futility of remaining, pleads in vain for his mother to come away from it all.

This was representative of hundreds of mothers about me, who, driven to the primitive and elemental emotions, clutched their young to them, beneath shielding arms and their own bodies, threatening to claw and bite, with the full fury of wildcats, anyone who might venture dangerously near. A still picture of the incident was given farflung publication. It justly incensed people throughout the civilized world.

Suddenly, from out of the west, came some Japanese war planes. Were these godless ruins we were now standing in the midst of, just the evidence of practice slaughter? Evidently so! For now these returning planes swooped low as their machine guns spat deadly fire, and proceeded to strafe everything left living.

The wretched fugitives didn't have a Chinaman's chance. Hemmed in this high-walled box canyon, herded like sheep on a slaughterhouse runway, they jostled and struggled. It was a mad nightmare, Grand Guignol on a wholesale scale, as back would swing the planes, again and again, death-dealing pendulums. Innocents ran screaming and stumbled, dying, over already smoldering bodies.

Joe and I dropped back to avoid the full fury of the stampede. Once, a half-mad coolie made a wild lunge at me, thinking my hand camera, which was shouldered up to my eyes in shooting position and beaded on him, was some sort of a machine gun. Joe jumped into the breach, yelled something at the poor devil in Chinese, and bowled him aside at the same time. After that little incident, I dropped my camera to my side; made it incon-spicuous.

When the Nipponese fliers had done one of two things—ex-hausted their ammunition, or thought the job was complete enough—they flew away. Now, we watched the long, tedious, and heartbreaking progress of the still living, as they wended their way, literally, over the bodies of the mangled, dying and dead. They were two and three deep in many places, and overlapping. It was more than I could stand, but I *had* to stand it—as we waited, wisely, for the great mass to thin out.

Little by little, Joe and I edged out, cautiously, worked our way out of this canyon of death . . . and we, too, had to step over bodies, and on them!

At dinnertime, I couldn't eat. I had to get out into the air, and I walked alone. I stopped in at the Navy Club and the best in the house took a thorough beating. I don't remember walking back to the Italian Embassy, nor do I remember going to bed; but, thank God, for a few hours at least, I was able to forget the slaughter of the innocents at Pukow.

Before the end of that terrible day, Alley and the other Americans were warned by the embassy that evacuation might come within a matter of hours. Chinese units were retreating fast.

EMBASSY OF THE
UNITED STATES OF AMERICA
NANKING, DECEMBER 4, 1937

CONFIDENTIAL:

THE EMBASSY CONSIDERS IT ADVISABLE AT THIS TIME TO WARN AMERICANS WHO ARE PLANNING TO BOARD THE "U.S.S. PANAY" THAT THEY SHOULD BE PREPARED TO EVACUATE AT SHORT NOTICE. THE EMBASSY HOPES THAT THE EVACUATION MAY BE EXECUTED WITH AS LITTLE INCONVENIENCE AS POSSIBLE AND, BARRING A SUDDEN EMERGENCY, WILL ATTEMPT TO NOTIFY AMERICANS SEVERAL HOURS IN ADVANCE. SINCE DECISION TO EVACUATE AT A PARTICULAR TIME MAY DEPEND UPON VARYING

FACTORS, INCLUDING CONDITIONS IN THE CITY, COMPLETE PREP-
ARATIONS FOR EMERGENCY EVACUATION SHOULD BE MADE AS A
PRECAUTIONARY MEASURE. DUE TO LACK OF SPACE, THE COM-
MANDING OFFICER OF THE "U.S.S. PANAY" HAS NECESSARILY
LIMITED BAGGAGE TO ONE SUITCASE AND ONE BEDDING ROLL PER
PERSON. NO EXTRA BEDDING IS AVAILABLE ON THE "PANAY" AND
IT IS ESSENTIAL THAT EACH AMERICAN TAKE SUFFICIENT BED-
DING, INCLUDING BLANKETS, SHEETS AND PILLOW.

RELIABLE REPORTS INDICATE THAT SOME CHINESE UNITS FROM
THE CHINKIANG-TANYANG-KINTAN-LIYANG-KWANGTEH LINE HAVE
RETREATED TO A POINT NOT FAR EAST OF CHUYUNG (KUYUNG).
THIS DEVELOPMENT MAY MAKE EVACUATION TO THE NAVAL
VESSEL ADVISABLE BY TOMORROW.

The following day the final order came to assemble on the
bund, the vast trading embankment that ran along the edge of
the river:

EMBASSY OF THE
UNITED STATES OF AMERICA
NANKING, DECEMBER 5, 1937

THE EMBASSY CONSIDERS IT INADVISABLE THAT AMERICANS RE-
MAIN LONGER IN NANKING. ALL AMERICANS ARE URGED TO
FOREGATHER AT THE EMBASSY WEST COMPOUND TOMORROW
MORNING, MONDAY, DECEMBER 6, AT 9:30 A.M., TO PROCEED IN
A GROUP TO THE BUND AND EMBARK ON THE "U.S.S. PANAY".
AS PREVIOUSLY STATED, EACH INDIVIDUAL SHOULD TAKE BEDDING,
AND BAGGAGE IS LIMITED TO ONE SUITCASE PER PERSON. THE
EMBASSY WILL APPRECIATE PROMPT ACKNOWLEDGMENT, BY
TELEPHONE, OF THE RECEIPT OF THIS NOTIFICATION, IN ORDER
THAT MOTOR CAR TRANSPORTATION MAY BE ARRANGED FOR
THOSE REQUIRING IT.

A heavy thunderstorm broke over Nanking that night. It
was hard to tell the sound of thunder from the sound of
bombs. But the next morning the sun shone through clearly,
and a little group of half a dozen Americans gathered at the

embassy, each with a bedroll and a single suitcase, ready to transfer to *Panay*. The transfer was made without incident and Commander Hughes told his new passengers that although they should remain on the ship each night, they would have an opportunity to go ashore on business during the day, as long as the situation did not get considerably worse. For the time being the gunboat would stay anchored as she was, just off shore and in sight of the embassy compound.

The civilians were assigned sleeping space in the few spare bunks and in various compartments where a bed or two could be improvised. They were briefed by the ship's officers on what was expected of them during their time aboard and what they could expect in return. The instructions were basic and simple. Meals would be served on schedule and only then. There was to be no liquor broken out on board, regardless of what might be smuggled on the ship from any civilian supply. And during drills, alarms, and the regular routine of ship's business, the new arrivals were urged to stay clear of the crew, guns, passageways, bridge, and engine room. When someone remarked that there was nowhere else to go except bed, one of the *Panay* crew allowed that this was a good solution, too; as civilians, they were lucky they had that alternative.

The stray birds from shore having been nested, the embassy people returned to the compound for another apprehensive day's work. One of the new arrivals followed suit. He was R. W. Squires, an American born in China who was an agent for the China Import and Export Company. Squires had a considerable problem. He had acquired a yardful of lumber in Nanking in the late fall at an advantageous price as the situation had gotten worse. His concern over the lumber made some of his fellow passengers suspect that it was a heavy personal speculation that could make him or wipe him out. Apparently he had been betting on an early truce in the war and a quick return to what passed in China as normalcy. The odds on the bet were changing fast. As the Japanese approached, Squires made a roundabout contact with the invading authorities to try to make a sale. But the Japanese weren't buying anything they could reasonably expect to own as "spoils of war" in a few weeks at the most. The Chinese weren't interested either. The Chinese commanders at Nanking were already making long lists of useful supplies in the city they would have to destroy just before it was overrun. But the lumber tycoon wasn't giving up. He had a salesman's initiative and an American's drive. And as soon as *Panay*'s officer of the deck had finished his briefing, Squires was headed for shore to pursue a new scheme to find a buyer.

Two other Americans, who would eventually take refuge on *Panay* and play significant parts in the events to follow, also headed ashore soon after the briefing. They were newsmen. And they had come aboard that morning only to cover the evacuation story. Both intended at the time to ride out the occupation in Nanking, in spite of the urging of Atcheson. Norman Alley, who had filmed the terrible Pukow railroad station bombing, was a Chicago-born newsreel cameraman who had studied the business in a tough school. Alley had wanted to be a straight reporter. But early in the game he was struck by the photographer's better chance for carrying off big bylines by snapping a few pictures at the right time. Alley had learned his trade on the Chicago *Tribune*, had gotten shot at in that peaceful city more than once, had covered the expedition to capture the bandit Villa in Mexico, had flown the dawn patrol on the Western Front with Eddie Rickenbacker, had survived the hectic postwar years in Chicago under William Randolph Hearst, a demanding and unpredictable boss who used Alley as a combination troubleshooter and court photographer for the weddings and social rumbles of Hearst's influential coast-to-coast coterie of film stars and socialites. Alley's companion in Nanking was James

Marshall from Seattle, Far Eastern correspondent for *Collier's* magazine.

Marshall was a freelance writer who had been traveling in Japan when the Chinese war broke out. He had immediately applied to go to the battle area around Shanghai. The Japanese preferred to manage the news as well as they could and promptly put Marshall on a boat back to Seattle. The minute his ship had docked on the West Coast, he had flown south to Alameda Island in San Francisco Bay, eastern terminus of the *China Clipper*, and had booked passage back to China. The thousand-mile trip from Tokyo to Shanghai had taken him 13,000 miles out of his way. On the way out on the *Clipper*, Marshall and Alley had met, had sealed their incorporation with a pint of Scotch 10,000 feet over the Pacific, and had been traveling through China together. Both had a nose for news. But their biggest scoop would come when they thought they were going to miss it—in the next few days while they were fretting aboard *Panay* about being walled off from the capture of Nanking and what they thought was the war story of a lifetime.

On the way to *Panay* the morning of the evacuation Alley had shot film of the Americans waiting at the river's edge with their pitiful little bedrolls and suitcases amid the confusion of the Nanking waterfront. Then his camera picked up the sharp, white silhouette of *Panay* in midstream, showing the launches pulling alongside and the crisply uniformed United States sailors helping the evacuees come aboard to safety through a gleaming mahogany boarding gangway that bore a ferocious United States eagle carved on each side. The flag snapped out overhead. Aboard ship Alley moved about above decks and below, setting up a few staged shots that he had in mind to intersperse later with the film he hoped to get when the Japanese took the city. To create the feeling of action, sailors were asked to man the signal flags and lights, men ran to their battle stations, and machine gunners—still in their fresh-pressed blue uniforms—trained their weapons at imaginary targets. The men thought it was a lark. And Alley made a note to cable the film editors in San Francisco to be careful to edit out any shots that showed anyone laughing or horsing around in the background. Marshall talked with the officers to get the background material he needed about the ship and its mission. They all had some good Navy coffee and small talk in the tiny wardroom. Everyone the correspondents talked to seemed to be trying to plug his own name and home town, in hopes he might show up in a *Collier's* dispatch back to the States or flash for a moment of fame on the darkened screen at the Bijou between the Saturday night double features.

After about an hour, Alley and Marshall headed for shore. They were armed with some film, some notes, and a borrowed American flag to stretch over the top of their 1932 Chevrolet, which had been bought from the German embassy and still carried a large black swastika painted in a white circle on the roof. Embassy secretary Atcheson and military attaché Frank Roberts glared at the two strays from the rail of *Panay*; every time Atcheson apparently had collected all his chickens in one place, they would start to stray again.

With the United States embassy closed, in effect, the American correspondents were invited next door to bed down in the Italian embassy building that had been evacuated some time before. The hosts were Herbert Ros, an Italian vice-consul who had remained behind, and two Italian newsmen, Luigi Barzini and Sandro Sandri. Ros was a stiff little man who kept largely to himself; his father was an important figure in the Italian diplomatic service. Sandri, representing the Italian paper *La Stampa*, had an international reputation as a war correspondent. He was often called the Floyd Gibbons of Italy. He had fought in the 1914-18 War, had covered the rough street battles and maneuvers of the Fascist takeover in Italy, and had traveled with the Italian Army during the Ethiopian Campaign. Barzini was the son of a famous Italian war correspondent for whom he had been named. He was on assignment in China for Milan's *Corriere Della Sera* newspaper. Barzini spoke fluent English; he had graduated from the Columbia University School of Journalism seven years before. Sandri spoke nothing but Italian, was a staunch Fascist. Even in the presence of his older and more famous companion, Barzini made no attempt to hide his sympathies, which were obviously for the Chinese and the Americans. At the same time he could see his country was drifting slowly toward an alliance with Japan.

Because of his facility with the language and his easygoing personality, it was natural for Barzini to make friends with the easygoing American newsmen. He towed Sandri behind him. Once they moved away from any Italian-speaking community, Sandri had to depend on Barzini's linguistic ability to get much of his story.

The American newsmen were delighted to share quarters with Sandri, Barzini, and Ros. In addition to Norman Alley and Jim Marshall, two other Americans had moved into the old Italian embassy building. They were Arthur Menken of Paramount News and Eric Mayell of Fox Movietone. It was a lively and congenial group, in spite of the fact that the men were all essentially competitors. And the quarters were reasonably comfortable and extremely spacious. Luigi Barzini still remembers those last few days of "peace" with some nostalgia.:

The embassy had been evacuated long before. It contained a lot of furniture. This had belonged to an Italian Naval Mission which had instructed the Chinese Navy and had left a while before, and to some departed Catholic missionaries. We therefore had all the beds and mattresses we needed. We also had a lot of servants, all the original Italian embassy servants, plus a vague number who joined us every day and for whom we made armbands with the Italian colors, Chinese lettering (only God knows what it said), stamps, and our signatures. The armbands were supposed to save their bearers from being recruited by the Chinese to work on fortifications. The cook was excellent. All the servants from the other abandoned embassies sold us whatever stores had been left behind. I remember we had an enormous lot of raisins from Greece, enough Havana cigars to last a year, champagne, cognac, and tins of many things. Sandri spent his days reading holy books from the Catholic mission's library, lying on an Italian naval officer's bed; he ate raisins, drank champagne or brandy, and smoked cigars. Our only contact with the outside world was a very efficient long-distance telephone line to Hankow. It carried our voices thousands of miles through war-torn Chinese provinces. One asked for a number and got it in a matter of minutes. I remember I always asked for "urgent" communication, at triple rate. Who paid the bill? Good Scotch and gin could still be obtained. The total effect was a relative peace and plenty in the middle of the confusion, panic, and devastation. There would only be a few more days of it.

On December 9, the reporters received the last official communication sent by the Nanking embassy to the Americans who had elected to stay:

EMBASSY OF THE
UNITED STATES OF AMERICA
NANKING, DECEMBER 9, 1937

TO AMERICANS IN NANKING:

THE AMERICAN EMBASSY HAS RECEIVED A TELEGRAM FROM THE AMERICAN CONSUL GENERAL AT SHANGHAI, STATING THAT THE SENIOR CONSUL AT SHANGHAI HAS RECEIVED A COMMUNICATION FROM THE JAPANESE CONSUL GENERAL WHICH, IN SUBSTANCE, STATES THAT IT IS THE EARNEST WISH OF THE JAPANESE FORCES THAT ALL FOREIGN NATIONALS NOW REMAINING IN NANKING SHOULD STAY AWAY FROM THE ZONE OF ACTUAL FIGHTING BY EVACUATING THAT CITY WITHOUT DELAY.

THE EMBASSY HAS TELEGRAPHED, FOR COMMUNICATION TO THE JAPANESE AUTHORITIES AT SHANGHAI AND TOKYO, A LIST

OF THE NAMES AND ADDRESSES OF THE EIGHTEEN AMERICAN
CITIZENS NOW IN THE CITY WITH THE REQUEST THAT THE JAPAN-
ESE AUTHORITIES AFFORD THESE AMERICANS APPROPRIATE PRO-
TECTION AND FACILITIES IN CASE OF NEED.

The message was alarming. But the next day dawned on
relative quiet—and some of the alarmists thought they had
been just that. Then came one of the strangest incidents of
the whole siege of Nanking. The city seemed calmer than it
had been, though the stream of refugees going toward the
Hsiakuan Gate, the only remaining exit from Nanking, was
heavy. General T'ang Sheng-chih had warned the city that
he could not guarantee that the gate would remain open after
3 P.M. Suddenly from the northwest came the sound of aircraft engines. It was not the sharp, clean beat of a single
plane but the heavy, oppressive drone of a large formation of
aircraft. The air-raid sirens screamed with their doleful,
doomed wail. The Chinese in the streets scurried for shelter,
except for a few who were so numbed and tired and shell-
shocked that they had to be driven to cover by the auxiliary
police. The few antiaircraft guns still available cranked around,
elevated, and got ready to fire. Then as the spotting officers
on the northwest wall were calling out the first ranges, bearings, and elevations, one sharp-eyed officer spotted the large
red Russian star on the wings of each plane.

The word spread quickly through the defensive units. Hold
fire. There were 36 plans in all, twin-engined bombers with
escorting fighters. To the dispirited Chinese defenders below,
the meaning of this armada was simple. By some miracle, the
Russians had suddenly entered the war to save them. The
planes circled the city, spectacularly low. Some of the squadron leaders dipped their wings and then the aircraft broke
formation and went into a series of spectacular maneuvers.
From the antiaircraft units cheers went up here and there.
The people in the shelters, hearing no bombs but conscious
of the uneven tempo of the stunting engines so close over-

head, were edging out of the shelters. Then, on some signal above, the squadron reformed, made a wide circle around to the northeast of the city and headed back toward Russia.

The Chinese were mystified. It was a cruel trick—and a mercenary one. As the American correspondents found out later, the planes were Russian all right, scheduled for eventual delivery to the Russian Air Force. But they had been flown to Nanking as sales bait, part of a weird Russian scheme to tempt the Chinese government to buy aircraft from the Soviets. The Russians had picked their market poorly. Most of the high Chinese officials still left in Nanking would be dead within a few days, either in the final attack or in the rape of the city that would follow. It was no time to try to make a sale.

By Saturday, December 11, the situation around the city had deteriorated badly. The Chinese Army's last-man brigade seemed to be dwindling in troops and in resolve. The auxiliary police were completely ineffective and disorganized. Secretary Atcheson made one last swing through the international section, asking the few remaining Americans to change their minds and come aboard the gunboat. He stopped where Alley, Marshall, and the others were staying and pounded at the front door. From an upstairs window, the Americans watched him but played possum. If they stayed they did not want Atcheson to feel the responsibility was on his hands. They needed time to decide. They watched the embassy man move on, then called a huddle. If they wanted to, Alley, Marshall, Menken, and Mayell could go aboard *Panay* with no problem. They were not so sure about the Italians. But the Americans did not want to leave Sandri and Barzini behind. And the Italian Embassy in Hankow had telephoned, asking Barzini, Sandri, and Ros to clear out, to avoid the chance of any embarrassing incident with the Japanese. Reports were coming in of the harsh treatment Japanese troops were handing out to civilians in the path of their advance. Foreign nationality seemed to make little difference to the commanders in the field, regardless of what promises the generals and the diplomats made in Shanghai and Tokyo. Now with the gunboat about to move four or five miles upstream to stay clear of stray shells and bombs it was fish or cut bait. Though all the newsmen wanted to be on hand for the big story, their home offices had advised that they didn't want anyone to die getting it. After a long discussion, with Barzini doing the translation for Sandri, five of the six decided they had better go aboard the gunboat. Menken elected to stay. A flurry of wires from Nanking to Hankow and Shanghai finally obtained the necessary permissions to take Sandri, Barzini, and Ros aboard.

The reporters packed most of their small possessions. A few things were left behind, but none of the men was too optimistic about seeing them again; if the Japanese didn't loot the house, they figured Chinese stragglers would. Everything to be taken was loaded into Alley's old Chevrolet, with the Stars and Stripes now covering the swastika on the dented top. They started off toward the bund with Alley's Chinese driver at the wheel.

Alley still remembers the trip, the mob in the street, the despair, and the confusion. "We darn near had to drive up over the backs of the people to get to the river." On the way they spotted Squires, the lumber merchant. At the last minute Squires had arranged with a British river freighter to carry his lumber upriver to Hankow. But he was having a devil of a time getting the lumber from the yard to the river. Alley recalled:

There he stood in the middle of the mad traffic and as busy as a tobacco auctioneer. The street was loused up by his coolies lugging his two-by-fours on their shoulders. . . . Squires had much lumber that he wanted to have moved, very little labor that wanted to move it. It was comical to watch him singing mammy songs in pidgin English as he offered triple and quadruple wages to any Chinese passerby who looked as if he had a strong back.

The three American newsmen, along with Sandri, Barzini, and Ros, said good-by to Arthur Menken at the bund, got into a launch that was waiting there, and headed out to the gunboat. It was already some distance from the heart of the city. During the raid on the Pukow railroad yards that Alley had covered, several bombs had fallen near *Panay*'s anchorage. And several days later Hughes had moved upstream to a safer spot off a section of the city called San Chia Ho. There was a telephone in the Allied Petroleum Corporation installation there by which Hughes had been able to keep in touch with Atcheson at the embassy. Almost as soon as the newsmen climbed aboard with their gear, the order came to prepare to get *Panay* underway. Some shelling had started from the south bank of the river. Splashes and explosions were clearly evident along the north shore near where *Panay* was anchored. Between *Panay* and shore were three large Standard Oil river tankers, several Chinese steamers resting perilously low in the water with heavy loads of refugees, and two British gunboats, HMS *Scarab* and HMS *Cricket*. Army Captain Roberts thought the shells came from Chinese artillery searching the north riverbank for Japanese scouting parties that were reported to be operating there. But when the near misses were repeated, Commander Hughes decided it was Japanese fire sent over to annoy the ships and force them away from the Nanking area so the attack could proceed without any restriction. Before the whole flotilla could move, there ensued a weird "after you, no after *you*" situation with the American and the British commanders each signaling to the other to get underway first. It was something of a point of naval one-upmanship. With the British gunboats most endangered by the shells, Hughes waited for *Cricket* and *Scarab* to start up-river ahead of him. He was prepared to stay behind until the area was cleared, to pick up any casualities in case there was a chance hit among the merchant ships. But the British stood on ceremony. After repeated semaphore messages back and forth, with even the stilted "beg to suggests" of naval language getting a little impatient toward the end, Hughes finally gave up and ordered *Panay*'s anchor raised. It was 5 P.M. Atcheson ordered a message sent advising Shanghai of the move.

Just before she gathered way, lumberman Squires came puffing over the side from a water taxi. A sailor pulled him to safety as his rented boat skidded out from under him and the gunboat gained way. Squires wore a broad smile. The major share of his lumber was safe on the way upriver to Hankow where the Chinese Government had retreated. As far as he was concerned, the war could go on now any way it wanted to.

George Atcheson stood on deck calling the roll of displaced civilians. On board with him were Weldon James, an Associated Press correspondent from Greenville, South Carolina; Herbert Ros of the Italian embassy; Captain Frank Roberts, military attaché; Luigi Barzini; D. S. Goldie of Standard Oil; J. Hall Paxton, second secretary of the Nanking embassy; Eric Mayell of Fox Movietone; Emile Gassie of New Orleans, code clerk of the Nanking embassy; Sandro Sandri; Norman Soong, a Hawaiian-born Chinese who was a *New York Times* photographer and a United States citizen; James Marshall; Norman Alley; Roy Squires; and Colin M. McDonald, a London *Times* correspondent.

As the long string of ships started upriver in the late afternoon headed by *Panay*, the Americans looked back on the smoking city. "All of us," wrote cameraman Alley a few years later, "stood and watched the burning and sacking of Nanking until we had rounded the bend and saw nothing but a bright red sky silhouetted with clouds and smoke. Looking back at the carnage, I couldn't help but think of Francis Scott Key, when he was detained aboard a British sloop and witnessed the all-night assault on Baltimore's Fort McHenry in the War of 1812."

5

"They're letting go bombs! Get under cover"

THE MOVEMENT UPSTREAM was to be a routine one. Atcheson's 5 P.M. radio message telling of the move had gone to the top State Department officers in Shanghai, Peking, and Hankow. A copy had been routed to the State Department's radio room in Washington for the attention of Secretary of State Cordell Hull. There was no reason to believe that Atcheson's request to have the American embassy in Tokyo notify the Japanese of *Panay*'s new position would not be all that was needed.

Panay had steamed 12 miles upstream from Nanking jetty before anchoring shortly before dusk. The three Standard Oil river tankers had joined her. Their names were Chinese—SS *Mei Ping*, *Mei An*, and *Mei Hsia*—and they were manned by Chinese crews. But their captains were Europeans or Americans. They were run to American standards and were relatively clean, comfortable ships, compared to their Chinese counterparts. A number of Standard Oil shore personnel had taken refuge on them to wait out the capture of Nanking.

Among them were some Standard Oil security guards dressed in dark blue uniforms similar to those of Chinese regulars; this may have started a rumor that would have fatal results. Each of the oil tankers also showed a large American flag. Their silhouettes were not as distinctive as that of *Panay*. So they made a conscious effort to stay away from Chinese shipping and remain near the gunboat. The night passed without incident.

About 7:30 the next morning, the random firing that had troubled them the day before started again. Army Captain Roberts took note of it: "Japanese infantry guns—probably about 37 mm.—from the south shore began shelling a small fleet of junks anchored near the north bank and about half a mile astern of us. I observed some of this shelling in which three junks were hit and set afire, though in general the firing was very poor. Commander Hughes decided to move once more."

The Italian correspondent Luigi Barzini described the fierce artillery attack for his paper, *Corriere Della Sera*, with a strange and frightening beauty:

On the river's left bank, in the transparent mist, ten or twelve junks with exceedingly high, slender masts were anchored next to one another. The Japanese opened fire, gutting them, sinking them one by one. Sandro Sandri watched the scene through binoculars and observed what seemed to be a strange Chinese print: junks suspended between sky and earth in the pale water, quivering, bobbing spasmodically every now and then, dissolving into tiny pieces.

At 9 A.M. *Panay* raised anchor and headed upriver again against the sluggish current. *Mei Ping*, *Mei An*, and *Mei Hsia* followed. The convoy had been underway only about an hour when Hughes was flagged from the north bank of the river by a Japanese Army unit. The particulars of the message that the Japanese signalman was trying to put across with his nervously wig-wagging flags were not clear. But when Hughes spotted a stubby Japanese field piece being skewed around and trained on the gunboat, the tone of the message seemed clear. The captain ordered engines stopped. He did not anchor or make any attempt to move in toward the shore but simply let the ship slowly lose way against the current in the middle of the channel.

Shortly a motor landing boat put out from the group on shore with a party of soldiers aboard and headed for *Panay*. Hughes and his executive officer, Tex Anders, watched from the bridge, giving one engine and then the other a few revolutions at a time just to keep *Panay* in position in the middle of the channel. Crewmen who were not on duty formed in curious knots along the rail aft, but the word was passed that all hands should stand clear of the gangway and none of the crew should make any attempt to communicate with the Japanese when they came alongside. When the landing boat pulled close to the starboard gangway, Hughes could count about 20 infantrymen, a noncommissioned officer, and a lieutenant in the boat. A heavy machine gun was mounted on a swivel in the bow behind a steel shield. The lieutenant hailed the gunboat in pidgin English and said he was coming aboard. The fact that he didn't request permission galled Captain Roberts particularly: "No armed party comes aboard a United States warship unless they're asked." But the Army man was just a supernumerary on board and held his tongue. Hughes ignored the Japanese officer's rudeness. He and Anders put it down to a combination of ignorance and a poor command of English. Hughes was known for something of a quick temper, but he sat on his anger this time. "I had special orders from the Commander Yangtze Patrol," he explained at the court of inquiry, "not to be too sensitive about points of naval etiquette when dealing with the Japanese military—and above all else, to use my judgment in avoiding such complications as might arise." If there was to be an incident, the Americans were not going to start it. Hughes and Atcheson met the Japanese as he came up over the side. He was a fairly short man, made to look even more bulky by a wide-belted, mustard-colored overcoat. A pistol hung at his waist.

Like many Japanese officers, the lieutenant could speak little English, but he seemed to be able to write it with more ease. On a small pad he wrote "Where are you going?" Hughes wrote his answer, identifying *Panay* as an American gunboat assigned to protect United States merchant ships in that sector of the river. Then the officer demanded to know what Chinese troops and ships the *Panay* had seen and where they had been located. Hughes answered firmly, then wrote it out. The United States, he explained, speaking slowly and enunciating clearly so that the Japanese might be able to pick up his words, was a friend to both China and Japan and could take no part in furthering the military operations of either side; he could not answer the question. The Japanese seemed unsure what he should do next. Could he inspect all the ships of the convoy to assure himself there were no Chinese troops aboard? The captain refused. Would the captain come ashore with him, presumably to see a superior? Again Hughes refused; this time his temper was beginning to simmer. Norman Alley, who was standing nearby, said Hughes then seemed to draw his short frame up "until he was about nine feet tall." "And now," the captain said, "would you kindly leave my deck."

There was a rumor in American papers later that Hughes had slapped the Japanese officer's face and had him thrown over the side to swim ashore. But there were no such dramactics. With no show of emotion and no apology or word of departure, the Japanese landing party returned to its boat and shoved off for shore. On the north bank, where they had come from, three other armed boats were now visible. The crew of the artillery piece still stood by, but less militantly. On the bridge, Anders rung for both engines to go ahead and

Panay headed upriver again. "At no time," Commander Hughes testified later, "did the Japanese indicate we were proceeding into any danger zone." Nor was there any indication from the Japanese that *Panay* should turn back.

The Japanese shore party was soon out of sight. The soldiers appeared to have no more interest in the gunboat. But now at least one Japanese unit knew the American convoy was in the area. If they had had a radio, they could have passed the word to field headquarters. Probably they did. The message could have served two purposes: to warn all Japanese military units to be careful because neutral shipping was in range— or to pinpoint that same convoy for attack.

About 11 A.M. *Panay* reached a spot in the river known as the Hohsien Cutoff. It was about 15 miles above the anchorage of the previous night and 27 miles above the Nanking customs jetty. Here the river runs almost north and south and is divided by a series of islands. Vessels headed upstream will soon have to turn almost due southeast to reach the town of Tangtu. Or, to save time, ships may take a westerly channel, cutting off Tangtu, and proceed on to Wuhu. An island known to the Americans as May Queen is the first of several islands that a ship approaches going upriver. The ground on the east bank of the Yangtze at this point is firm and rises up to a series of low hills immediately beyond the track of the Nanking-Wuhu railroad, which parallels the water. But on the west side of the Yangtze there are large patches of marshland close to the water's edge, covered with ten-foot-tall seas of reeds, each reed about as thick as a bamboo fishing pole. The reeds rise out of the mud of the marshland like a young forest. Except for what cover the reedy areas supply, the ground is open on both sides of the river with no foliage that might hide troops. Hughes could scan the territory on both sides of the river with his powerful 7 x 50 binoculars. There was no sign of military activity—Chinese or Japanese. It seemed a safe place to anchor. *Panay*'s hook

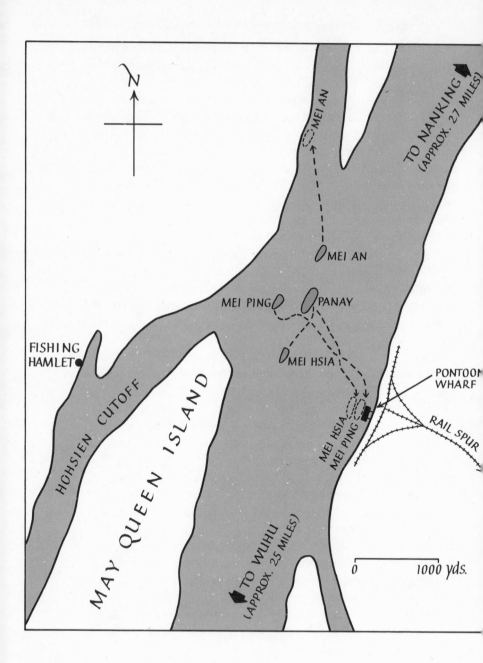

went down into about 45 feet of water. Bearings taken on points on shore showed she was just out of the channel, favoring the west bank of the Yangtze. May Queen Island was about 1,000 yards ahead. *Mei Hsia* moved ahead of the gunboat about 500 yards and anchored. *Mei An* took up a similar position astern. The third Standard Oiler, *Mei Ping*, moved in close off *Panay*'s starboard bow and anchored. A party from *Panay* had been invited aboard the last named ship for the afternoon and there would be less distance for launches to travel back and forth.

As soon as the gunboat was anchored, Atcheson advised the consulate in Shanghai and the embassies in Hankow and Peking of the ship's position. And again he requested that the Japanese be informed; he reported in the message they might have to move again. And he was already worried about getting back to Nanking to assist the handful of Americans who had remained there:

SHELL FIRE AT NINE OCLOCK THIS MORNING CAUSED THE PANAY TO MOVE FARTHER UPSTREAM AND VESSEL IS NOW ANCHORED TWENTY SEVEN MILES ABOVE NANKING AT MILEAGE TWO TWENTY ONE ABOVE WOOSUNG. STANDARD OIL COMPANYS STEAMERS MEI PING, MEI AN, AND MEI HSIA ARE ANCHORED NEARBY.

AS FROM THIS EMBASSY PLEASE INFORM JAPANESE EMBASSY OF PRESENT POSITION OF PANAY AND AMERICAN MERCHANT VESSELS NAMED, AND REQUEST THAT APPROPRIATE INSTRUCTIONS BE ISSUED TO JAPANESE FORCES. PLEASE ADD THAT CIRCUMSTANCES MAY AGAIN CAUSE PANAY TO MOVE EITHER UP OR DOWN RIVER AND THAT PANAY EXPECTS TO RETURN DOWN RIVER TO NANKING AS SOON AS FEASIBLE IN ORDER TO REESTABLISH COMMUNICATION WITH AMERICANS WHO REMAINED IN NANKING AND IN ORDER THAT THIS EMBASSY MAY AS SOON AS PRACTICABLE RESUME ITS FUNCTIONS ASHORE. PLEASE STATE THAT THE AMERICAN EMBASSY HOPES THAT APPROPRIATE STEPS TO FACILITATE THIS PLAN WILL BE TAKEN BY ALL FOUR AUTHORITIES WHO MAY BE CONCERNED.

SENT TO SHANGHAI, REPEATED TO DEPARTMENT HANKOW, PE-
KING. PEKING PLEASE REPEAT TO TOKYO WITH REQUEST THAT
EMBASSY TOKYO COMMUNICATE TO JAPANESE FOREIGN OFFICE.

ATCHESON

Then all hands settled down to wait out Japanese capture of the city they had left.

Sunday dinner on U.S. Navy ships, wherever they are afloat, is like Sunday dinner back home, the big meal of the day. And out of range of the Nanking bombardment, there was the time and the inclination of the *Panay*'s cooks to turn out a particularly good dinner.

With all the visitors to serve, the meal, which started at noon, took somewhat longer than usual. But nobody had anything particular to rush through it for. Even Sandri—who was particularly dubious about American food and would question Barzini suspiciously about the content of each dish—ate heartily. About one o'clock Captain Frank Roberts, Dr. Grazier, and the *Collier's* correspondent, Jim Marshall, went over to *Mei Ping* to listen to the scheduled Shanghai radio news broadcast. *Panay*'s equipment was busy on Navy frequencies. Chief Machinist Mate Vernon R. Puckett and Chief Pharmacist Mate Thomas A. Coleman had taken a small party of men over to *Mei Ping* "on liberty" to set up a temporary "Navy club" where the men could enjoy a few bottles of cold beer. *Mei Ping*, not being Navy property, could serve as legal repository for the brew bought by a slush fund the crew had contributed. It wasn't exactly Ship Street in Hong Kong. But it was better than nothing.

The radio news relayed from Shanghai hadn't seemed encouraging, except that it sounded as if the Japanese success was coming so rapidly that *Panay* could head back for Nanking soon. Captain Roberts and Dr. Grazier returned to the gunboat shortly before 1:30 P.M. The Army officer went to his cabin on the port side to complete a War Department report.

Dr. Grazier met cameraman Alley along the deck and the two decided to walk off their dinner. The stewards were still washing mess trays and wardroom dishes. In the radio shack on the upper deck, just aft of Commander Hughes' quarters, Radioman Third Class James T. Murphy had just started a routine transmission to the Patrol flagship, USS *Luzon* in Hankow. Embassy Secretary Atcheson, in the cabin he had been given by Lieutenant Geist, was deep in State Department paperwork. In the best Navy tradition, a number of Navy men were already "sacked out" in various corners of the ship where they weren't likely to be disturbed.

About 1:35 the spotter on the bridge passed the word down to Commander Hughes that planes were in sight high overhead. They were coming from a southeasterly direction. They could have been Chinese. While the captain was on his way to the bridge, the spotter had a chance for a closer look. He concentrated on a flight of three machines. Bombers, from the size of them. They were too high to make out any insignia. Hughes picked up his uniform cap and headed for the bridge with Chief Quartermaster John H. Lang. It was something he had done many times in the past few weeks. But there was obviously less danger of an accident now than there had been in the crowded anchorage off Nanking with Chinese shipping crowded in close around them. As Hughes left his cabin he could see the oversized Stars and Stripes hanging from the gaff at the after mast. There was not much breeze and the flag dangled, limp. He knew, however, that the colors painted across the upper deck awnings fore and aft could be clearly seen.

The captain reached the pilot house, picked up a pair of binoculars, and started the climb to the open bridge above. Now he caught his first clear sight of aircraft. What he saw were about six planes strung out in a line ahead of the ship. The leading three were rapidly losing altitude as they came in toward *Panay*. Almost immediately they appeared to go into power dives. Hughes was alarmed. Lang shouted a warning, "They're letting go bombs! Get under cover." Hughes and Lang ducked back into the pilothouse as the first bomb struck. "It seemed to hit directly overhead," Hughes testified. The time was 1:38 P.M.

6

"No flags were seen . . ."

LIEUTENANT SHIGEHARU MURATA of the Japanese naval air service peered through the windshield of his big, Mitsubishi type 96 bomber at the wide, muddy Yangtze about 11,000 feet below and slightly off to his left. A quick check showed the two other bombers of his flight in position behind and on either side of him. He ordered the three aircraft to open up their formation a bit. If his two wing men had to maneuver to drop their bombs, he did not want a collision. Murata's flight had taken off from the captured airfield at Changchow about 100 miles due east of their current position. Their area of operations that day was like a giant triangle, with their airfield at Changchow marking the right of the triangle's base and the Yangtze River city of Wuhu marking the left. Nanking was at the triangle's apex, with the river running northeast from Wuhu to Nanking where it turned eastward and heads towards Shanghai and the sea.

Stretched out behind Murata's flight were 21 other dive bombers and fighters divided into three groups. They had purposely hit the river near Wuhu, upstream of where they expected to find their targets. Then they had swung right,

parallel to the river, intending to follow it to Nanking. Somewhere between Wuhu and Nanking they knew they would
find what they were looking for.

From the 11,000-foot level the Yangtze Valley looked rich
and peaceful. Only a large pillar of smoke rising up from Nanking about 30 miles off Murata's right wing—and a smaller
column of smoke behind and to the left, from the vicinity
of the highway leading from Wuhu toward the coast—showed
evidence of the war. The fighting was still somewhat remote
to the flyers. Lieutenant Murata had been in China for only
eight days. His unit was part of Rear Admiral Teizo Mitsunami's 2nd Combined Air Group still based in Shanghai. But
parts of the group had just been moved up to Changchow,
halfway between Shanghai and Nanking, to support the attack on the Chinese capital. In the eight days they had been
operating in China, Murata could see the Japanese were in
complete air command in the area. They rarely saw Chinese
planes—or even Japanese Army aircraft, for that matter; Lieutenant General Iwane Matsui, supreme Army Commander,
had only a dozen or so Army planes in the area, all primarily
for use in infantry reconnaissance and artillery spotting. Most
of Murata's action to date had been against ground positions.
In that kind of bombing you were lucky enough to find the
right spot, much less see the enemy. But today's assignment
was better. This was the sort of thing they had all been
trained for. Intelligence had reported that several Chinese
vessels, loaded with troops fleeing Nanking, were pushing upriver above the city. Murata's group and the three behind
him were racing hell-for-leather toward the spot. This was
their first real chance to bomb enemy ships. Each pilot wanted
to get a chance before the targets were obliterated. Murata's
group was winning.

About a mile or so behind him and coming at top speed
were six single-engine biplane dive bombers commanded by
Lieutenant Masatake Okumiya. Early that morning they had

taken off from their base in Shanghai and dive-bombed Chinese positions near Nanking's East Gate, where heavy fighting was taking place. The squadron then had landed at the Changchow field, instead of going all the way back to Shanghai. Once on the ground in Changchow and after seeing to his planes, Okumiya had commandeered a car and headed for Army headquarters to see if he could get information on targets for the next attack. As he was careening along the rough road that circled the airdrome, he almost collided with another staff car coming in a hurry from the other direction. Okumiya was flagged down by the occupant of the other car, Lieutenant Commander Motoharu Okamura, an intelligence officer, who signaled him to turn around and follow at top speed back to the Navy hangars. The news was as good as a pilot could have hoped for, Okumiya wrote later, recalling what happened next:

Arriving at our station, we were informed that an advance Army unit had reported seven large merchant ships and three smaller ones fleeing the capital, loaded to capacity with Chinese troops. They were on the upper reaches of the Yangtze, the most advanced being about twenty miles from Nanking. Ground forces were unable to reach them, and so it was requested that the naval air arm make an attack. It was rumored that a successful attack might earn a unit citation.

The pilots had a short briefing. There was not much more information. No description of the ships. What little intelligence existed had resulted from a telephone call that came in to naval air headquarters from Liuetenant Commander Takeshi Aoki, who was acting as liaison officer with the Japanese army that was charged with the capture of Nanking. Aoki was well known and well liked, was considered to be one of the top officers in the naval air service, and had been picked off by Vice-Admiral Kiyoshi Hasegawa's staff to handle the sensitive liaison job with the Army. Like every interservice job, it was loaded with situations that could worsen the natural interservice rivalries if handled poorly. Friction between the two services on the advisability of the war and the conduct of it was already causing difficulty.

Considering Aoki's reputation and the souped-up temper of the naval pilots, no one was in a mood to question Aoki's intelligence. If he said there were targets, the flyers were sure they were there. The men were itching to go. Okumiya explained later:

There had been a standing order to avoid bombing of vessels on the Yangtze because of the danger of involvement with foreign neutrals. But learning of these obviously legitimate targets, we were thrilled when Captain Miki gave the order for all available aircraft to participate in the attack. We naval officers were eager for the opportunity to attack a target that floated. We had made many runs against sea targets in practice, but in actual combat had been limited entirely to land objectives. Excitement was further increased by the prospect of a unit citation, a thought particularly appealing to men newly arrived at the front. It did not take us long to get ready.

The 24 available planes were divided into 4 groups: Murata's 3 medium bombers, 6 dive bombers under Okumiya, 6 more under Lieutenant Ichiro Komaki, and 9 fighters led by Lieutenant Ryohei Ushioda. The attacking instructions were left flexible in the rush of departure. Each squadron leader was free to act on his own, utilizing to best advantage the particular strength of his own type of aircraft. Okumiya had a brief chance before he took off to remind his pilots to dive with the sun at their backs and aim first for the largest ship in the group. Then the aircraft roared into the air, two or three careening dangerously down the runway in the slipstream of the planes ahead in their eagerness to get into the air and head inland.

The planes covered the 100-mile westward flight between Changchow and the Yangtze in about 40 minutes, then turned to the northeast to follow the river. Lieutenant Murata spotted the ships first. There appeared to be four or five ships, possibly still underway. Even at that height, the Japanese pilots could see small boats moving between several of them. Probably this was Captain Roberts and Dr. Grazier coming back from hearing the Shanghai news broadcast on *Mei Ping*, then the "liberty party" heading over for their afternoon beer. But to the Japanese pilots, the small boat movement seemed to confirm the report that these were Chinese vessels with troops aboard. Some of the troops were probably being put ashore in small boats to fight again.

Okumiya wagged his wings and pointed the ships out to the other pilots in his squadron, who seemed to go "wild with joy." "I looked for possible enemy aircraft," Okumiya said, "and seeing none, banked my plane as the signal to prepare for attack. As my squadron lined up in single column behind me, I surveyed the ships below, observed the second one from the north to be the largest and selected her as our target."

Okumiya had spotted *Mei Ping*, a fat and tempting quarry.

Murata's three high-level bombers were already going in. Each of his planes had six 120-pound bombs. Their approach was straight. There was no evasive zig-zagging. They had all the aiming time they needed. Their flight path took them at a slight angle across the group of anchored ships. It was the sort of classic attack pattern they had been taught since flight school. Murata's planes scored what looked like two direct hits on *Panay* on their first pass. Then the three big bombers circled off in a big swing to the right to clear the way for the dive bombers and wait for their chance for another bombing run.

Okumiya's dive-bomber group was diving in now, strung out behind the leader like a string of migrating ducks. Okumiya remembered:

I lost sight of the distant horizon, then the far reaches of the river. And by the time our 60-degree dive had brought me down to 1,000 meters [about 3,300 feet] my vision was completely filled with the ever-growing target on the yellow surface of the water as it filled and overflowed the viewer of my primitive bombsight. At 500 meters [about 1,500 feet] I released the bomb and pulled out of the dive.

Okumiya's bomb was a 500-pounder. It went whistling down toward *Mei Ping*. Okumiya's pull-out forced him deep in his seat. But as he eased off into a more gradual climbing turn, he looked back over his shoulder and was surprised to see only a big water ring behind *Mei Ping*. A miss! As he watched, the remaining five planes from his squadron dropped their bombs, too. One other dive bomber in Okumiya's group had a 500-pounder; the remaining four aircraft carried two 130-pound bombs each. But to Okumiya's dismay, not another hit was recorded on the first dive. The five planes from his flight joined Okumiya back in the sun and grouped for another attack, as the second dive-bomber group under Komaki went in. Komaki had maneuvered his planes around toward the south, waiting their turn. Instead of dropping in and raking the ship on the diagonal, Komaki chose to come in from closer to dead ahead. They dove in two tight groups of three planes each, concentrating the attack on *Mei An* and *Mei Hsia*. Then from the west Ushioda's nine fighters swooped down in three waves of three planes each. Each of the fighters also carried two 130-pound bombs and each dropped one bomb on the initial dive then moved down lower to strafe.

Murata's high-level bombers made one more high-level run over *Panay*, dropping their remaining bombs. To the Japanese pilots it looked as if the ship they had hit first—*Panay*—was slowly moving upriver, badly damaged. Okumiya had seen a violent burst of steam from one of her funnels as a result of Murata's first salvo. It could have been a hit in the boiler room, he thought. Later, when he looked again, she seemed to be sinking slowly while one of the other vessels—it was

Mei Ping—attempted to come alongside. The Japanese pilots began to concentrate their bombs and guns on the three apparently undamaged Standard Oil vessels. There was a good deal of confusion both above and below. Okumiya cannot remember seeing any more major bomb hits, though another ship was now showing signs of being hit. Years later Okumiya said his most vivid memory of the attack was that "the decks of the ships were crowded with men, many of whom were wearing black suits." Or was it U.S. Navy blue?

Gas was running low in Okumiya's group. Although he felt the attack had not been an unqualified success, they could still point to two vessels damaged in the river. Two others seemed headed for grounding on opposite sides of the river. Okumiya's squadron headed for the base first, as the remaining aircraft pressed home a last strafing attack against *Mei An*, headed for the west bank, and *Mei Ping* and *Mei Hsia*, which were soon crowded in against a pontoon hulk moored on the other side of the river at the foot of a rusty spur of railroad track.

In the meantime Okumiya and his pilots were pushing hard for Changchow, to refuel and return.

The report the Japanese pilots filed was laconic. It—or a cleaned-up version—would later be submitted as evidence to United States authorities. It was full of inconsistencies;

Four vessels in company were proceeding up the Yangtze River near Kaiyuan at a speed of approximately four knots. No flags were seen although one plane flew as low as 300 meters [about 800 feet] to try to identify the vessels.

The Japanese claimed at first that only five bombing attacks were made.

First . . . three bombers made attacks, appeared to make several hits, and the vessels of the convoy appeared to be on fire. At 1330, six pursuit planes made an attack and sank one vessel. At 1340, six bombers attacked one vessel which had come alongside the hulk at Kaiyuan. The vessel listed badly. At 1350, three bombers made an attack against two vessels which had come alongside each other. Both vessels were sunk.

When Lieutenant Okumiya's squadron landed on the field at Changchow, he reported that when he had left the scene, two of the four ships still seemed undamaged. Okumiya requested permission to refuel, rearm, and return. He was in the air again before the others were back. By the time he returned to the river, there were no ships in sight in the channel. (*Panay* had gone down and the three tankers were beached.) Okumiya was furious. The enemy had escaped. He swung south toward Wuhu, but the search was no more productive. Then he led his group back to the north and east, following the course of the river toward Nanking. Only then did a quarry come into view ahead. Okumiya, thinking he had caught up with the survivors of the first attack, led his five planes down in another screaming dive. Each pilot had orders to let go one of his two 130-pound bombs. It wasn't until Okumiya had pulled up after another near miss that he noticed a bright red, white, and blue Union Jack snapping from the mast of one of the ships. For the second time in one day, Okumiya had attacked a neutral warship. His bombs had narrowly missed HMS *Cricket* and HMS *Scarab* as they maneuvered in the Yangtze about ten miles upstream from Nanking.

A frantic wave-off by Okumiya caught the last three planes before they could dive. In disgust—and thankful for once that they had not scored any hits—the lieutenant reformed his squadron, with nine bombs remaining in their racks, and headed for Nanking. This time they bombed inside the city and returned to their field by dark. Okumiya felt downcast and suddenly very tired from the day's flying. He didn't know what sort of trouble he had started. But he suspected it would be a lot.

7

". . . it seemed it would never end"

ON BOARD PANAY, the lookout's hail of "Planes overhead!" had made those already on deck look up and had brought others out of their cabins or up from below.

Frank Roberts stopped the War Department report he had just begun, grabbed his binoculars and hurried to the open upper deck behind the sick bay, to spot the type of planes passing over. As military attaché, he had more than an idle observer's interest in who was up there. If they were Japanese, the Army would want details on whether or not second-line aircraft were now being put into the fight. If they were Chinese, it was important to know whether they had started to use some of their long-husbanded planes or whether these were new aircraft supplied by the Russians. Roberts found Alley, Marshall, Colin McDonald, and Weldon James, already gathered at the rail, peering up into the sun. Before Roberts could focus his field glasses on anything, he was knocked off his feet by a tremendous blast and concussion behind him. Jim Marshall spun toward the bow, saw the radio mast sag forward, and heard what he described as the *ssst* of other bombs falling. He and Roberts dived for the door of the sick bay immediately behind them just as another blast came.

Alley, the cameraman, looked up just in time to spot planes, heard the sound of a whistling bomb, then saw a tremendous explosion just to the port of *Panay*'s bridge. Dr. Grazier, from his spot on the starboard side of the main deck, spotted the planes, too. Then before he realized they were attacking, he was "deluged with water and falling debris." The bomb had hit on the other side of the ship but had flung solid water all the way over the top of the bridge.

Probably the man best qualified to say he had seen the first bomb actually hit was Ensign Biwerse. This young officer stepped out onto the port deck forward, glimpsed aircraft, thought he heard "a burst of machine-gun fire"—and then . . .

The next thing Biwerse knew he was sitting dazed on the deck, his uniform and tie completely blown off and his shirt in rags. In addition to stripping the ensign nearly bare, the first bomb had knocked out the bow 3-inch gun, wrecked the pilot house, damaged the radio equipment, and wounded the captain severely. "Even though we weren't moving," Engineering Officer Geist still remembers, "it was a good shot in those days for a bomber."

It was Lieutenant Murata's high-level bombers that had done this part of the job, though most of the men on *Panay* thought the first salvo had come from the dive bombers. When Murata had released his bombs, his aircraft were almost 11,000 feet up and nearly two miles distant from *Panay* on a straight line of sight. Only the lookout on the bridge, who sounded the initial alarm, and a few others on *Panay* had seen the aircraft at this point. And none of these people was expecting bombs to be released or trying to spot their fall. The first thoughts of alarm had not come until the dive bombers started to drop down toward the ship. Hughes and Lang clearly saw bombs fall away from these planes just about the time the heavy bombs from Murata's aircraft reached the surface of the river. They couldn't understand how impact had come so quickly.

The first reactions aboard *Panay* were shock. Then disbelief. Then anger.

Cameraman Norman Alley was no military man, but his "Chicago eye" had made him accustomed to looking in several directions at once and committing as much detail as possible to memory, so that long after any event was over and the film was shot he would still be able to remember impressions and facts that could be written into picture captions or newsreel commentary by some editor halfway around the world. Alley was one of the few who noticed the high-level bombers apparently retreating downriver after their initial attack. Later Alley said:

My first reaction was that the Japanese, mistaking the *Panay* for an enemy ship, had then realized their error and were leaving. This was wrong however, as almost directly thereafter a squadron of six small pursuit-type bombers came over at a much lower altitude and immediately began to power-dive and release what seemed to be 100-pound bombs.

Even today Alley is still sure it was no mistake.

Hell, I can believe those babies flying level up there at 7,000 or 8,000 feet might not be able to tell who we were. But when they started dive-bombing, they would have had to see our flags. They came straight out of the sun. And they came over and over again.

Alley was already cranking away with his hand-held Bell & Howell.

Photographer Norman Soong was on the top deck, dozing in a sunny, secluded spot. He heard the roar of planes, then the frightening crash of the first bomb. Wood, steel splinters, glass, and water rained down all around him. Soong didn't know what had happened, but he knew it was good for some pictures. He grabbed his camera and also headed for the open deck aft, where Roberts and the others were gathering. Soong's first thoughts were not about death but about capture. Though he was an American citizen, he was obviously Chinese. And he suspected the Japanese in their current mood might well ignore his American passport—or refuse to believe it—and torture or kill him.

Ensign Biwerse, with most of his clothes blown off in the first blast, was momentarily in no good position to make observations of any sort. But one of the first things he remembered was looking aft to see if the American flag had been aloft. It was still there. "I could not believe that we were being attacked when American flags were painted and plainly visible to aircraft on the canvas awnings both forward and aft, as well as one flying at the gaff."

Chief Machinist Mate Peter H. Klumpers was comfortably sacked out in the engine room in a nice warm spot atop the port cylinder heads. He was jarred awake by the first explosion and then couldn't decide whether the noise was part of the dream world or the wide-awake one. Everything was black. He realized he was awake, but the lights were out. So he stumbled down to try to start the generator before somebody came down and raised hell about no juice.

Chief Watertender Emery F. Fisher was also following Klumpers' lead in good Navy tradition, with a Sunday afternoon nap in the Number 1 fireroom. He woke up thinking that someone had turned a warm shower on him. It was fuel oil. The main fuel line had been ruptured by the first bomb.

On the bridge, Commander Hughes and Chief Quartermaster Lang had barely made it inside the pilothouse to the meager protection its steel walls offered. The steel plating there was heavier than in most of the other deckhouse bulkheads. The bridges of the gunboats were often targets for pot shots from bandits and troublemakers ashore. And all the bridge windows, though open at the time, were equipped with bulletproof steel shutters that could be fastened tight against rifle fire. The first bomb hit the water just off the port bow, slightly forward the bridge. Hughes was thrown hard against the engine-room telegraph, which stuck up like a fire plug on the left side of the bridge; his left leg was painfully fractured and his face badly cut. Lang remembers reaching for the general alarm and yelling to anybody who could hear, "All hands take cover, we're being bombed!" Lang, a 37-year-old Minnesota man, had been in action before, 20 years before. He had served in the Canadian Army in World War I, had been wounded once. But he liked the military life. And on his discharge in 1919 he enlisted in the U.S. Navy. "It seemed to be the only place at the time where there was any action." Lang had come aboard *Panay* seven months earlier when the old USS *Palos* was decommissioned at Chungking.

He was getting plenty of action now. A spray of bomb fragments laced into his right arm, lodging at the elbow. Blood started pouring down to his hand as the wounded captain sagged against him. Lang, half-supporting Hughes, started for one of the doors at the rear of the pilothouse and the ladder that led down to the main deck. They met Radioman First Class Andy R. Wisler coming out of the radio room. Wisler remembers Hughes saying, "Damn it, I'm hurt. Help me down." The captain was obviously in pain, but he sounded more mad than anything else.

Wisler was a 30-year-old career Navy man from Nashua, Missouri. He had been in the Navy for nine years at the time of the *Panay* attack—and eight of those nine years had been served on the Yangtze Patrol. Like Lang, Wisler gravitated to the Yangtze because "that was where the action was." To Wisler, as well as to others, the routine in the Fleet was too boring. A military tradition was strong in his family. A grandfather, Isaac Wisler had been a sergeant in the Western Territory during the Civil War. An uncle had been with Dewey at Manila Bay.

When the first bomb hit, Wisler had been in the chief petty officers' washroom gazing out the window. Then *wham!* From instinct, he headed for the deck. "I started to open the door to get out, but the door was jammed, due to the warped and buckled bulkheads. The next attempt I *did* come out—along with the door, its frames, and anything else that could come adrift with it." It was a stout door and he remembers thinking later he ordinarily would have had a devil of a time breaking through it.

Wisler had immediately hurried forward along the upper deck to the radio room, where he knew Jim Murphy was on duty. On the way forward, Wisler ripped the canvas cover off one of the machine guns, intending to come back. He noticed on the run that the forward mast was down, which probably meant radio transmission was no longer possible. One look at the wreck of the radio shack was enough to convince him the equipment was out of action for days. He mentally wrote off Murphy as a casualty—probably dead. Then Wisler made his way through the debris of the radio room and out onto the deck on the starboard side, where he found Commander Hughes and Quartermaster Lang.

The two petty officers helped the captain down the ladder to the main deck and into the narrow passageway forward that ran the width of the ship separating the officers' cabins from the main galley. There was some shelter there, except from bomb fragments that might come from directly on either side. Wisler and Lang propped the captain up in the meager shelter against one of the galley bulkheads. The word was passed for the doctor. Executive Officer Anders hurried up. Anders himself was already severely wounded in the throat by bomb fragments and could not speak. And when Wisler requested permission to man the machine guns, the executive officer could only nod his assent. Radioman Wisler took off at top speed up the ladder to the upper deck and headed for the first machine gun on the port side, which was just opposite the wrecked radio-room door. The canvas cover was a tight fit and Wisler was tugging and cursing it loose when a hand with a knife reached out from somewhere and slit the canvas from top to bottom. A box of .30-caliber machine-gun ammunition appeared on the deck beside him. Wisler snatched a pan of of ammunition, fitted it to the top of the Lewis gun and was in business.

Finding a target was harder. The machine guns were mounted four to a side and were slightly recessed into the upper deck. Although they could elevate to the vertical to bear on aircraft on either side of the ship, they were primarily intended for dealing with sniping bandits ashore and for covering pirate river junks. Their field of fire went in a wide arc from about 15 degrees behind the bow of the ship to 15 degrees ahead of the stern. Now the planes were coming in from directly ahead. And they could not swing the guns far enough forward to bear. Wisler remembers the frustration.

Bombs were released two at a time, and they would come sailing down. Quite a thing to remember. About three or four feet long, and about a foot in diameter—or at least that's the way they looked. Painted red on the forward end. They would sort of whistle as they went over the ship, hit the water—and explode. That whistle was not the long, drawn out thing you hear in the movies, but a sort of high-pitched rushing sound . . .

The gunners had to hold their fire until after the bombs were released. The best shots came when the planes turned to one side after releasing their bombs and started to climb. Wisler recalls:

They would present a target going away. But the speed was over 200 miles an hour—even in those days—and the target was available only a few seconds. I don't know how many rounds I fired. I would let bursts go at planes, move the gun to lead them, fire and let them fly into the stream of bullets. The only thing wrong was that no plane ever fell into the river. Speed Adams was the one passing me ammunition. He was robbing the ready locker and all the other places where he could find it. At gun one the spent brass was about ankle deep. I evidently had my mouth open most of the time and it was filled with a lot of burned powder. Also the full beard I was sporting in those days was also catching its share of smoke and dirt.

Speed Adams was just beginning his wars with the Japanese. He was a 35-year-old radioman second class from Campti, Louisiana, who had been in the Navy since 1922. A tour of duty in China convinced him he would like it and he eventually promoted a transfer to the Yangtze Patrol. Adams had served on *Guam* and *Oahu* before coming aboard *Panay*. Four years later he would ride the bucking, rolling gunboat USS *Mindanao* from China to Manila just before the war broke out, and just in time to be taken prisoner at Corregidor. For three years, four months, and two days he would be a prisoner of war of the same enemy that was trying to sink his ship now. Adams and Wisler were working around the Number 1 machine gun within a few feet of each other. During the attack, Wisler never received a scratch. But Adams, right next to him, would be hit with bomb fragments in five places—none serious—and his dungaree trousers would be shredded with near misses. Some of the others were not so lucky.

Fireman First Class Robert R. Hebard of Sparta, Wisconsin, had received a very embarrassing wound: a hunk of shrapnel in the right buttock. Hebard wrapped a large towel around his rear, looking like some Fiji Islander, then went back to firing his machine gun. He figured he was lucky. He had been kneeling low behind the gun at the time. And he could only figure that the velocity of the fragment had been partially spent by hitting the superstructure behind him. It was going to be a rough afternoon, Hebard decided. The first bomb had thrown him out of his bunk, where he was taking a quiet Sunday afternoon siesta, onto the top of one of the finely scrubbed, white teak mess tables. Hebard headed for the machine guns immediately and kept firing until ammunition was exhausted and the abandon-ship order was finally given.

If the suddenness of the surprise attack was confusing to the crew, they at least were ready for it in theory, with a battle station assigned to each man and drills well practiced. For the civilians, there was nothing much to do but cower and wait.

The newsmen—Alley, Marshall, Soong, Mayell, Sandri, and Barzini—were the best off. They had something to concentrate on. Each knew he was in the middle of a monumental scoop—if he lived through it. Alley's Bell & Howell was whirring with the first of the thousands of feet of film he would take during the attack. And Soong's Sunday afternoon had providently begun with three rolls of unexposed 35-millimeter film crammed into a pocket of his leather jacket.

Sandro Sandri had been through Ethiopia and some rugged fascist revolutionary battles. He was no gun-shy recruit. But both he and Luigi Barzini felt strangely alone and apprehensive now in the middle of this sudden new combat, on a foreign warship, surrounded by shouting men speaking a different tongue.

Shortly before the attack had started, Sandri, Barzini, and Ros had joined Weldon James and Colin McDonald for an after-lunch cigarette on the after end of the upper deck outside the tiny *Panay* sick bay, which was serving as a temporary press room during the forced evacuation. Barzini's wireless report back to *Corriere Della Sera* told the story of what happened next the way he saw it:

. . . a plane flew over us, motors roaring. A second later, the first bomb exploded. . . .

At the time we did not understand what had happened. We were stunned by the blow and by the ship's frightening shudder, by the din of shattered glass. I could not believe we had been bombed.

I don't know why we threw ourselves on the floor of the sick bay; we were surrounded by a metal barrier which would not have stopped a knife, only a wooden roof above us. We were stunned, stretched out on this floor which shuddered like an animal, while glass, fragments, bottles, medical supplies, books from bookshelves rained about us, like dust shaken from a carpet.

Two cots collapsed, the door collapsed, and the uproar was by now so intense we could not hear our own voices. The planes power-dived with an anguished howl of motors, followed by the hiss—like steam escaping from a boiler—of the bombs. Then came the deafening blast.

There were giant hammer blows, which beat against the deck with a superhuman violence. The flooring gave way beneath us.

There were no longer any doubts: we were the target of an aerial bombardment—a small white boat, smaller than the ferry which plies between the Venice Lido and Riva degli Schiavoni every 20 minutes, anchored in the middle of a freezing river and a rapid current which would have carried far adrift anyone who might have jumped in. The next bomb would enter the Santa Barbara [as Italians called the ammunition room] and blow us all to bits; if not the next, the one after. Escape was no longer possible. Now bombs began to fall on the loaded oil tankers anchored around us. One ripped through the roof of the officers' deck on the *Mei An*, killing everyone present: the captain and his European guests. We saw it through the caved-in door of the sick bay. We were counting off the seconds of our lives with a strange inner rebellion, with disgust for our futile end: this was surely some sort of misunderstanding which would be cleared up in a few hours. It seemed incredible. We did not want to believe it.

The thin, tin-can walls of the sick bay had looked deceptively protective to almost everyone on the stern at that moment. Captain Roberts had been adjusting his field glasses when he heard the first bomb whistle down and explode. He was smashed to the deck, trying to curl up protectively around his binoculars like a quarterback being blitzed; a good pair of glasses was one of the most essential tools of his trade. Two more bombs exploded close by, each rocking the ship and showering down bomb, wood, and glass fragments in a cascade of water. Roberts was conscious of a loud hiss of steam, a somewhat alien sound to an Army man in combat. He didn't know what such a sound meant on a ship, but he doubted it was good news. Then there seemed to be a vacuum of sound. The whine of airplane engines was receding. The ship was strangely quiet. It was the lull of shock—before the moans of the wounded begin. Roberts got up and made a dash for the sick-bay door. Then the second salvo of bombs came crashing down, exploding close aboard. The concussion laid Roberts flat on his back on the deck again, only a few feet from where he had started. He remembers a helping hand:

Weldon James from the sick bay pulled me, considerably shaken up, inside the room. I crouched with the others while two more bombs fell, knocking the ship's medical supplies all around us, breaking the windows, and generally wrecking things. Then I got to my feet and looked out the door at the planes. I saw two light bombers at an altitude of not more than 2,000 feet and climbing. I called to McDonald to look too. "Mac," I said, "look at those red circles. You'll probably need to testify that these planes are Japs."

Several times in the next few days both Roberts and McDonald would wonder if they were ever going to make it out alive for a chance to testify. McDonald took a long look at the last plane to pull away. "I see it. It's a Jap all right. Like those at Nanking!" The silhouettes were familiar after the last few days. Roberts and McDonald had spotted Lieutenant Okumiya's dive bombers pulling away.

As Okumiya's flight climbed to reform for a second pass and while Komaki's six planes were maneuvering to attack, there was another brief lull. For the first time the men had a chance to look around them, to see who was wounded, to see if they themselves were.

Commander Hughes was in considerable pain from his fractured leg and was propped up now in the galley, so covered around the face with soot from a fractured galley stovepipe and with blood from his own wounds that some of the men recognized him only by the two and a half stripes on his uniform coat. Tex Anders was bleeding and speechless from shrapnel wounds in the throat. To issue his orders, he would scribble them on scraps of paper and on the white bulkheads. Engineering Officer John Geist, also wounded in the leg, stood nearby, relaying Anders' instructions.

Geist toured the ship, checking casualties. Embassy clerk Gassie was being shoved up through a hatch to the main deck from the ship's office below. Gassie had a broken leg and was in considerable pain. Geist then spotted Chief Watertender Fisher, one of the men who had forecast an afternoon of good sleeping, emerging from the engine room. The engineering officer first thought Fisher was horribly wounded. The chief was covered from head to foot with a glistening substance that, at a quick glance, might have been blood. It was oil from the ruptured main fuel line. Now, even had there been time to get under way to try to dodge later attacks, *Panay* was finished. She could get no fuel to steam.

Geist headed aft. Because the ship was at anchor, his duty was to keep under cover those men who did not have air-raid stations. As he chased half a dozen gawkers into the crew's shower, he could see three heavy bombers of Lieutenant Murata's flight apparently retreating downriver. Then he saw the dive bombers pulling up. They were climbing but were still incriminatingly low. "They came low enough for us to see the red suns on their wings distinctly," Geist says, "and we could see the pilots of some of the planes. Even in the excitement, they would have had to see our flags."

Fireman First Class William A. McCabe of Harrington, Delaware, still can't figure out when he was hit. McCabe was in the crew's quarters on the main deck immediately below the sick bay, sitting at the crew's mess table, playing a little poker. The cards were flying, but no money was visible on the table, as the Navy insisted. Just matchsticks. The ship shook from the first explosion. Somebody yelled, "The Japs have bombed us." And a head popped through the crew's quarters' door to shout, "We're being attacked. The Japs have hit us. Take cover." Nobody stopped to scoop up the matchstick pot. McCabe sprinted for his station in the engine room. Somewhere along the way he took a hunk of shrapnel in the left shoulder.

Machinist Mate Second Class Karl Johnson of Arlington Heights, Illinois, was already in the engine room when the first bomb hit. He had been aboard *Panay* only three months. Johnson's first reaction, when he heard bombs and machine guns, was to head topside. He remembers yelling to no one in particular, "Let's get some .30-caliber ammo up to the guns on the deckhouse." He too got a load of shrapnel in the shoulder almost as soon as he hit the deck.

Chief Machinist Mate Klumpers, who had awakened in the dark of the engine room with a first thought that he'd better get the generators started before somebody raised hell, was not really surprised when he found that the source of the trouble was not generator failure but Japanese bombs. After the shelling they had experienced at Nanking, Klumpers personally expected more trouble from the Japanese.

After working briefly with the generator, Klumpers' first thought was to wonder if *Panay* could get underway. He soon found the answer to be no. The main stream line was out. That had been the strange hiss Roberts had heard. He did not know then that the main fuel line was severed, too.

Somewhere along the line that afternoon Klumpers would pick up shrapnel wounds in the left knee and right wrist. Like most of the less seriously wounded men, in the excitement he could not remember just when he got hit. But also in the excitement, Klumpers still remembers one particular bit of overlooked bravery. At one point a flitting shadow caught his eye at the engine-room skylights above him. Machinist Mate First Class Gerald Weimers was calmly dogging closed the bulletproof steel skylights to the engine room. Klumpers could hear what sounded like machine-gun bullets striking the deck around the man above. Weimers would have several close brushes with death that day. The first *Panay* man to die would be machine-gunned in a boat Weimers had volunteered to run to shore.

During the next brief lull while the third flight of Japanese bombers was maneuvering for their attack, Lieutenant Geist and several of the petty officers tried to get their passengers to some spot where there was at least a minimum of cover. What cover there was was mostly psychological. Sandri and Barzini started to head below from the sick bay on the upper deck. Only one of them would make it. Barzini wrote in a dispatch to Milan:

I got to my feet with Sandri during a lull in the bombing. We dashed through the sick bay door toward the small stairway which led to the lower deck. The shriek of diving motors, increasing like that of a siren, sounded again. We raced to the petty officers' wardroom; another two or three bombs exploded. Outside antiaircraft guns began to fire a few yards away from us, a deafening roar. A naked petty officer, who had been taking a bath when the bombardment began, directed the fire. It was a futile Don Quixote-type gesture, but it was worth as much to die on one's feet firing as to die huddled, crouched in a corner.

It seemed strange that no bomb had yet scored a direct hit. After the first, all exploded several yards from *Panay*, pockmarking it with fragments like a colander. After ten minutes of this nightmare, however, we were still alive. Immediately after an explosion, several of us ran to the small stairway, squeezed into the engine room, where the walls were slightly thicker, presumably machine-gun proof. Sandri did not follow us. The stokers had opened the valves to drain the boilers and avert the danger of an explosion; the steam escaped with an impetuous roar, the motors rumbled; the machine guns blazed wildly, bombs exploded with metallic, lacerating sound. The wounded, at our feet, moaned and those who had been hit by flying fragments screamed with pain.

We lit a cigarette offered us by a sailor, passed the match to McDonald, who had none. There was nothing to do except wait until it was over. We had nothing else to do except wait to die or live, and only fate would determine this. Between one onslaught and another by the Japanese planes, Norman Alley of Universal news and Eric Mayell of Movietone News rushed on deck with cameras glued to their cheeks to record a moment, stolen here and there, of that inferno, then raced back to the engine room as soon as the plane motors neared. . . . The ship was filling with water, listing to one side. The attack had been going on for 20 minutes, it seemed it would never end.

Captain Frank Roberts had tried to leave the questionable safety of the sick bay to get down to the main deck before the third flight of bombers hit the ship but had been driven back to the shelter of the chief petty officers' quarters just forward of the sick bay where he'd started. Later he recalled:

I attempted to get down to the main deck by the port ladder, but as I got opposite the door of the CPO quarters, I heard another power dive coming and stepped inside the room. I had taken only a couple of steps when a shower of fragments hit me in the back and knocked me to my hands and knees. At the same time I heard the sound of a machine gun and the splatter of bullets against the ship's side. Almost simultaneously another bomb exploded just to port, knocking down some of the bunks and breaking more glass. Being dazed and dizzy, I remained on the floor for some moments while two other bombs exploded somewhere near. Then I was aroused by the sound of cries from the Italian, Sandri, who had been hit through the side by a machine-gun bullet and was in great pain. Seeing that Ros, the secretary of the Italian embassy, and Weldon James were with him, I went to the starboard door and looked out, observing the two after machine guns being operated by their crews and firing tracers at the planes, which were climbing away from the ship toward the north. The fire was fairly accurate, and the stream of bullets was coming close to the nearer plane. I went back to the doorway and looked to see if more planes were coming. They were. But I had time to notice the steel shield opposite the doorway; it had several bullet holes in it, and then I understood what had struck me in the back; probably a spent bullet and fragments of the steel shield.

Later I discovered that a bullet or a metal fragment had torn a three-inch rip in my left trouser leg just at the top of the pocket. That steel shield saved my life; Sandri, who was opposite an unshielded window, got his death wound from the same burst. Still later, I found holes in my coat, the largest at the left shoulder, and there was a severe bruise, although the bullet or fragment did not penetrate.

Sandri was badly hurt. Machine-gun bullets or a bomb fragment had ripped into his left rib cage in two places. He had been standing calmly, cigarette in hand, when he was hit. Above the uproar, some of the Americans nearby thought they had heard him cry out in English: "They've hit me. I'm dying." Then clutching his side with his hand, he slid to the floor.

Sandri's English exclamation was a source of some controversy later. When they heard about it, some of the Americans who had not particularly liked Sandri's somewhat haughty manner and his rough fascist reputation felt the Italian newspapermen had been stringing them along—pretending to know little English, asking Barzini to translate everything, but in the meantime eavesdropping on all that was said. But to an American acquaintance Barzini explained recently that "Sandri spoke no English whatever. People might have heard me say, 'He's hit,' and unconsciously transferred the words to his mouth in their memory."

Perhaps the best luck that befell the *Panay* crew on that bad luck day was the fact that Dr. Grazier emerged unhurt. The doctor had been strolling on deck when the first bomb hit. But his position, fortunately, was on the opposite side of the ship from where the bomb hit the water and where Ensign Biwerse had been stripped bare by the first concussion. Dr. Grazier had first attended to the captain where he had been deposited in the galley by the badly wounded Lang and the puffing Wisler. Then he had moved quickly to set up an emergency aid center. The sick bay on the upper deck might be a great place in normal times for a man who needed light, air, and quiet to get over a case of fever. But Grazier knew —just from looking at the rest of the ship—that the sick bay was probably riddled already with bullets and bomb fragments. Moving aft from the galley, the doctor headed for a steel door that led off the main deck into an "air lock" that then led into the upper part of the boiler room. A man stepping into the boiler room through the air lock entered from the deck at a level about even with the top of the boilers. From a narrow steel platform by the door, a ladder led down to the boiler-room deck. A grating began at the platform and circled the boilers near their top, so the engineers could inspect the upper works. From bilge frames to the boiler room overhead where the stacks emerged to become funnels was a 20-foot-high space. The plating was thicker here. Lockers and machinery fitted in along the boiler-room bulkheads gave added protection. And below the level of the main deck, the fuel bunkers nestled against the hull on either side of the boilers provided an additional barrier against bullets and splinters. Grazier ordered the most seriously wounded brought in and stretched upon the metal gratings above the boilers.

Barzini and several of the other noncombatants were in the boiler room, helping the doctor make some of the wounded comfortable on the hot steel gratings when Ros came down from the CPO quarters on the top deck.

"Where's the doctor?" Ros asked. "Someone's been wounded above in the petty officers' quarters. Where's the doctor?"

"Who's been wounded?" Barzini asked, and at the same time, he knew the answer to the question. He doubted that Ros would have been the man sent below if the wounded man was not Sandri.

Ros spread his arms and replied, "Sandri."

"Badly?" Barzini wanted to know.

"I don't know," Ros answered. But he looked at his fellow Italian as if he did know. And as if it were bad. They followed Ros back to where he had left Sandri. Barzini described the scene when they got up into the shattered CPO flat:

Sandri was lying on the deck, his jacket open, his shirt raised above his wounds; two red holes that did not bleed. He told me, "This time they've killed me."

We tried to put something under his head. It seemed so profoundly illogical and unjust that one of the two of us should die from a Japanese attack on an American gunboat; we could not believe it was true.

The machine guns, a few yards away from us, spit entire rolls of ammunition, angrily, uninterruptedly. One could hardly hear above the uproar. The ship was already listing to one side. "What an end," Sandri said. "On another nation's ship, here in this country." He was pale, frowning, morose. He was suffering intensely.

The doctor arrived, panting, examined him. There was nothing much to be done on the spot. He was not losing blood.

He descended the steps on his feet, supported by the rest of us. We were all hoping that the dual wound had been caused by a single bullet, entering, exiting, not touching anything except the lung. We encouraged him. "Look at how many wounded you've seen who've pulled through," we told him. He made no reply.

Up on the top deck the defense was better organized now. The general alarm had never sounded throughout the whole ship. Anders had tried to ring it; all he could get after the concussion of the first bomb was a weak tinkle. But the machine-gun fire had started almost immediately. Nobody needed to be told this was not another drill.

"All the gun crews were operating with splendid coolness," Alley testified. "And I believe several hits were made, even though not on planes' vital points." Ensign Biwerse, recovering from the concussion of the first bomb, was heading topside toward the radio shack when he noticed Wisler manning the forward portside machine gun. "I'm sure he hit one plane," Biwerse reported. The officer had reached the top deck, where Wisler stood just in time to see part of the radio room crumple in on itself from the blast of another bomb. The mast above the radio room went completely over the side with the same explosion and Biwerse was knocked back down the ladder to the main deck.

James Murphy, the duty radioman, who Wisler feared was dead, had simply decamped by the time the second bomb hit the radio room. His receivers had been knocked to the deck. The transmitter was disabled, too, stopping the message to *Luzon* that he had started to send. (There would be no immediate alarm aboard the flagship. Often generator trouble on the gunboat had stopped transmissions before. A major generator repair might mean *Panay* would be off the air 24 to 36 hours. That much time could go by before she was really missed.) Murphy had moved to one of the machine guns right outside his radio-room door. It jammed on the first shot and he moved to another. He was lucky to find a gun open. Boatswains Mate First Class Homer W. Truax, whose air-raid station was captain of the forward 3-incher, had to wait in line for a chance at one of the other Lewis gun mounts. Truax had tried to man the big gun but had found its muzzle bent down toward the deck like a limp hot dog and all its swivel and elevation gear wrecked. So he spread his crew around among the machine guns to help load and carry ammunition.

All the enthusiasm on the part of *Panay*'s gunners, however, wasn't scaring anyone away. "You'd just get rid of one plane and you'd get hit with another," Lieutenant Geist still remembers. "The bombs were probably 100-pounders. When you get hit square with a couple of hookers like that in a ship the size of *Panay*—which is not much bigger than today's large ocean-going tugs—you can't last long."

The 3-inch guns were never to get into action. *Panay*'s air-raid bill called for both guns to be manned and trained. They would be fired if "ready ammunition" were available on deck. But in air raids or when planes were in the vicinity, the air-raid bill also called for all watertight hatches and doors to be closed. This meant the doors down through the hull to the 3-inch magazine had to be closed, too. No ammunition could be passed up. Hughes considered the 3-inchers basically ineffective and regarded the watertight integrity of his ship as far more important than whatever fire could come from these guns. So hatches to the 3-inch magazine stayed dogged tight during the whole fight and all ammunition for these guns stayed below.

The first three or four bombs probably did the major damage to hull, guns, radio gear, and machinery. Chief Boatswain Mate Mahlmann was below deck forward when the bomb that blew the clothes off Ensign Biwerse struck the water and exploded—probably not more than 20 feet from where Mahlmann was standing inside the hull. "The bulkhead seemed to give and water started to rush in," Mahlmann said later. "Everything—all the gear—fell to the deck. Water was rushing in forward, the office was flooded, and the forward area I was in was flooding. Water was coming in aft, too. It seemed like the whole ship was struck at one time, all over every place I went." Getting to the deck, Mahlmann almost fell over Gassie, the clerk from the embassy, who was now lying in the protected passageway between the galley and the officers' quarters. Mahlmann stopped only long enough to strap a life jacket onto Gassie. Then he ran to his battle station at the aft 3-inch gun. It was still immobilized for antiaircraft use by a wood and metal awning frame. So Mahlmann, too, headed for one of the machine-gun positions.

In spite of orders to stay under cover, there was considerable

movement along the narrow main deck as men ducked outside
to try to get a look at the planes. Watertender Fisher, on the
way back to the engine room after reporting the broken fuel
line to Lieutenant Geist, collided hard with Quartermaster
Lang. Fisher tried to pull Lang into the protection of the air
lock going down to the boiler room. "Get in here," Fisher
remembered yelling. "You'll get hit." The quartermaster
shook him off. "What the hell, I'm hit already." As Lang
moved aft, his own blood had begun to widen the deep red
circle on his shirt and trousers that Hughes' wounds had left.
A gash in Lang's arm was pumping blood at an alarming rate,
and cuts on his cheek and chin added to the flow. All the more
reason Lang wanted a chance to fight back. In another few
minutes he was crouched behind one of the machine guns on
the deck above, banging away at the Japanese.

About 20 minutes after the first bomb had dropped, water
was a foot and a half deep below deck forward. The pumps
were unable to keep up with it. Cameraman Alley saw the
situation from a layman's eye only. But even he could see
the severity of it. "The vessel was shipping water over the main
deck and seemed to be in imminent danger of sinking. There
was barely a square foot of surface on either side that was unscarred by fragmentary explosions." The cabins under the
forward gun had been pretty well wrecked by the same blast
that disabled the gun. Embassy Secretary Atcheson, working
in one of them, had just stepped out of it when the inner
wall was blown in. Bridge and radio shack were wrecked. The
tiny two-bed sick bay, with most of its supplies, had been
riddled, the steel walls shot through with fragments that
would have killed anyone remaining upright. Most of the
guns were still in action. But ammunition was running low,
and water had reached the main ammunition magazine below.

Several large holes in the hull along the engine-room and
fire-room walls were admitting not only water but also air. In
order to steam, _Panay_'s fire room had to be put under pressure

so there would be a forced draft through the boiler fires. But no pressure could be held with the engine-room bulkheads like good Swiss cheese. Even slipping the anchor chain to try to beach the ship seemed useless without power to steer. *Panay* was now so close to the center of the river, she probably would have floated aimlessly with the current for miles. A sitting duck. And a mortally wounded one.

8

"Get all small boats alongside"

To Tex Anders, the reports that were coming in from all over the ship sounded ominous. *Panay* was taking water fast. The small homolite pumps spotted through the hull that were supposed to handle a flooding situation either could not be started or could not keep up. The machine guns were rapidly running through the drums of ready ammunition kept in boxes near each mount, and the spent drums could not be reloaded fast enough to keep up with the speed at which the ammunition was being shot up. It was discouraging to the gunners that they hadn't been able to bring down any of the Japanese. But perhaps the persistence of the fire was at least making the aviators more cautious.

Some of the gunners felt sure they were scoring hits, but it would have done a lot for morale if they could have seen even one of the Japanese spin down, trailing smoke.

Seaman First Class Stanley McEowen, a 25-year-old Ohio man who was known as one of the best athletes on the gunboat, was also sure they had scored some hits. McEowen had been rummaging around in the carpenter's shop in the forecastle when the first bomb hit a few yards away. If he had been on deck, rather than shielded by the steel plate of the hull, he probably would have been killed. McEowen remembers knowing instinctively that the explosion came from a bomb. Someone shouted, "Christ! Those fools are attacking." The first warning cry heard by many throughout the ship had to do with something "they" had started. And there was the immediate assumption in most minds that "they" were the Japanese. McEowen headed topside fast enough to step out on deck in time to receive the impact of another blast and take shrapnel wounds in the jaw and groin. But they didn't stop him from winning a Navy Cross for his conduct later on.

Norman Alley, who had had a chance in World War I to observe antiaircraft fire both from the ground and from the observer's seat of a reconnaissance plane over the Western Front, thought *Panay*'s return fire was more accurate than some of the gunners gave it credit for. But his first concern was to get the planes into his camera sight. There was almost too much to shoot. The attacking aircraft. The other ships. *Panay*'s gunners. After the excitement of the first few moments of the attack, Alley was conscious of the need to conserve his film. Each roll carried only 100 feet, after which he'd have to stop and reload. Hurry! No telling what was coming next. He circled the gun positions, watching for the men who appeared to be the coolest and most accurate gunners. Several times he focused on their targets for long exposures when he was certain the stream of Lewis tracers would bring something down. But each time the Japanese would pull up at the last minute and climb away.

Everyone wanted a turn at the guns. It was frustrating just to stand around and not be able to fight back. As a result, most of the eight Lewis guns changed hands several times during the bombing. Even Tex Anders had taken a crack at the invaders early in the attack, until both hands were raked with bomb fragments as he reached up to lock a new drum of ammunition onto the top of his gun.

The most evident gunner—if not the most accurate one— was Chief "Swede" Mahlmann. Most American heroes are framed in suitably romantic, though often inaccurate, pictures in the American mind: Farragut in full uniform, sword at his side, leaning out of the rigging of the *Hartford* at Mobile Bay to shout, "Damn the torpedoes, full speed ahead." Molly Pitcher manning a field gun at Monmouth with fire in her eyes and perhaps a trace of décolleté. Paul Revere, cloak flying out behind him and horse hoofs striking sparks on cobble through every Middlesex village and farm. Sergeant York, looking more like Gary Cooper, bringing in his 132 German prisoners single-handed. But Ernest Mahlmann is mostly remembered as the man who went into action without his pants. How it happened, Mahlmann recalled for another old Navy man recently:

Before the capture of Nanking we made room for the evacuees. They expected about 30 of them. Only 13 came aboard. The officers and crew had to move or double up. Some of the officers slept in the wardroom. Us chief petty officers gave up our quarters, so it was up to us to find a place to sleep.

There were six of us in all; two slept in the engine room on cots, one in the dead fire room, one on the bridge, one in the crew's compartment. And myself on a cot in the forward hold on the boatswain's locker. I was pretty cold in this hold as it was below the water line, with just room enough to spread a cot—with room to get in or out only at the head or foot. This cot was between the ship's side and the forward magazine. The magazine was my most serious worry at that time.

Just as the first bomb struck, I was getting up and starting to get dressed while sitting in my cot half-covered with a blanket, slipping on my shirt and tie.

As I was about to get into my trousers, the crash came. Everything started to fall, cases of soap and soap powder with many other things that were hung up. The water started rushing in. Instead of finishing the job of getting into my trousers, I thought it would be faster to get them off as there was a ladder to climb.

At about this time the water was knee deep. There were two wire doors that led to the ladders. The first one I tried was barred; several long poles that were used to swab out the guns had fallen down and across the door. This made it impossible to get out that way. I went to the other door and found it blocked with a chair. This I managed to be able to reach out and clear. All this time I was waiting for the magazine to go; but luck was with me there. I started up the ladder. About this time another bomb landed. This was a direct hit. I realized then that we was the target.

Mahlmann hit the deck clad only in a long, wool CPO shirt and a life jacket. In that dashing outfit he would appear before millions of Americans in darkened newsreel theaters and from the banner-headlined front pages of hundreds of newspapers. "The Pantless Gunner of the *Panay*," as Mahlmann came to be known, eventually inspired a poem by Vaun Al Arnold, a Kansas City sometime poet. The verses appeared first in the Associated Press and eventually were reprinted in civilian and service newspapers and magazines, to be circulated in dog-eared clippings. Some took it for humor. But Arnold meant it straight:

> Commend me to that noble soul
> Who, in the battle's heat,
> Rushed to his post without his pants,
> The bombers dive to meet;
>
> Who stood upon the rocking deck
> In careless dissattire,
> With shirt tail flaunting in the breeze,
> To deal out fire for fire.
>
> Old glory's color deepened
> As she floated o'er this son—
> The man who had no time for pants
> But plenty for his gun.

Come, name a million heroes,
But to me there'll never be
A finer show of nerve and grit
On any land or sea.

Then dwell upon your epics
Should you feel an urge for chants
Recall the sinking *Panay*
And the gunner minus pants.

But this unarmored Horatius at the Bridge had more to recommend him before the day was over than being out of uniform. If two or three outstanding Navy men can be singled out from the many whose conduct that day was "above and beyond the highest traditions of the naval service," Swede Mahlmann, Tex Anders, and Doc Grazier are perhaps the men.

Years later when even the most vivid memories of the incident were growing a bit dim, the names of Anders, Grazier, and Mahlmann still jump to mind when many of the old *Panayers* are pressed to name the hero of the attack. Mahlmann's Navy Cross citation puts it in official language:

For distinguishing himself by his display of heroism on the occasion of the bombing and loss of the U.S.S. PANAY on December 12, 1937, Mahlmann manned three machine guns at different times. It was due to his efforts that the boats were successfully lowered and manned during the abandon ship operations; he was continuously exposed to heavy bombing and machine gun fire from attacking planes. He made all of the trips in the sampan while abandoning ship and voluntarily returned to the sinking PANAY for supplies after she had been abandoned.

But Quartermaster Lang may have summed it up best for all of them: "Mahlmann was the spark plug of the crew. And later when abandoning ship, he got everyone off, picked some men out of the river, and brought ashore bandages and medicines, plus the records from the sick bay. He helped the wounded and was a tower of strength during the long march inland."

The time for that long march was coming closer, though most of the crewmen were still so intent on firing at the attackers, tending to the wounded, or trying to rig up emergency systems to take care of the damage that there was not much thought of abandoning ship and making it to shore. That was Hughes' and Anders' concern. And they were keeping a wary eye on a losing battle with water below deck. Water was a foot and a half deep in the ship's office, one deck down. And the floor of the office was at least three feet higher than the boiler-room floorplates. Anders' quick calculations told him there was probably four to six feet of water in most of the ship. The bulkheading would not keep it for long from flowing from one compartment to the next. The boilers were out. To minimize the danger of an exploding boiler early in the attack, Fireman First Class Ernest C. Branch had lifted the safety valve of the one boiler that had been kept fired up when the ship anchored; that was the burst of steam the Japanese aviators thought indicated a hit. With no steam in the auxiliary lines, the main steam generator was useless. There was only emergency power through most of the ship.

Panay's abandon-ship procedure assigned each man to one of the two launches and gave him a trip number. Under the best conditions each launch would have to make five runs to shore. With wounded to be carried and the large number of supernumeraries on board, the time involved on each trip would be greater and the number of men who could be carried each time would be smaller. Fortunately the boats seemed to be in fair shape with no major damage. There was a 26½-foot motor sampan, which doubled as the captain's launch, and a 22½-foot pulling sampan that could be rowed or run with an outboard motor. Anders quickly calculated the time he figured Panay could remain afloat and the time he thought it would take to get everyone off. Then he pulled a Yangtze

River chart to him with one bleeding hand, flipped it over, and on its back wrote his orders. The blood from the wounds kept dropping on the chart and blotting the lettering. He had to shift repeatedly to a fresh area of the paper until the words were spotted all over the back. His order was a little hard for Lieutenant Geist to read at first:

<pre>
                              alongside
           Get all
                      boats
           small

           Can we run
           ship aground
              if not
           Abandon Ship
</pre>

With no power, grounding was out of the question. And it was even doubtful if *Panay* would stay afloat long enough to get to shallow water. They would have to abandon ship. Geist ordered the word passed through the gunboat. Some of the men, to whom the ship had been "home" for years, found it hard to believe. Those manning guns on the upper deck felt *Panay* was now holding her own in the fight. They couldn't see how bad the damage was below.

The order was repeated, and Swede Mahlmann and several of the senior petty officers began to move the men along. Army Captain Frank Roberts and some of the others who had no battle stations or abandon-ship duties set about the job of collecting supplies and getting the wounded into the first boats. Then Roberts looked to his own needs.

When I went into my cabin I found it knocked about pretty much, water pouring through leaks in the pipes and a mess generally. I got my overcoat, my pistol, some handkerchiefs—which later went for bandages or tourniquets—some matches, a flashlight, and some other things. I recall thinking about whether I should try to rescue my file of messages and deciding against it, because they would do no one any good.

Norman Alley figured he had nothing much worth saving now except his camera and film. During a lull in the attack after the abandon-ship order was given, he made a round of the decks to get shots of the damage to the ship. "There was barely a square foot of surface on either side of the vessel which was unscarred. She was shipping water over the main deck at this minute and appeared in imminent danger of sinking." As Alley rounded the stern near the badly riddled crew's quarters, he came on four sailors heaving mattresses and table tops over the fantail in preparation for their own abandon-ship effort. Three of the men had just given up their life jackets to some of the civilian passengers. The fourth, Watertender Second Class Fon B. Huffman, a 24-year-old Iowa man who had been in the Navy since he was 16, spotted Alley with no life jacket on, stripped off his own, and tossed it to the cameraman. Huffman had a shrapnel wound in the right shoulder that was beginning to hurt as the numbness of the first shock wore off. He remembered hearing somewhere that a Navy mattress would hold you up in an emergency. Huffman heaved a mattress into the river and went over after it. The mattress promptly started to submerge—and then Huffman remembered for the first time that he couldn't swim a stroke. With the help of his three shipmates he stayed afloat on some other debris until Swede Mahlmann pulled him to safety in the first boat heading for shore.

For the crew, there were the final duties, the sort they had practiced for months at drill, but never really expected to have to perform. Dr. Grazier made ready to abandon his first-aid post set up on the steel gratings over the boiler room. During a lull in the bombings, he and an assistant had searched through the demolished sick bay on the upper deck. There they salvaged all health records and as many medical dressings, drugs, and antiseptics as could be crammed into a sturdy Navy Hospital Corps pillowcase. Then Grazier started loading his wounded into the boats.

Lieutenant Geist, dragging one wounded leg, headed for the ship's office, where the payroll records were kept. He strained futilely at the lugs fastening the overhead hatch, but they were jammed. In the wardroom was another safe, which had all the ship's money—about $40,000 in cash and vouchers. Its doors, too, were sprung hard shut by the bombs. Water was beginning to come into the wardroom now, and it was at deck level. That meant *Panay*'s hull was almost awash. Geist had to back out empty-handed.

In the improvised first-aid post in *Panay*'s boiler room, Luigi Barzini bent over the wounded Sandri, who would be going ashore in one of the first boats.

Supported by Barzini and several of the others, Sandri was taken to the motor sampan that was now alongside *Panay*'s gangway and he was laid in the bottom. Sandri gave his countryman a weak salute.

Ahead of the gunboat, Captain Mender of the tanker *Mei Hsia* saw the first *Panay* boats go over the side as the abandon-ship order was given. *Mei Hsia* had been lucky. She had escaped with only minor damage in the first bombing and strafing attacks; she could still steam. Although there was really no place to "run and hide," Mender decided that with *Panay* going down, the only chance to save his own passengers and crew seemed to be to run for shore. The tanker *Mei Ping*, obviously badly hit, was already headed for the south bank of the river. *Mei Hsia*, still able to give some assistance, moved in close to *Panay*'s starboard bow. Captain Mender intended to put her alongside the gunboat and take off as many men as possible. Aboard *Panay*, those who watched *Mei Hsia* move down with the current thought at first she was out of control and drifting. All they needed now to add to their troubles was to be rammed by the tanker.

There were hails across the water from *Mei Hsia* that she could take off some crew. The men aboard the gunboat realized then that the tanker could still maneuver. There were shouts across the narrowing gap of water. "Keep off! Keep off, for God's sake!"

Up above the Japanese planes were forming for another attack. *Mei Hsia,* filled with gasoline and oil, was a monstrous floating and fused bomb that could be touched off with a lucky hit from one of the planes—or by an internal explosion from *Panay.* Captain Mender saw the danger, too, and ordered *Mei Hsia's* engine ahead. By the time the big propeller caught the water her stern was only a foot or two from *Panay's* starboard bow. *Collier's* correspondent Jim Marshall was standing near the bow rail. The abandon-ship order had been given. As far as Marshall could see, he was just a fifth wheel in an operation that was having trouble functioning with four. The *Collier's* man had just come from a last search through the cabin he shared with Dr. Grazier. He had gathered up his pipe, some tobacco and matches, a camera, and all the traveler's checks he still owned. The few other personal objects he had brought aboard didn't seem worth weighing himself down with, especially if he had to swim. Marshall patted his back pocket to make sure the traveler's checks were still there. He buttoned his coat tight, measured the distance between *Panay's* rail and *Mei Hsia's* after deck—and jumped.

As *Mei Hsia* pulled away, Norman Alley caught the last sight of his fellow correspondent that he would have for a long time. "I saw Jim Marshall on deck [of the *Mei Hsia*] trying to lower a lifeboat. It isn't easy to lower a lifeboat alone. He'd work one rope and lower one end of it a bit, then go to the other end and work that rope. He was there on deck all alone." *Mei Hsia* moved off toward the south shore, where the burning *Mei Ping* was already headed.

By now the two *Panay* launches were returning from their first trip ashore. And the complement for the second trip was being gathered along the rail. Although *Panay* seemed to be settling fast, particularly to the starboard side forward, there was a reluctance on the part of some of the men to leave the ship until they were individually ordered off. Frank Roberts thought ahead of what would have to be accomplished once they got to shore and began to make some decisions of his own. Aboard ship, as an Army man he was just a passenger. On land, there might be a number of things he would have to do—and do right the first time. George Atcheson, he noticed, was still on board. Atcheson, as secretary of the embassy, would be the logical man to try to get back through the combat area with word to the outside world of what had happened. As a diplomat, he would have a better chance of moving through the country than any of the military people would, though it would be chancy at best. Roberts insisted that Atcheson get into the next boat ashore. Atcheson argued that he should stay to the last, but Roberts was firm, making it clear to the secretary that he thought he was authorized to use force to get Atcheson off the gunboat, if necessary. Atcheson gave in.

Roberts looked at his watch. It was a little after two o'clock.

The planes had wheeled away—at least temporarily—and the men used the respite to gather the last supplies they thought they could use. "I remember thinking it was a terribly long time the boats were taking to get back, and there was some talk of swimming to shore if the ship started to go down under us. Looking at the 600 yards of cold water, I thought, 'I'll never make it.'" Then Roberts spotted the boats returning. Both boats looked low in the water and seemed to move slower than before; but with no passengers, he knew that was a nervous illusion. Roberts and Colin McDonald of the London *Times* helped Tex Anders and three wounded sailors into the smaller of the two boats, the sampan that was powered with the outboard. Anders had lost so much blood he could not be on his feet for any length of time. Roberts urged him to get ashore and save his strength. Lieutenant Geist and Ensign Biwerse could see to the last men off. The remaining places in the sampan were taken by nonwounded men assigned to that trip. Gerald Weimers was in the stern running the outboard. One Chinese boatman helped him. They tossed in their supplies, an odd lot of equipment. Some of it was very useful and carefully thought out. But much of what was packed in the boat at that last minute was the sort of inconsequential junk that people always grab first in emergencies. Nevertheless, it *was* all packed in and they pushed off for shore. According to the abandon-ship bill, each man had certain items to bring ashore: a signal pistol and ammunition, rifles, charts, matches, gas, water, ponchos and blankets, cooking utensils. One vital piece of Navy equipment would be missing because the man who was to bring it was "on liberty" on *Mei Ping*: Seaman First Class John Dirnhoffer was assigned the coffee pots.

Roberts could see now why the boat had looked so low in the water. She was leaking badly from three or four bullet holes. She had been strafed on the first trip to shore. McDonald began to bail with the only thing at hand—a steel helmet. Then he tore up his handkerchief to stuff into the splintered holes to try to stop the water. To Roberts, it was a long trip:

Some 200 yards from shore the outboard motor on our boat became overheated and stopped. The coxswain and the bowman and I pulled on the oars and McDonald bailed with a tin hat, and finally, after being carried about 600 yards downstream from the main party, we made shore, somehow got our wounded up the bank and into the shelter of the marsh reeds, unloaded our duffel, and tied up the sampan. I gave my field glasses to a sailor and asked him to keep a sharp outlook for the planes, which we felt sure would return. Then I looked at the wounded of the party, found I could do nothing for them, and so went along the shore until I came to the main party and found the doctor. As soon as possible he went off to attend the men I had just left. The other sampan put off for the ship to get needed supplies of water, food, and blankets while Atcheson, the captain, and I discussed the situation.

On board *Panay*, the men who would make up the last boatload were going about their last assignments or, in some cases, just killing time when there was nothing more to do. It seemed an interminable wait. Just before he left the ship, Tex Anders had scrawled on his blood-stained chart one more reminder: "confidential publications." And now Communications Officer Biwerse was making a last search of the shambles, to see if he had overlooked anything. The table that held the safe with the code books had collapsed and the safe was wedged between the table and a bulkhead. Biwerse thought of trying to heave the whole safe over the side, but then figured he couldn't budge it. He was right, even allowing for the incredible strength man can muster in emergencies. Tex Anders figured it would have taken half a dozen men with plenty of tackle to move it. Later, there would be some concern about the safe at the board of inquiry; as long as the Navy couldn't be certain all the confidential publications were safely beyond recovery, several important U.S. Navy and State Department codes would have to be considered "compromised."

Radioman Wisler had been through the wrecked radio room, too. Wisler had found the Navy call book, which listed confidential call letters of all ships and stations. He had heaved it into the river and had watched with awful fascination as it seemed to float for about 20 feet before its weighted covers finally took it under. What Navy genius had designed that? Wisler had been told everything would sink like a rock. He was glad there was nothing else lying around loose that he was supposed to get rid of. If the other confidential material didn't sink any better than that, they were in trouble.

Wisler looked out the radio-room door at the distance be-

tween the ship and shore. He figured he *could* swim it if the
water weren't too cold. The ship didn't seem to be settling
so fast now. Maybe the boats would be back in time, and
maybe he had time for a little planning. Wisler took a flashlight from the drawer of the wrecked radio-room desk, put in
some fresh batteries, and pocketed $90 he had squirreled away
in a stationery box in another drawer. He picked up a heavy
waterproof jacket he kept in the radio room and then headed
aft for the crew's compartment. His own sleeping space was
below the water line and it had probably long since flooded.
But with the ship being abandoned, he figured if he could
scrounge what he needed from someone else's locker, nobody
could object now. A jackknife and some matches were the
first necessities that came to mind. He found what he was
looking for in the locker belonging to a buddy, Fireman First
Class Newton Davis. Davis, he knew, was already ashore so
he figured it was all right to "requisition" the things. Wisler
found a talcum-powder can, emptied it, placed the matches
inside, and stuck the whole thing in his jacket pocket up-
side down. It was the most waterproof rig he could devise.
Wisler remembers:

Around this time, another member of the crew and myself spotted
Mr. Biwerse, still without his pants. We remarked that it was going
to be sort of cold on the beach without them. He nodded and when
I saw him again, he had put them on. I was standing near the
engine room with John Lang when a plane—a sort of Johnny-
come-lately—came overhead. I remarked to Lang that if I thought
it would do any good, I would go up to my machine gun and take
a few shots at him; I knew there was still one pan of ammunition
left on the gun I had been using when the attack stopped. A
bomb fell somewhere. And I think Lang muttered something.
Cussing. I know I was.

But Wisler didn't go back to the gun on the top deck. It
seemed so futile now.

At 3:05 P.M., with the last boat alongside, Wisler stepped in and raised up the lifeline for Biwerse to duck under after him. The young ensign was the last man off the ship. With flags still flying, *Panay* was abandoned—the first ship of the U.S. Navy ever lost to enemy aircraft. And, in a sense, the first American naval casualty of World War II.

9

"Let's get this bucket moving"

As THE LAST LAUNCH headed for the north shore, every man, at one point or another, must have looked back at the slowly settling gunboat. Her main deck was almost awash for the length of the ship. The raised forecastle was still about three feet above the river. But the ship was down by the head, with most of the water coming in through the holes in the bow made by the first bombs and then overflowing in turn to each section of the ship farther aft. *Panay* was like an ice tray, with water pouring in one end and slowly seeping under, around, and over each baffle, to fill up one compartment after another. The white paint work of her cabins was scarred everywhere with pockmarks and punctures where bomb fragments and machine-gun bullets had gone through the metal or ricocheted off it. An hour earlier she had been spick and shipshape. Now she was a forlorn sight. The men felt suddenly very lonely. Several of them remembered later forcing their eyes back into the boat where familiar faces were at least one familiar link with the warm, tight, peaceful little world they had waked to that morning.

Across the river to the east another group of Americans wasn't so fortunate. The beer drinkers who had gone aboard the *Mei Ping* were starting their most adventurous liberty ever. *Panay* was obviously sinking in the middle of the river. Their "club," *Mei Ping*, was aground and on fire on the east shore. And now they were surrounded by excited or panicky Chinese. The eight American sailors felt very much alone.

It had all seemed to happen so quickly. Aboard *Mei Ping* Fireman First Class Joseph L. Hodge of Siluria, Alabama, had just uncapped his first bottle of cold beer when he became conscious of the drone of aircraft engines increasing to a diving whine. Hodge turned to Chief Machinist Mate Vernon R. Puckett and said idly, "Do you hear what I hear?" Borrowing the binoculars from Captain Jorgensen, the Standard Oil skipper, Hodge looked skyward just as the river between *Mei Ping* and *Panay* exploded. Hodge could never remember whether or not he finished the beer. The second bomb hit almost immediately just aft of *Mei Ping*'s stack. It must have been a small one, because the explosion seemed nowhere near as violent as the one they had just witnessed in the river off *Panay*'s bow. There was a pause—and then they could hear moans. Three Chinese had been badly hit.

The first instinctive thought of most of the liberty men was to try to get back to *Panay*. But the hundred yards of water they had shouted across a few minutes earlier suddenly looked like an ocean—and a mean one. The third salvo of bombs was ripping it up in ugly brown eruptions that seemed more like solid mud than water. The first moments, numbing moments of shock and surprise, had already begun to wear off. The shouts and cries of pain and panic from the main deck of the big tanker were already becoming loud, undisciplined, and unnerving. Gunner's Mate Third Class John A. Bonkoski of Conshohocken, Pennsylvania, appeared on the bridge. Bonkoski would get a Navy Cross for his conduct in the next few hours but would never live out the war. Now he offered his services to Captain Jorgensen, too. Jorgensen shouted some orders in Chinese to his crewmen. No one seemed to pay much attention. Then he turned to the Navy men on the bridge. "Let's get this bucket moving." Now the men had something to do. There was some light damage forward, and more aft of the stack. But *Mei Ping* still had full power and a crew. By the time the first flight of dive bombers finished its attack, her anchor was slowly coming in. Bonkoski was on one wing of the bridge, relaying orders in pidgin. And though he had never handled anything larger than a motor whaleboat before, the job was getting done. Bonkoski was concerned that the anchor chain would get kinked or that something might go wrong in the engine room, and then they would be left drifting on that miserable time bomb. And even though he suspected *Mei Ping* going flat-out could probably knock off only eight or ten knots—hardly the sort of speed you needed for dodging dive bombers—it made them all feel better to get going. Anything was better than just sitting there. The planes seemed to be gunning for *Panay* now, with less attention to the tankers. Maybe they thought she was a Chinese warship. If so, the more distance between the ships, the better. But damn it, *Mei Ping*'s Stars and Stripes were flying in full display. Why couldn't they see the flag? Maybe if some speed were gotten on *Mei Ping*, the flag would stand out a little in the wind.

Mei Hsia, *Panay* and *Mei An* had been anchored in a straight line, one behind the other, facing into the current. About 300 yards separated each ship in line from the next. *Mei Ping* had been to one side of the line a hundred yards or so off *Panay*'s starboard bow, close enough, Bonkoski reflected, so that lousy aim at the gunboat could send the tanker gurgling to the bottom—or more probably blow her sky high, with all the gas and oil she carried.

As soon as the anchor was up, Jorgensen rang down for full speed ahead and got about a fifth of what he asked for. He cut the wheel to port so *Mei Ping* would pass well ahead of *Panay*'s bow and headed for the south bank. As *Mei Ping* headed across the current she seemed to lose power. Bonkoski, looking on from the bridge, groaned; those goddamn Chinese motor macs couldn't keep a coffee pot perking. The tanker started drifting down on the gunboat. Down below, Mario Blasini, *Mei Ping*'s Italian engineer, shouted, shoved, cussed at his gang and his engine and got things going again. From aboard *Panay* there was frantic waving to keep off. The tanker's screws seemed to bite into the water again. Jorgensen had some steerway now, and he swung her away from *Panay*. She picked up a little speed. Ahead on the south bank of the river, there was a fairly good-size wharf of some sort. A rail line led into it from the low hills. If they could get *Mei Ping* alongside the wharf, they could take refuge on shore, away from the danger of all that gas and oil. Overhead, Bonkoski could see and hear the planes again. It was a sweaty situation and was going to be close.

The "wharf" that *Mei Ping* was headed for turned out to be a leaky pontoon moored at the foot of a rusty railroad spur. Jorgensen put his ship alongside it. Pretty hard. But nobody cared at that point. It was better than being in the middle of the river, a tempting target for everyone. The small fire that had started aft when the first bomb struck near the the stack had spread now to *Mei Ping*'s deckhouse. *Mei Hsia* came alongside about that moment and the two crews concentrated on the fire fighting, with the *Panay*'s liberty party doing most of it. Half the Chinese were already streaming off toward shore; the others were in some confusion below.

For the time being the Americans seemed safely out of it. "We put out the fire," correspondent Marshall reported later, "so we all had a drink. Then I took some pictures of the ships and after a while we looked across at *Panay* and saw her sink. There was a series of small explosions but no big ones. She went down by the head, rolling over on her starboard side, still anchored."

To the liberty party, it looked as if one terrible episode was over. Actually, trouble was just beginning. Up above the Japanese bombers could see that *Panay* had gone down. But they could see, too, that one fat target—*Mei An*—now lay grounded on the west shore of the river. And two other tempting targets were tied up at the pontoon on the east bank. The planes started down again.

The arrival of the *Mei Ping* and the *Mei Hsia* at the pontoon had not escaped notice on shore either. The fire fighters were almost too busy at first to spot the patrol of Japanese troops getting into position along the bank. The soldiers were cautious. The Chinese were terrified. But as soon as the Japanese caught sight of the American flags through the smoke of *Mei Ping*'s deckhouse fire, they moved forward with less of a menacing air. There was a good bit of yelling back and forth. The soldiers found it confusing. And with some reason. They could see the neutral flags—and yet there had obviously been firing between the other ship in the middle of the river and their own planes. Bonkoski tried to shout an explanation: "She's the *Panay*—an American Navy ship. An American warship. They sunk her."

The Japanese were still bewildered. "If American gunboat, why it shoot?" one of the Japanese officers called back. He shook his head. Infantry school hadn't included problems like this one.

To Bonkoski, the smartest move appeared to be to get off the tankers. The others agreed. A quick head count indicated that a couple of the sailors had already left the ship. The remaining Americans jumped down to the rusty old pontoon and started ashore, to find themselves eyeball to eyeball with the Japanese soldiers. They were ordered back aboard roughly. The Japanese soldiers looked madder now, probably because they couldn't quite figure out the situation. There was nothing to do but do as they said.

Back aboard *Mei Ping*, Chief Pharmacist Mate Coleman

got his shipmates busy gathering all the tanker's medical supplies. There were about a dozen wounded Chinese on board and Coleman gave them what treatment he could with the drugs and dressings that were available. Overhead they could hear the Japanese planes again. Back on deck, Bonkoski saw one of the aircraft circle low over the tankers. Two Japanese soldiers had moved to the end of the pontoon and were waving small Japanese flags to identify themselves and warn the plane off. The pilot seemed to catch their signal, pulled up, and made a wide, lazy circle, then headed back again at an even steeper angle. But this time, as he pulled out of his dive, two black egg shapes detached themselves from the bottom of the plane, almost in slow motion. As they fell away from the aircraft, they seemed to pick up speed—finally slamming with tremendous velocity into the side of *Mei Ping* just along the pontoon. The explosions seemed surprisingly small compared to some of the earlier bombs, but the fires flared up immediately. The two Japanese soldiers, who had stood frozen in place with their flags still in hand, keeled over on the decks of the pontoon as if someone had knocked them flat in a subway rush. They never moved again. Both were dead. Several more Chinese lay dead on the stern of *Mei Ping* and Jim Marshall was clutching a wound in his neck, which spurted blood alarmingly.

Ashore the Japanese soldiers dashed for cover. Seeing that, the Americans took the chance to run for it too. The planes made several more passes. Then with both tankers burning hard, the planes pulled away like satiated vultures, formed in rough formation and climbed toward the east.

Now the Japanese soldiers on shore seemed intent only in getting clear of the area. They were hurrying back inland in the direction from which they had come, paying no more attention to the survivors from the tankers. The Chinese passengers were spilling off the ships and spreading over the countryside in three directions. They were badly frightened, leaderless, and pathetic. Any wounded who could not go with them were left behind on the burning ship or at the shore's edge, if they could struggle that far. The *Panay* sailors and the members of the Standard Oil crews who had stuck together made one last search of the two burning tankers. The fires were fiercely hot now and spreading fast. A number of compartments were impossible to get into and the Americans could hear the screams of Chinese wounded trapped inside as the fire got to them. The others who could be reached and moved were manhandled ashore. The fire and numerous small, ominous explosions were just a step behind the rescuers, hurrying them on. The Americans moved the wounded into the protection of some small, half-ruined, wharfside buildings a short distance from the pontoon and then took stock of themselves.

Jim Marshall and Fireman Hodge were for starting for Wuhu at once. The others felt they had a better chance by sticking together near the area where searchers might look for them. Marshall and Hodge were resolute; they pushed off. The remaining seven Navy men—Puckett, Bonkoski, Coleman, Dirnhoffer, Joe Granes, Bill Hoyle, and Ray Browning—struck off inland along the rusty railroad line with several of the Standard Oil men. They had no idea where they were. But the railroad would probably lead to some sort of "civilization" and help. Then perhaps they could follow the rail line back to get the wounded.

Darkness came on them quickly. And after walking and stumbling for what seemed an interminable time in that awkward, hobbled gait that the spacing of railroad crossties forces on a man, they spotted a Chinese hut. It was mean, abandoned, dirty. And it looked absolutely beautiful.

The Americans put in a restless night, squatting against the walls inside, where there was a little warmth at least, or finally collapsing on the dirt floor until the hardness of it and the cold of the night jarred them awake.

As soon as dawn came, Browning, Dirnhoffer, and Bonkoski pushed on for help. The first group they came upon almost finished them. Half a dozen Chinese farmers, thinking the ragged trio of Americans straggling through the dawn light were Japanese separated from their unit, charged them with heavy sticks. It wouldn't have lasted long. But one of the Chinese, who might have put in a stint in Nanking, recognized good American curses—"Fa crissakes, we're Americans!" With many and profuse apologies and much back-peddling, the farmers took them back to a nearby village and fed them rice, fish, and cup after cup of hot tea. "I hate Chinese chow," Bonkoski told a shipmate later, "but boy, did that taste great!"

The village was miserable, but a damned sight better than the hut where they all had spent the night. The best thing would be to bring the others in from the hut. The three men started back with several of the Chinese to guide them. Coming around one bend, they spotted a four-man Japanese patrol. Like a well-drilled infantry-squadron exercise, Chinese and Americans scattered over a low rise. Thinking about it later, the Americans realized it was a stupid thing to do. The soldiers were not 50 yards away. A few shots by even poor marksmen would have brought down all the runners. And running was almost guaranteed to bring shots. But for some reason the Japanese just watched in amazement and plodded on. Crazy Chinese farmers.

About 15 minutes later the little group of fugitives emerged from hiding and started down the railroad line again. An hour later they spotted another group of armed men. Through the haze of shock and fatigue, the instinct was the same. Head for the hills. But their reactions were slower now. As Bonkoski looked over his shoulder, he realized the familiar spots and white and blue were British naval uniforms. It was an armed search party from HMS *Bee*. They were found. They were safe.

10

"Go and see my children in Italy"

IT WAS BAD GROUND from the standpoint of what was underfoot. Mud mostly. Some of it was frozen and some of it was simply gumbo. There were a few patches of soft spongy ground that looked high and dry at first—until you settled anything on them for a few minutes or sat down. Then it was just as if you had sat on a sponge. The seat of your pants sucked up water that felt icy enough to have come from 100 feet underground. But the reeds were 10 to 12 feet tall in most places and they offered good protection from observation from both the river and the air.

Tex Anders had sent the boats toward the west riverbank primarily because it was a good bit closer. When he gave the abandon-ship order, he wasn't at all sure how much time he would have before *Panay* slipped under, and he wanted to get in as many boats trips to shore as possible. First priority was to get everyone off. Then, with what time was left, they could try to save whatever they could from the ship that might come in handy. The charts had marked the area correctly: low, swampy ground. But until you actually set foot on it, it was hard to tell what it really would be like. Not good.

First there was a difficult scramble from boat to shore for the walking wounded. And there were more walking wounded than Anders had at first thought. The men had to make it up the four-foot mudbank between the edge of the river and the beginning of the reeds. There was a lot of slipping and sliding and cussing, with some men getting almost to the top, hitting a particularly slick spot, and skidding back down into the water again. They came ashore soaked and cold and miserable to start with. Then it was obviously going to be difficult to get the stretcher cases handed up out of the boats. The depth of the water fell off rather sharply just off the bank. One man had to scramble first to the top of the bank. Two others in the boat would pass up one end of the stretcher and one or two more men had to be standing in water up to their waists to keep the boat from sliding back out into the river. It was slow work. And sometimes brutally painful to the badly wounded when the stretchers were jarred or almost dropped. Chief Mahlmann had acquired a pair of pants from Coxwain Rider, who always kept spare clothes in the boat. And now the chief set about to supervise the unloading. "It was very hard to land the wounded," Mahlmann remembers. "The bank was steep and made of soft mud that broke away as we stepped on it. The bow of the boat had to be jammed into the bank and held there. And that meant some men standing in water most of the time." Spotting a bowed head struggling to support the offshore rail of the small sampan when it unloaded, Mahlmann splashed around to the far side of the boat to lend encouragement and muscle. He found Norman Alley. "Where the hell is the crew that's *supposed* to be handling this boat?" Mahlmann roared. Two more men jumped in beside Alley immediately.

Storekeeper First Class Charles L. Ensminger of Ocean Beach, California, who had been wounded by a flying fragment aboard the ship, was brought up the bank in bad shape. The boat in which he had been traveling to shore had been strafed and Ensminger had been hit again. Coxswain Ed Hulsebus of Canton, Missouri, had been hit in the spine by another machine-gun bullet while manning one of the Lewis guns. Hulsebus was totally paralyzed from the waist down. He did not appear to be in great pain and kept up a banter with the men who were handling him. But the paralysis looked bad. Motor Machinist Second Class Alex Kozack of Ansonia, Connecticut, had also been hit on the way to shore. Kozack's wounds were less serious.

Fortunately, Dr. Grazier was still on his feet unhurt. He had his hands full. Grazier ordered the wounded spread out in as much cover as he could find on the occasional patches of "dry" ground. Then he started making his rounds to see how his charges had weathered the trip. The list of men down was formidable: Captain Hughes, Anders, and Geist. Biwerse was up but suffering from concussion and wounds in the back and legs. Of the men, Ensminger, Hulsebus, Kozack, Davis, Ziegler, Cecil Green, Ken Rice, Charles Shroyer, and Carl Birk seemed to be in the worst shape. Among the civilians, Sandri and Gassie were bad off. And Squires, the lumber merchant, had a nasty-looking wound. There were plenty of nicks and bangs among the others. But they could wait.

Out in the river *Panay*, strangely enough, seemed only slightly lower in the water than she had been half an hour earlier. In the meantime, Dr. Grazier still needed medical supplies. If there was a chance to get off some additional water, food, and blankets, it could help. More supplies would mean more gear to carry. But there was not much thinking ahead at that point. Nobody had stopped to figure how much he might have to carry—or how far he might have to carry it.

When they saw that the ship was not going right to the bottom, officers and men began to have second thoughts about the "essential" things they had taken out in the first emergency. Jim Murphy had abandoned ship carrying his own personal Morse code–sending key in his peacoat pocket. It was just about the only thing he grabbed. He hefted it now and felt sort of foolish. The key had a heavy iron base and weighed about six pounds. It would have hardly been helpful if he had had to swim. And it was not going to be a very useful object in the swamps of China either. Denny Biwerse had ordered one of the crew to put in the boat a bushel baskel full of fresh eggs along with a Lewis machine gun. It was a strange combination. The gun would have to be buried later to prevent its capture. But the eggs would come in handy before the night was out. One sailor had grabbed a dress blue jumper as the most valuable article he could salvage at abandon ship. He was going ashore, but it was hardly the sort of uniform-of-the-day needed at that point. Some men like Wisler were analytical about it and gathered up a small packet of survival gear. Others scooped up a few letters, some photographs, a book being read at the time, an uncompleted correspondence assignment for a petty officer's advancement course. Now with time to sort things out in the relative security of the reeds, there were obviously a great many vital supplies missing. Mahlmann volunteered to take the motor sampan back for whatever else he could find.

The men on shore watched as Mahlmann's blunt little white launch chugged once more out across the long, cold expanse of brown water. It was getting on toward four o'clock and the look and feel of an early winter evening was in the air. The discomfort of the riverbank and the knowledge that tonight there wouldn't be the warm bright comfort of *Panay*'s wardroom and mess, with good chow, hot coffee, and snug bunks, came individually to each man. The chatter primed by nervous excitement tapered off. The bad jokes stopped. There was not too much now for most of them to do. Dr. Grazier, his corpsmen, and a few of the others worked with the wounded. Most of the rest of them just had to lie low and wait and think—and watch their home of a few months or a few years slip lower into the muddy river.

Frank Roberts, Tex Anders, and Commander Hughes took stock of the situation. The captain kept trying to sit up in his Stokes stretcher and Doc Grazier kept having to come over and order him down again. Hughes was first concerned about the men who had gone aboard *Mei Ping*. Was there a chance to get them back? Whatever happened, all the Americans would probably be better off if they could stay in one party. As far as the *Panay* group could tell, *Mei Ping* and *Mei Hsia* were still intact, tied up on the other side of the river, though there was some smoke coming up from that point. Maybe there was even a chance of getting one of the tankers to tow *Panay* aground before she sank. Maybe they could even do the job with one motor launch borrowed from each of the three tankers, coupled with *Panay*'s own motor sampan. Hughes resolved to try if *Panay* was still afloat when Mahlmann's boarding party got back.

If the ship could be beached, the shore party could be much better equipped. They could take what they needed for several days of hiding out inland and then get a couple of men to take the motor launch and try to make it through to some town farther up the river. The best information they had was that Wuhu was now in Japanese hands. They would have to avoid that. The more they talked, the more they realized that any Japanese contact at this point was probably dangerous. Maybe the United States and Japan were *already* at war. If not, if the attack had just been a mistake, then the Japanese might desperately try to find and wipe out all the remaining survivors so word of what really had happened would never get out.

As Hughes, Anders, and Roberts were conferring, something happened that made them suspect that their fears of the Japanese were probably well justified. Roberts remembers:

As we were talking, someone excitedly pointed out two launches coming down the river. Recognizing them as the same type of Japanese motor landing boat we had seen that morning, I took it upon myself to order the wounded carried well back into the reeds, and with one or two others remained at the riverbank in observation. The two boats came slowly down the river and just at this point our sampan started back for the shore. I was terribly anxious; it seemed to me she would never make it.

Roberts didn't have his field glasses. At that distance he couldn't tell whether or not Mahlmann had spotted the Japanese boats. And there was no way now the party on shore could warn or help the launch crew. The Japanese craft could easily overtake *Panay*'s heavily loaded sampan in a race for shore. And if the two Japanese boats coming downriver were equipped like the one that had boarded *Panay* that morning, they probably had machine guns in the bow. If Mahlmann hadn't armed himself with a .45 somewhere along the line, then the *Panay* boat couldn't retaliate with anything bigger than an oil can.

It wasn't long before Roberts' question was answered. "The Japanese held straight for *Panay*. And when they were about 300 yards from her and our small boat was still 200 yards from shore, there were several bursts of machine-gun fire from one or both of the launches." If the guns were like the ones he had seen that morning, Roberts figured they could only fire more or less directly ahead. There was only one conclusion. They were shooting up the gunboat.

Roberts saw the two boats pass around *Panay*'s stern and along the port side, where they boarded her amidships. Now the Japanese were hidden from the observers on shore. "After several minutes, during which our sampan got to shore and the two men made her fast and scuttled into the reeds, the Japanese boats left the ship and cruised slowly upstream, so slowly that they hardly seemed to move. We waited tensely, thinking they would surely head toward us." Because *Panay's* flags were still up and the boarding party would have seen her name on the stern and on the nameboards along the bridge, there was no doubt that they knew they were boarding an American vessel. Also, with the gunboat abandoned, the officers would know the American crew couldn't have gotten far. Now, Roberts figured, they would probably start to fan out and hunt the Americans down, following the launch to the west shore, where they had certainly seen Mahlmann heading.

Atcheson joined Roberts in the edge of the reeds. There was a hurried consultation. "George," Roberts said, "if they start toward us, what can we do?" Roberts would never forget the State Department man's answer or the look on his face. "There's only one thing to do," Atcheson said. "Go and meet them."

"All right," Roberts answered, "I'll go along with you." As he said it, he hoped that his legs would survive the trip. The Army officer was armed only with his Colt .45; he was one of the few in the shore party who had any sort of weapon. He knew the pistol wouldn't do much good in that sort of situation. He knew, too, that as an intelligence officer—if they truly were in a war situation—he should *never* fall into Japanese hands. If he did, he had an inkling of the treatment he might get. But he also knew he couldn't let Atcheson go out there alone. Roberts had only two choices. Both were lousy.

Suddenly the two Japanese launches seemed to pick up speed and head upstream again. They made no move toward the west shore, where the *Panay* party hid. Atcheson and Roberts watched until the launches were out of sight. Then they looked at each other in relief. There was not much to say. No doubt the Japanese would be back. But at least it looked as if the survivors had a bit of a breathing spell.

Deep in the tall reeds where Hughes lay in his stretcher,

Roberts reported what had gone on along the riverbank. He spoke too of the strong suspicion both he and Atcheson had that the Japanese would be back soon to hunt them down and wipe them out. The three men reviewed the condition of the survivors and the equipment they had. As far as the ship was concerned, Mahlmann reported that she was pretty well finished. There certainly was no chance to tow her to shore. Several small fires were burning through the main deck compartments. There was water everywhere below. Mahlmann remembered his last dismal visit:

We gathered up all the medical supplies, food, water, clothing, bedding, and cigarettes we could. Nothing else looked worth salvaging. The galley was as bad. Large pieces of beef on deck, coal black with soot. All dishes and stove pipes down. There was not anything that was fit to carry water in. The sick bay was also a complete wreck. I opened the hatch leading to the office and it was flooded to the top of the hatch. After this I went to the crew's bulletin board and broke the glass to get the watch, quarter, and station bill with all the names so we could check up and see who was missing. It turned out I didn't need it. The yeoman we had remembered each man's name and initial as well as most of their service numbers.

Yeoman First Class John Weber was the "memory bank." He went right to work on a new muster roll as soon as they hit shore.

To Hughes, the situation wasn't particularly rosy. And they needed to move fast. The captain was in more pain now; he knew there was no chance that he would be back on his feet soon. Anders couldn't talk and the bleeding from both hands and his throat was making him increasingly weak. Geist was wounded in the leg; he could probably keep up with the group, but he was in no position to take over command. Biwerse was on his feet, but he was suffering badly from blast and concussion. Grazier had his hands full with the wounded. Hughes turned to Roberts.

"Well, Captain, in joint operations, the Navy retains control until the shore is reached. Then the Army takes over." Hughes beckoned Atcheson to lean over the stretcher. "Don't you think, George, it would be wise if Captain Roberts took over charge of the whole party in view of the fact that I and my executive are both badly injured?"

Later, there would be some squabbling about that decision behind the scenes in the court of inquiry by a few old shell-backs who couldn't abide the idea of a Navy officer "turning over his command" to an Army man. But to the men on the scene it was a wise decision. Possibly the one that saved them.

Atcheson approved immediately. Roberts could speak excellent Chinese. He was familiar with land operations. He had studied the Japanese Army for years. If anyone in the group could put himself in the mind of the Japanese soldiers who would be looking for them, try to outguess their tactics, and outmaneuver them, then Roberts was the man.

Roberts then and now dismisses the controversy over Hughes' giving up his command.

I said I was willing to do anything I could. I understood very plainly, however, that Captain Hughes was not relinquishing command of his crew. I recall that he said, regarding his men, that I should have authority to tell them to do anything necessary, that I was authorized "to speak with his voice." I never considered that I had command in a strict sense over the crew of *Panay*. But I did, either by explicit or tacit consent, take command of the entire party, which included not only the crew, but embassy personnel and civilians, including four foreigners. Quibbling over details never entered the heads of any of us. The thing was to get our wounded and the rest of our party to shelter and safety. Lives were at stake. Someone had to assume command. And I should not have hesitated, if necessary, to break every regulation ever heard of in any service to accomplish the ends in view.

Roberts' first job was to get them out of there as fast as

possible. Nobody was sure of the countryside. Anders had brought ashore some charts, but they were the ones he was using to write his orders on and did not show in detail that section of the river. Anders knew where they were and roughly what the terrain was like on either side of the Yangtze at that point. But the details that stuck in his mind from trips up and down through that spot centered on the river itself—bars, currents, snags, markers, ranges to stay in the channel—not how far back the marsh might extend on either side or whether some passable country road paralleled the river at that point.

Roberts looked at the crewmen still on their feet and picked a couple of the stoutest and most reliable looking. They were to scout for some firm ground that the party could follow inland. Radioman Wisler was one of the men Roberts picked. Wisler had wanted to strike out as soon as he reached shore in an attempt to reach a town where there might be some sort of radio facility through which he could send back a message to the *Augusta* in Shanghai. But Biwerse had told him to sit tight. Now, with Roberts' authorization, Wisler could explore all he wanted to.

"I struck off inland and in about 50 yards ran into shallow standing water. Another 100 yards and the water was knee deep." After sloshing and sliding around for about 20 minutes, Wisler knew it was no good. He finally pulled himself up on firmer ground, just in time to hear the tormented pitch of an airplane engine. Wisler dove into a pile of reeds that some Chinese farmers had cut and pulled them over his head to hide, hoping like hell he wouldn't find some nasty Asiatic varmint already in the reeds with him. The plane roared in overhead and kept going. Shaking off the debris, Wisler retraced his steps toward the river until he found a rough sort of path. That was better. Instinctively he started downriver in the direction of Nanking. Before he had gone 100 yards he ran into deep water again. No good. Discouraged, he headed back toward the main group and reported to Captain Hughes. Hughes nodded. "Are you all right, Wisler?"

"Yep," the radioman answered. "I guess I must be living right." Hughes grinned through the soot and caked blood. The captain had been particularly close to his radio gang aboard ship. Not chummy. But close. Hughes had done post-graduate work in communications and felt that radiomen were a breed apart—and should not forget it. Hughes ran them hard. But Wisler forgot all that at that moment. He didn't know how bad the skipper was wounded. But he hoped Hughes would pull through.

Roberts still remembers the terrible hunted feeling that came over them when the planes that buzzed Wisler flew over them:

By the time we had finished churning up the area, the mud was about six inches deep most places where we were. We had to bur-row in the mud and reeds like a bunch of field rats. One plane circled our hiding place very low and we thought surely we had been discovered. But it went away. Then two flights of planes passed downriver at some distance inshore, and later we heard the sound of bombing about where we thought the British flotilla was anchored.

In spite of their own problems, Roberts and the *Panay* officers could still be concerned about the British group. They had all started upriver together on Saturday. The Americans knew the British steamers and the old Jardine-Matheson hulk were crowded with women and children.

It was a few minutes before 4 P.M. when *Panay* finally rolled slowly over on her right side, stuck her squat, stubby stern in the air, and slid, bow first, under the surface of the Yangtze. Some of the *Panay* crew had been watching her closely since the Japanese boarding party had left. Accounts differed. But several men reported hearing two muffled ex-plosions shortly before the gunboat sank. Charges set by the

Japanese? Hot engine-room equipment exploding when the cold water hit it? Or maybe nothing. Some men didn't hear any sound at all. But she was gone.

A few men remembered being so overcome at the sight of their ship sliding under that they doubted they would have heard anything. Instinctively one or two of the crew removed their caps as *Panay* started her final plunge. Others followed suit like the crowd on a street corner when a funeral goes by, each man a little uneasy about the etiquette of the situa- tion but each feeling a bit self-conscious and knowing that some gesture is called for. They all might have stood there watching for a long time, hoping perhaps that she would, by some miracle, surface again—if the planes hadn't come again.

They were peeling off from the southeast once more, the direction of the original attack; they could only be Japanese. But this time the *Panay* men were clearly not the target. As the planes crossed the south bank across the river, there was a loud crump—and *Mei Ping* and *Mei Hsia* seemed to dis- appear in a puff of flame that went up and up. A series of explosions followed almost immediately, each one bigger than the last. The *Panay* men could not tell if the blasts were more bombs or the cargo of the two tankers going up. But both ships were obviously finished. Along with *Panay*'s liberty party?

Anders could remember passing along the deck a few hours earlier when the liberty party was shoving off for *Mei Ping*. There was no reason then to take a "last look" at old familiar faces or register any part of the incident in his mind, except to unconsciously take note of who was going off the ship: Puckett, Coleman, Bonkoski, Hodge, Dirnhoffer, Granes, Browning, Hoyle. Now as Anders looked at the angry flames and black, greasy smoke, he doubted that he would ever see any of them again.

When the planes were gone, it was suddenly oppressively quiet. And then faintly they began to hear cries from across the water. The sound got you down in your spine. There was no way to help. The *Panay* survivors stood silently on the bank, staring across the stream. Was it Chief Puckett? Coleman? Who? A sudden putt-putt-putt from upriver sent them hurrying for cover. A small Japanese patrol boat appeared, following the sound. It had almost caught them by surprise, coming around the bend so close to shore that the last man had hardly had time to get under cover again. Roberts cautioned them all to be quiet. This was the closest any of the enemy searchers had come. There was nothing to do but hug the ground. The Lewis gun that Biwerse had brought ashore had been dismantled and the pieces buried in the swamp to prevent its capture. First Roberts longed for the gun, then he realized that it was probably just as well the weapon was gone. With the temper of the men the way it was, it would have been easy for some hothead to rip off a burst at the patrol boat and expose where they all were hiding.

The arrival of the partol boat and her slow hunt up and down the north shore convinced Roberts that he should abandon until dark his plan to move the party out of that location. The Japanese hadn't discovered them yet. In the meantime they had some meager protection. The minute they crossed the swamp and got into the open country beyond it, they could be easily spotted from the air. In addition, the problem of moving the wounded made striking directly inland almost out of the question. Negotiating the swamp behind the riverbank would be hard enough if everyone were fit and there were no men to be carried. Considering the condition of the men who should stay on a stretcher and those who could barely move, walking upstream along the riverbank where the ground was firmest seemed the only way out. And that would expose them to full view of any traffic on the Yangtze as well. To wait for the cover of darkness seemed the only sensible tactic, even though the wounded were suffering a great deal now from their wounds, the want of water, and the damp, growing cold.

"This period of waiting," Roberts still remembers, "was one of the worst of the whole experience. I was burning with rage and anxiety and impatience. But there was nothing to be done."

Ensminger was slowly dying. He was very quiet. Occasionally he would speak to the doctor or a shipmate, asking for a sip of water. That was about all. Sandri was in great pain. He lay on one side where he was more comfortable. He had hardly moved when Barzini came ashore and found him, covered with a sailor's jacket and several blankets. Barzini recalled:

He asked me to cover him because he was cold. He was extremely pale. We gathered four or five blankets among the reeds, where the sailors had tossed them as they landed, and placed them over him. One was his own: it was one of four we had "borrowed" from the Hotel Metropolitan at Nanking several days before, leaving a $50 deposit. At the moment of departure, Sandri had decided to take them with him. "We can never have too many! And besides, we've paid for them," he had said. Sandri was suffering atrociously. There was no morphine. Sandri asked only that we carry him to a higher point along the shore since the presence of so many men around him had softened the mud and he kept sinking deeper into it. Eight of us lifted him up by the plaid blanket lying under him and moved him several yards. "This is fine," he said. There was nothing more we could do. Except wait.

But if Roberts couldn't move out his whole group until dark, at least he could try to get a message out ahead of them.

Yuan Te Erh, a mess attendant first class who had been born in Shanghai and had some slight knowledge of the country around the river, was one of the men Roberts had sent fanning out earlier to scout a way out. The Chinese messman returned with the information that the little walled town of Hohsien was only about eight miles farther upriver.

And two miles from where they were now was a hamlet where they might get some help. Erh had brought back some villagers with him who could show the way. They could also help handle the *Panay*'s boats. Mahlmann and Rider retrieved the motor sampan and the outboard sampan from where they had been hidden in the reeds. In addition, the sailors had an Allied Petroleum Corporation launch they found in a small cove a short distance up the river. Roberts figured the boats would have to be pulled. The noise of the motors would be sure to bring a patrol down on them. The wounded could be put aboard. That would be the easiest way to move them.

Roberts decided to ask Paxton, who knew the countryside better than most of them, to go on to Hohsien ahead. Paxton would try to get a telephone message through to Hankow and then make any arrangements he could in Hohsien for the arrival of the wounded. With his knowledge of the country, the people, and the language, Paxton was a good choice for the job. But there was a problem. The State Department man had twisted his knee at some point in the attack. And it was beginning to swell, stiffen, and hurt painfully in the cold. In addition, he had received an arm wound that he hadn't told anyone about. As he walked around the little campsite on shore, he tried to move very slowly on his bad leg so no one would know he was hurt.

Roberts, seeing only Paxton's slight limp, thought little of it. Paxton was his best bet.

To go with him, Paxton picked Andy Wisler and Mess Attendant Far Ze Wong. Wisler could operate just about any sort of communications equipment. "Fuzzy" Wong—a Hankow boy—had spent some time in the area. Wisler and Wong had "requisitioned" a spavined old farm horse from a curious farmer who had strayed along the shore path. They mounted the half-lame Paxton on the half-lame nag and started off. The owner of the horse tagged along behind to keep an eye on his property. Paxton, Wisler, and Wong didn't mind. One more person—even a frightened Chinese farmer—gave the expedition a little more feeling of confidence.

Wisler still remembers every detail of the lonely start for Hohsien. Before moving off, he searched out a friend, Radioman Second Class Reginald Peterson, to say a few words of good-by and exchange a parting handshake. They passed some wisecracks about Wisler going on liberty. But Peterson was sure, as he watched Paxton's group move off into the dusk, that he would never see Wisler again. It wasn't a very aggressive-looking landing force. To Peterson it looked more like Don Quixote.

"We started upriver following a path through the reeds," Wisler remembers, "and just after it was fully dark, we came to a gravel road that ran inland from the river. Stepping onto this road in the darkness, I managed to twist *my* ankle." Now there were two lame men. Wisler could have used a ride, too. But Paxton's charger looked so frail, Wisler figured that if he climbed aboard that horse both riders would probably sag to the ground like a leaky balloon. The radioman decided he would just have to keep on walking.

"We could move rather fast along the road and it was good and dark. Once we were hailed by Chinese soldiers. We identified ourselves and one of the soldiers accompanied us. I think maybe another followed at a distance and maybe there was one ahead. It was too dark to see. They were sort of suspicious of us. But they let us keep moving."

There wasn't much conversation. Even when riding, Paxton's twisted knee began to hurt like the devil as the cold got to it. And Wisler spent most of his time watching the road to make sure he didn't step into another pothole and aggravate his throbbing ankle. Occasionally Wong would say something to one of the soldiers or the horse's owner. There would be a brief and alarming loud crossfire of Chinese; it's a hard language to whisper. Then silence.

"After walking for a while," Wisler recalls, "the can of matches in my pocket began to get in the way." The talcum powder can he had put the matches in to keep them dry was bulky. He figured since he was ashore he probably wouldn't need them again. "I asked the soldier in Chinese if he wanted the matches. He was surprised but he took them. Matches would be hard for a fellow like that to come by. He probably thought he was dealing with some kind of a nut." It added to the suspicion and the uneasiness.

Both Chinese and Americans were apprehensive about running into a Japanese patrol. If they did, Paxton and Wisler had developed a plan. The radioman could speak some French and had an impressive beard. In addition to Wisler's radio skills, one reason Paxton had picked him to come along was the fact that Wisler reminded the State Department man of the bearded French Catholic priests who worked in the area. In the event of meeting a patrol, Wisler was to spout French only; while Paxton—equally bearded and (he hoped) ecclesiastical looking—would try to convince the Japanese they were priests. "It probably wouldn't have worked," Wisler speculates, "but at the time it seemed like a good idea. I told Mr. Paxton I had two years of high school French. And while no one in France could understand me, I could spout it on command and throw in a few *pax vobiscums* if that would help."

But there were no incidents and no challenges. Behind them, the two Standard Oil tankers still blazed up. And occasionally they could hear the sound of a new explosion. But they could not see the ships any longer, only the reflection against the sky, which brightened and darkened as the fire blazed up through a new fuel compartment or died down after burning itself out in another part of the ship.

They plodded on in the darkness. The eight miles to Hohsien seemed twice that distance. The gates of the little town had been locked at dusk. There was a good bit of pounding and shouting before they were finally opened.

USS *Panay* (PG 45) on standardization trial, doing a brisk 17 knots off Woosung, China, in August of 1928. (*U.S. Navy photo*)

USS *Panay* at summer moorings, Chungking, 1932. The easy life on the Yangtze Patrol, as far upriver as the gunboats normally operated. (*U.S. Navy photo*)

USS *Augusta*, flagship of the Asiatic Fleet, at anchor in China waters and the victim of another "incident." (*U.S. Navy photo*)

The officers of USS *Panay:* (left to right) Geist, Hughes, Anders, Dr. Grazier, Biwerse. (*Photo by Norman Alley*)

Coffee in the captain's cabin: (left to right) Marshall, Hughes, Barzini, Biwerse. (*Photo by Norman Alley*)

Captain Frank Roberts. (*Courtesy of General Roberts*)

owning, Klumpers, and ahlmann on Panay *at ankow. (Courtesy of eter Klumpers)*

Headed upriver Sunday morning: (center) Mei Ping; (left) Mei Hsia; (far right) Mei An bringing up the rear. (*Norman Alley*)

Steamer packed with chinese refugees fleeing Nanking. Some of these ships were also bombed on Sunday. (*Norman Alley*)

The attack. These stills, taken by Alley through a normal lens on his movie camera, show almost the same proportion as the actual visual observations by the survivors. Altitude is estimated at 100 feet! Note bombs in the racks on the planes. These pictures were censored by President Roosevelt and are published here for the first time. (*Norman Alley*)

TOP *Panay* fights back: (left) Rider; (right) Mahlmann. BOTTOM: Near miss hits the water between *Panay* and Mei Ping, where the liberty party was trapped. (*Norman Alley*)

Abandon ship order just passed. TOP: Some men go over stern with wooden gratings for support. All were picked up later by boats. BOTTOM: Wounded being loaded into outboard sampan. (*Norman Alley*)

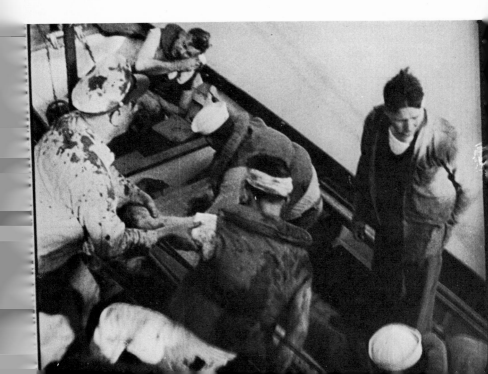

Going under. TOP: *Panay*, decks awash. Note flag stretched over awning just behind bridge. Forward mast, which carried radio antenna, is broken off just above splice. BOTTOM: *Panay* starts to roll over on starboard side and slide under by the bow. Time: About 3:55 P.M. (*Norman Alley*)

TOP: Mahlmann—still without pants—supervises unloading from motor sampan. BOTTOM: On shore immediately after the attack. Note height of reeds. (*Norman Alley*)

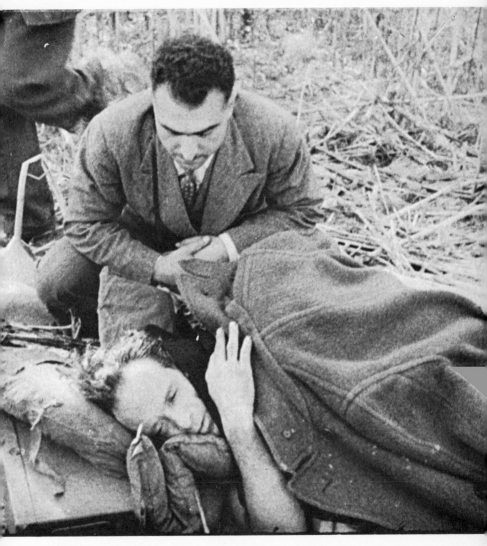

Luigi Barzini leaning over mortally wounded Sandro Sandri. Sandri continued to lie on his side until he died the next day, in an attempt to ease the pain of a wound in the abdomen. (*Norman Alley*)

Captain Hughes resting after the party of survivors reached the bank of the river.

TOP: Tuesday morning at Hanshan, December 14. Lieutenant Geist naps with head on cap in school courtyard. BOTTOM: Chinese soldiers act as litter bearers; they are heading back to Hohsien, Tuesday afternoon. (*Norman Alley*)

TOP: Coffin comes aboard USS *Augusta* with honors.
BOTTOM: Coffin containing body of Ensminger is brought aboard *Oahu* on Wednesday morning, December 15, by British naval launch. (*Norman Alley*)

The rescue force—USS *Oahu*, HMS *Bee*, and HMS *Ladybird* upriver.
(*U.S. Navy photo*)

Colonel Kingoro Hashimoto of the Imperial Japanese Army. (*Wide World*)

"We went into the streets," Wisler recalls, "and ended up at the local Army headquarters. There Mr. Paxton explained that we wanted to get word out that *Panay* had been bombed and sunk."

Americans in China had a pidgin expression, "walla walla," that stood for the barrage of excited talk most Chinese seemed to indulge in before starting out on any major project or decision. There was plenty of "walla walla" when the little group of local officials in Hohsien heard why Paxton, Wisler, and Wong were there, muddy, tired, and injured. These Chinese had no grasp of the international repercussions that would vibrate through the world when that word got out. But they knew something was badly out of balance. Wisler watched the confusion.

A message was finally written out, it was translated into Chinese, the Chinese version was encoded into a five-numeral code, and this was sent by the Chinese by telephone over a line to *somewhere*. We could hear the operator shouting these code groups into his telephone. It would be next day before it got to Hankow. We also learned there was a motor road about 100 kilometers [60 miles] away where a car might take Mr. Paxton to the embassy in Hankow. We decided to push on there by rickshaw; the local army commander said it could be arranged.

Paxton had come ashore without any money, so Wisler's 90 Chinese dollars were pressed into service. The plan they settled on was for the State Department man to get on to Hankow as soon as possible and report to Ambassador Nelson T. Johnson. Wisler would get back to the main party and guide them on into Hohsien.

When Wisler got up to leave the little headquarters building, his ankle had stiffened so much that he could hardly hobble. Paxton would have a rickshaw and then a car from here on in, so Wisler inherited the tired old horse.

Fuzzy Wong was left in town, and I was escorted to the gate. And me on the horse with the owner leading it, left the town and started back down the road we had traveled up an hour or so ago. In about a mile, I commenced running into groups of *Panay* survivors. Now they knew they were not going to be hunted down by Japanese soldiers—at least not right then. Later on Huffman told me he couldn't figure out how anyone as ugly as I was could look so good looming up in the pale moonlight that night.

The group that Wisler met had started moving off from the riverbank for the hamlet Yuan Te Erh had discovered as soon as dark had come. One of the main problems in moving had been the lack of litters to carry the wounded who could not walk. Only two regular stretchers had been brought ashore, one lightweight wood and canvas one and a metal Navy Department basket stretcher in which Hughes had been strapped for the trip in from the ship. Coming off Sandri had been able to walk to the boat with a little aid. Hulsebus and Ensminger had been carried off the ship, one after the other, using the other stretcher. Kozack and Green, the other two seriously wounded sailors, had gotten their wounds in the strafing that was given the boats on the way to shore. Now Sandri could not move at all, and the four sailors also needed to be carried. Most of the other wounded were still navigating more or less under their own power. But Doc Grazier could see that with every hour that passed a few more wounded would become stretcher cases.

As soon as it had gotten dark, Hughes, Sandri, Ensminger, Hulsebus, Kozack, and Green were moved from their hiding places in the reeds down to the shore and into the three boats. The most seriously wounded were to be stretched out on top of the cabin of the oil company launch. Seeing that space was tight, Ensminger insisted on crawling below to make more room for the others. It didn't matter. He must have known then he was about to die. With the cold, the darkness, and the mud underfoot—freezing in some places now—it was a difficult job. Roberts called it "devilish slow work." For the wounded, who occasionally were bumped and jarred and almost dropped, it was often painful. Once they were all loaded, Atcheson and Roberts went ahead to the little hamlet to make what arrangements they could for stretchers and bearers to get them all into Hohsien.

It was slow going towing the boats along the shore. They didn't dare start the engine of the motor sampan. To Roberts, waiting in the village for them, the trip seemed to take hours. "When the boats arrived, we transferred the wounded to the farmhouses, using bamboo beds, doors, sections of a pigpen, springs from the seat of the launch, even planks. Then we got the supplies off and finally cut the three boats adrift so that the Japanese would have no evidence of our landing at that point."

It seemed a somewhat symbolic decision and a hard one for sailors to make. But from there on, they could make better time on foot. While they were getting ready to move, welcome news came through. Some policemen and soldiers arrived at the hamlet asking for Roberts and Atcheson. They were from Hohsien and had been sent back to the hamlet by the local magistrate; Paxton had obviously gotten through. The Chinese urged them to move on to Hohsien as quickly as possible. The facilities there were slim. But Japanese patrols would probably give the town a wider berth until they were stronger in the vicinity.

There was time for a meager meal. Hot tea was brewed for all hands. Biwerse's bushel basket of eggs was supplemented by some eggs from the village; these were boiled so each man could have one. A little Chinese wine turned up from somewhere. It wasn't very strong. Or very good. But it was passed around. A swallow or two brought a welcome warming sensation into cold bodies after the damp of the swamp.

Roberts returned to the house where he had left George Atcheson and found the State Department man trying to bring some order out of the terrible confusion of hiring some Chinese to help with the wounded.

The bearers we had collected were proving difficult. They had objected that four men to a stretcher were not enough; and they wanted more than the $5-a-man agreed on at first. They also wanted a safe-conduct return to their village. In a scene of typical Chinese confusion, everyone talking at once, we wrangled and argued for minutes on end, but finally got off the first of the wounded—the captain. I detailed one sailor or civilian to accompany each stretcher.

With 13 wounded who really should be carried now, they would need at least 52 bearers. But when they thought everything was arranged and were ready to move out, they found that 16 of the bearers, who were still dissatisfied with the arrangement, had slipped away into the night. That left 4 wounded without the Chinese needed to carry them. Roberts asked Dr. Grazier, Ensign Biwerse, Lieutenant Geist, and 3 or 4 sailors to remain behind with the 4 wounded. He would go on toward Hohsien to get help.

Roberts and Atcheson gave the orders to shoulder up the gear. The bearers and the crew were told off in fours and sixes around the improvised stretchers. In the darkness there was a pocket of grumbling. One group of three or four men had gotten more wine now and weren't moving. Roberts remembered the .45 strapped to his side. He hoped he wouldn't have to use it. It was the sort of situation where one or two moves made rashly or wrongly could quickly make discipline go to hell.

Roberts knew the men were strung out to the end of their stamina. For the first time in about six hours there was a chance to let down their guard. They all felt better, now that they knew the Japanese would not find them immediately. The fire in the hamlet was warm and the wine was good. Why not stay right here until morning, when they could get some proper gear to carry the wounded? Maybe then it would be safe to take the injured men on to Wuhu in the boats. That would be a lot better than slipping and sliding around in the dark with a 180-pound shipmate on top of a goddamn chicken coop door. To hell with it!

George Atcheson didn't raise his voice often. He raised it only once that night. But what he said was stern. And he obviously meant business. "Atcheson gave 'em hell," Roberts still remembers with a grin. Roberts' .45 would hang useless at his hip. He hadn't had time to move before the embassy man lit into the reluctant sailors. In a few minutes, the stragglers were formed up and moving out of the village. Atcheson and McDonald pushed out ahead toward Hohsien. That was the end of it. About 15 minutes later, they all felt as if they had been on the road for hours. The hamlet was well behind them. The incident was forgotten. And there was never again any question of authority.

If there had been any light, it would have been a strange procession to observe. A sliver of a moon came up later. And the glare of the burning tankers warmed the sky behind them. That was all. Norman Alley wrote later:

We were draped in blankets. That made us look like a processional of sorry ghosts of some long vanished Indian tribe. Besides this, we were still wearing our life jackets, because the padding afforded additional warmth. I found myself walking beside the stretcher on which poor Sandri was being carried [a peasant's bed, really, carried by four coolies]. I was walking at his unwounded side, the side he had to lie on. He glanced up and recognized my face in the moonlight. He smiled wanly, and groped out to reach my hand. He clasped it, squeezed it with fast dying strength. "Okay, Sandri," I encouraged, as though he understood what I was saying. "It won't be long now."

About three miles from town the column, plodding along in the pale moonlight, suddenly ran into a string of armed men across the road ahead of them. If he had been leading a column of U.S. Infantry, Roberts would have known just what to do; a signal would have sent them immediately into skirmish lines on either side of the road. But his motley assortment of unarmed sailors, wounded, and plodding Chinese was like some unwieldly serpent stretched out behind him. It had taken a lot of momentum to get it going and no infantryman's whistle would send it scurrying now. Roberts just prayed the armed men weren't Japanese.

The soldiers turned out to be a Chinese river patrol that had gotten word of the sinking and had come ashore to investigate. There was more "walla walla." But after half an hour it terminated in permission to proceed. Roberts pushed on ahead to set up the arrangements in Hohsien. "Long before I got there, my feet were blistered, for—humiliating as it is for a doughboy to admit—I had been caught in silk socks, which promptly wrinkled, with painful results." Roberts, walking at a fast pace, soon left the column behind.

Somewhere back toward the tail of the group, Alley was still walking beside Sandri's stretcher. The Italian had said something when the column stopped for so long, but the American had no way of understanding or answering. "As we proceeded along the road, I held tight to his hand, and he kept whispering something in Italian," Alley remembers. Sandri was from Friuli, flat country crisscrossed by rivers and canals, and Alley suspected the sight of the Chinese countryside, becoming clearer under the rising moon, reminded the Italian of home.

To Luigi Barzini, also walking behind Sandri, the countryside seemed more like Lombardy, with waterways, canals, willow trees, and the odor of river mud. The four Chinese padded on ahead carrying Sandri's stretcher. It jounced, not too gently, from the flexible bamboo yoke they supported on their shoulders. Barzini could hear Sandri call out from time to time:

"Sandri begged them to go slowly and he asked me at each stop if we had arrived. 'Piano,' he said to the coolies in Italian. And the coolies obeyed immediately, as if they understood. Twice he called me over to him. He wanted something to drink. Before our departure we had given him two sips of tea donated by a peasant who lived near the houses where we had stopped and who had nothing else to give." By then, all the wounded were suffering from thirst. But the doctor was reluctant to have them receive any water that hadn't been boiled first. Barzini reminded his companion that the only water they had come to was not really safe to drink.

"Not even safe enough for a dying man?" Sandri asked. They all tried to assure him that he was going to pull through. But Sandri knew.

Then came a strange incident that the others did not understand. To Barzini it made perfect sense. The way the correspondent described it to his readers back in Italy was moving and emotional to a fascist nation that thought it was bracing for a new struggle with communism:

He called me a second time to tell me, "The planes that bombed us were Chinese. Russian-made, of course, with Russian pilots, and Chinese flags painted on the wings."

Weldon James who was walking next to me, asked, "What did he say?"

We translated. James said, "He's probably feverish. We all saw the planes were Japanese."

Sandri was not raving. I knew what he wanted to say. He was hoping to die as a soldier, in the service of *Il Duce*, killed by an enemy he had fought. He wanted his death to take on an even higher significance. He had gone aboard *Panay* and had convinced me to join him three days before, when our intention had been to await the arrival of the Japanese in Nanking, telling me: "We can't provoke an incident. Suppose something happens to one of us. Suppose a grenade hits the embassy villa. There would be international repercussions. We can't embarrass the government or the ambassador."

If the planes which sunk *Panay* and set fire to the Standard Oil tankers had been Russian or had been flown by the Russian pilots we had seen lunching at the hotel in Nanking several days ago, he would have died happy to have sacrificed his life to his country even aboard a ship belonging to another nation.

We told him, "You're right. Maybe they were Russian. No one

could see very well. They're the same ones who bombed the *President Hoover* last August." [Chinese planes—reported to have been flown by Russian pilots—had bombed the American liner near Shanghai, wounding ten on board. The ship, explained the Chinese, had been mistaken for a Japanese troop transport.]

From somewhere in the night came the sound of Chinese. bells. Sandri said something in Italian to Barzini and Alley. Barzini translated: "He thinks they are convent bells." Sandri didn't know the difference. But one thing he did know was that he was dying. Alley watched him.

Sandri lay silent for a while, his eyes gazing straight up at the moon. I guess he was thinking of his part of the wars in Morocco, in the Sahara against the Arabs, against the enemies of the fascists in Ethiopia, and for nearly a year in Spain. Then he was caught up with a convulsive cough. He looked up again, weakly shook his head, and muttered to Barzini, "This is a stupid end!"

It was about midnight when Roberts reached the Hohsien gate to meet a party of soldiers and Red Cross men starting back toward the hamlet. Roberts found that McDonald and Atcheson, who had arrived first, had turned up a Chinese official of Standard Oil who was based at Hohsien. They had also found the local magistrate, a former Syracuse University graduate named Wang Tien Chih. The connection with America was a tenuous one. But it seemed particularly strong and welcome that night.

Even though the threat of Japanese retaliation hung over them, the two Chinese indicated immediately that they would do everything possible for the Americans. With at least two large groups of survivors strung out along the road to the hamlet, there was still a great deal that had to be done, and limited facilities with which to do it. Plus distractions. Plus harassments. In the middle of their conversation, an air-raid alarm sounded and for almost an hour all activity stopped as everyone took shelter. Somewhere up there they could hear the Japanese pilots searching for them. The high up, steady hum of the reconnaissance plane. And then low and nervous, here and gone—the sharp whine of the low-level fighter.

Roberts was impatient to get on with it. "When the air-raid release sounded, I went up to the little emergency hospital building in the public park and found the wounded just being carried in." Roberts, stumbling through the pitch-black streets, found what the Hohsien magistrate proudly called a hospital was really no hospital at all but simply a small, one-story brick building with a thatched roof and no beds or any real hospital equipment. It had been one of the outbuildings connected to an old temple. But since the war had moved closer to Hohsien, it had been cleaned out some-what and converted for use by wounded soldiers. "I got the old caretaker to boil plenty of water, for which the injured were suffering, and with a quilt draped over my shoulders—somewhere along the line I had given my overcoat to one of the wounded men—I spent the rest of the night getting water to them, keeping them covered up, and helping them into less uncomfortable positions."

Except for some limited first-aid experience, Roberts hardly knew where to begin. Dr. Grazier had stayed behind with the final group of four wounded men who were the last to get on the road. Until he or one of the corpsmen arrived, there was not much more that could be done. "At about 1:30 or 2:00 in the morning, Ensminger died. He must have been unconscious for some time, for I didn't know when he went, only discovering it when I went to move him, poor fellow. He was one of those that came ashore in my boat, and I never head a whimper out of him at any time."

Even inside the building with the heat that was available, it was, as Roberts still remembers, "cold as Billy Hill." Out on the road where the other groups were straggling in it was getting really miserable. But the walking, though slow work, tended to keep some heat up in their bodies. Radio-man Wisler, who had passed the first group coming in toward Hohsien, had kept on back toward the hamlet. He had only a vague memory of the way he had come—and the glow of the burning tankers—to guide him. The Chinese farmer who owned the horse still tagged along, now more concerned about his animal and the lateness of the hour than where they were headed. For all he knew, these crazy foreigners would never let him get back home again.

Finally Wisler came to the last group of men headed by Engineering Officer Geist. Geist had a leg wound and was making heavy weather of the walk, but he and the others were taking turns carrying one of the wounded crewmen. Geist assured Wisler there was nobody else behind them. "I paid off the owner of the horse," Wisler remembers, "and started walking in with this group." With Geist's wounded leg and Wisler's twisted ankle, they would move at a compatible pace. But now the radioman developed another more interesting problem. "My ankle was sore, but it soon loosened up and only throbbed a bit. But I had not sat on a horse for about 15 years and I was SORE. SORE. SORE." For a sailor, it was the sort of injury they had never trained him to cope with in boot camp.

It was almost five in the morning before Geist, Wisler, and their little contingent got in through the Hohsien gate, found a place to sleep in another one of the old temple buildings near the "hospital," and turned in. To Wisler, there was abruptly a strange let-down feeling the minute he collapsed. He had been so busy since the sinking that he hadn't experienced the loneliness many of the men felt as they watched *Panay* slide under the Yangtze waters late in the afternoon. "Suddenly I was alone. No lights anywhere. There was a pile of straw nearby, and I crawled into that, pulled some of it over me, and went to sleep. Passed out would have been just as descriptive." At least they seemed safe for the time being.

Dr. Grazier had barely gotten into Hohsien ahead of Geist and Wisler. But there was not even the cold comfort of a straw pile for him. His work was just starting again. Roberts had been the "gray lady" around the hospital since midnight. But there was little he could do that was medically helpful. Now Roberts watched the doctor go into action, with two volunteers, Truax and McEowen, helping him:

He was tired and haggard. But he rolled up his sleeves, washed his hands, and went to work—first giving morphine shots to Sandri, to Gassie, who was in great pain with his badly broken leg, and to Anders, who had lost a great deal of blood and was very weak, yet unable to sleep.

I told Rider, the sailor who had been helping me, to get some sleep and he dropped off at once. At 5:30 I lay down myself and slept for nearly an hour. Two Chinese who had some medical training had come in to help the doctor. By 6:30 he had done about all he could and was all in. So I put him to bed in my place, asked the two Chinese to keep an eye on the wounded, and went off to see about the rest of the party. I found most of them in a couple of Chinese inns in the center of town, doing fairly well for themselves, with the assistance of the Chinese messboys and boatmen from *Panay*. I went on to the house where George Atcheson and McDonald had spent the night and got a wash, and we all had tea and peanuts for breakfast. Then George went along to see the magistrate and make tentative arrangements to go on toward Hofei, where we knew there was a mission hospital in which we might leave our wounded.

Hofei was some 65 miles away. But it seemed the best bet. In fact, it seemed the only one.

There was one bright note. Atcheson had gotten through on the telephone to a Dr. Taylor, a missionary at Anking, about 120 miles away. He had also reached a Dr. Burch at Hofei. Both had relayed messages from Atcheson to Ambassador Johnson in Hankow. At least the rest of the world knew what had happened to them now, and American relief parties would know roughly where they were. Even if the

Japanese tried to hunt them down and kill them, the secret was out. They knew, too, that Paxton was on the way to Chaohsien. From there he could probably call Ambassador Johnson direct with the rest of the details.

As morning came, most of the *Panay* men woke from an uneasy sleep and began to take stock of their situation. Coxswain Maurice D. Rider of Southampton, Massachusetts, snapped upright from where he was dozing in the "hospital" and immediately thought of his patients. Rider's Navy rate meant his specialty was seamanship and small-boat handling. But he realized with satisfaction that he made a pretty fair hospital corpsman, too. Until Doc Grazier had arrived, he and Captain Roberts had handled all the wounded between them, and yet he doubted that their combined previous experience totaled anything more than blisters and hangovers. Looking at his torn and suffering shipmates, Rider started building up a hatred for the Japanese that wouldn't be improved by the remainder of his duty in China—or by a Sunday at Pearl Harbor four years later when *Arizona* would go down beneath him entombing a thousand shipmates.

John Geist woke up that morning cussing. One of the petty officers who didn't know Geist very well, but who always thought of him as a rather quiet man, was surprised to hear the engineering officer suddenly announce that he felt like "blowing the boilers." To everyone's surprise, Geist began to "voice his opinion of the Japanese, his leg, and a few other items, in well-chosen words." Then, as if he'd never blown off a syllable, Geist got busy checking the whereabouts and condition of the survivors.

Norman Alley got up, strolled around the town, decided it was not much better in his estimation than the little fishing hamlet they had been in the night before, and looked for a place to sack out again.

Andy Wisler woke up shortly after dawn to hear excited Chinese voices. He could understand enough to hear one

villager say, "Who is he?" "American," another answered.
"Is he dead?" "He sleeps." Wisler decided to reassure them
He brushed aside the straw and got up. It was, he remembers,
"a painful, creaking process." He went outside. The first
person he encountered was "Doc" Rider. The coxswain took
one look at Wisler, commented that he looked worse than
most of the wounded, and led him back inside to a cot.
Wisler flopped on it and slept soundly for two or three more
hours. When he awoke and looked in a cracked mirror, what
he found didn't seem to show much improvement.

My face was covered with smoke and burned powder. My full
beard was full of straw, and in general I could be considered a mess.
I noticed my dungarees were split in the seams of the seat and
down one leg. Hardly presentable in polite society. I still had a few
dollars in Chinese money, even after lending Mr. Paxton the $90.
So for a dollar or so I obtained a pair of padded Chinese coolie
pants. Not exactly the best-looking attire. But it was December and
where we all thought we were going, I knew they would be warm.
    At a Chinese eating place for a few cents I bought a bowl of
rice and some other food. Vegetables and meat. I had always liked
Chinese food. And long ago I had learned to use chopsticks, so
food was not going to be a problem. I didn't smoke so I didn't
have to worry about cigarettes. The hot tea with the meal took care
of the water problem. And except for the slightly swollen ankle, I
was ready for a long walk.

    Swede Mahlmann had spent an uneasy night at the town's
"hotel." It had been almost too cold to sleep.

The upstairs part was not so bad. There were a couple of wooden
beds with straw matting for a mattress and there were about four
or five men to a bed. The rest of us slept downstairs and shared
what blankets we had. As I recall, me and one of the Chinese
boatmen shared a blanket—and it was pretty thin. The Chinese
gave us all the assistance possible. I never thought we would have
to eat coolie chow or drink river water. But this was a time that we
were glad to get it. We had rice cakes, dough balls, and some kind

of hard bread. The water was boiled and drunk warm. Pretty bad.

Luigi Barzini had spent the night sharing a Chinese pallet with an American sailor. The town had never had more than a half-dozen visitors at a time before, and the men were doubled up everywhere. Filthy, half-frozen, famished. But they were tired enough to fall in their tracks and sleep. Barzini didn't sleep long. At dawn he awoke, worrying about his companion. Their arrival the night before had been depressing. When they had gotten to the little hospital building, the stretchers were laid down in the garden, awaiting the arrival of a magistrate, who, with typical Chinese thoroughness, was recording the name of each man.

"Where are we?" Sandri had asked.

"We've arrived," said Barzini.

"What do you mean? Is this the hospital?"

"It's very small," Barzini answered.

"Then," Sandri said simply, without changing tone, "I will die tomorrow because if they have no oxygen to give me they cannot save me." He dropped off again into unconsciousness.

In the morning Barzini found Sandri still unconscious inside the little hospital.

A crowd of curious Chinese civilians and soldiers hovered over the stretchers. The doctor, exhausted, was still medicating and bandaging one of the wounded. We seized a Chinese soldier by the arm, walked him to the door, stuck a rifle in his hand, and made him keep the people at a distance. Sandri was sleeping in the identical position of the evening before, lying on his good side, his fists clenched next to his chin. He was paler, thinner. His face had grown austere, the eyebrows furrowed. I remember thinking he looked quite noble.

Barzini also remembered a request Sandri had made of him the night before. "Go and see my children in Italy."

The correspondent made himself a promise to do it.

11

"Panay unheard since 1342"

On Sunday afternoon the USS *Luzon*'s radio watch had duly noted that *Panay* had gone off the air in the middle of a transmission. For a while the duty radioman on the Patrol flagship waited for the message to start again. When nothing further came in, he turned to other routine, logged in the incomplete message, and let it go at that.

The radio officer of the watch noted the entry later. No great surprise. Generator trouble or battery difficulty had stopped transmissions before. But it was somewhat inconvenient now with Atcheson and Paxton both aboard the gunboat incommunicado—and the Nanking situation as bad as it was.

A few Americans were still inside the city. *Panay* was the only link between them and the American ambassador in Hankow. The radio blackout, depending on the cause of it, might go on for 24 to 36 hours. It had in the past. Inconvenient. But hardly critical. And now that *Panay* had cleared out and gone upriver with all who would go, it was reasonable to assume she would be all right.

But with still no word by late afternoon and with warnings coming of increased Japanese air and ground activity in the Nanking area, Yarnell on *Augusta* endeavored to track down his Nanking station ship. At 4:33, when *Panay* had already been on the bottom for half an hour, Admiral Yarnell's first search message went out to the commander in chief of the Yangtze Patrol and all his ships:

PANAY UNHEARD SINCE 1342. WHAT IS NATURE OF CASUALTY. ARE YOU IN CONTACT WITH PANAY VIA BRITISH.

Oahu, in Kiukiang, about 200 miles upriver and the closest ship to *Panay*, was not much help. She had heard nothing either. They had all been listening on the same frequencies. *Luzon* radioed back:

NO COMMUNICATION SINCE 1335 WHEN DURING PANAY TRANSMIS-SION NITE DISPATCH SIGNAL CEASED. BRITISH ENDEAVORING DE-TERMINE NATURE CASUALTY, BUT BELIEVE NO BRITISH SHIP NOW WITHIN SIGHT.

The hunt wasn't on yet, but a little uneasiness was begin-ning to show. Some disturbing reports of other types were coming in. USS *Luzon* had received word that Japanese Army units had just gotten orders to fire on all ships in the river, regardless of nationality. Then, late Sunday afternoon, the Americans had heard there had been two incidents involving the British. HMS *Ladybird* and *Bee* had been shelled by Jap-anese artillery near Wuhu, killing one man and wounding four. And the British gunboats *Cricket* and *Scarab* had been dive-bombed near Nanking, where they were protecting British nationals evacuated on the Jardine-Matheson ships.

Yarnell and his staff began to wonder if *Panay* had run into some sort of a dust-up too. If so, she might need the help of *Oahu* sent down from Kiukiang or a destroyer dispatched from Shanghai. *Luzon*, working through the radio room of the American embassy at Peking, asked again that Tokyo be notified of the earlier move of *Panay* and the Standard Oil vessels so there would be no chance of confusion. *Luzon's* message went off at 10 P.M.—at just about the time Paxton, Wisler, Fuzzy Wong, and the reluctant Chinese farmer who owned Paxton's bony mount were making it through the gate into Hohsien.

Most of the rest of the night, the wireless rooms of *Augusta*, *Luzon*, and *Oahu* were busy with official reports, rumors, and rumors of rumors. Each word seemed to get a little more confusing or alarming. On hearing more information about the Wuhu shelling of the British ships and discovering that Americans were also on board the Jardine-Matheson vessels, Nelson T. Johnson, in Hankow, sent another urgent message from *Luzon's* radio room to Secretary of State Cordell Hull in Washington, the embassy in Peking, and the American consulate in Shanghai. Johnson outlined all he had heard and ended with an urgent request:

JAPANESE INFORMED BRITISH AT WUHU TODAY THAT JAPANESE MILITARY FORCES HAD ORDERS TO FIRE ON ALL SHIPS ON YANGTZE. UNLESS JAPANESE CAN BE MADE TO REALIZE THAT THESE SHIPS ARE FRIENDLY AND ARE ONLY REFUGE AVAILABLE TO AMERICANS AND OTHER FOREIGNERS, A TERRIBLE DISASTER IS LIKELY TO HAPPEN.

The first full account of that disaster did not come into United States hands until three minutes after ten on Monday morning. Paxton's various telephone calls had gotten through from the back country into Hankow. Yarnell received the news in an "URGENT" message from the commander in chief of the Patrol:

PANAY BOMBED AND SUNK AT MILEAGE 221 ABOVE WOOSUNG. FIFTY FOUR SURVIVORS. MANY BADLY WOUNDED, NOW ASHORE AT HOHSIEN ANHWEI. HMS BEE WILL PROCEED THIS POINT TO ASSIST AND BRING SURVIVORS TO WUHU. USS OAHU FUELING KIUKIANG PREPARATORY DEPARTING WUHU. NAMES OF PERSON-

NEL LOST NOT KNOWN. ATCHESON SAFE, CAPTAIN HAS BROKEN
LEG. FURTHER INFORMATION WILL BE FORWARDED WHEN RE-
CEIVED.

With the first full news of the terrible disaster, many of
those in Shanghai felt a strange sense of relief. The ship had
gone down. Now they knew how. What had happened to
the Standard Oil vessels was still vague.

As for the reference to "bombed," there was no doubt in
anyone's mind who was responsible. It was inconceivable that
any of the planes from China's limping Air Force had done
the job. They were rarely seen in the air now. In typical
Chinese fashion, they were always being "pulled back for
the big battle," where they could be thrown in to turn the
tide decisively. That would never happen, because the battle
for which the Chinese were always husbanding their arms
and men and ammunition never got fought; it was always
the battle scheduled to come *after* the one that ended the
war.

From Monday morning on, in agonizing bits and pieces,
the story filtered back down the river. Yarnell was tight-lipped,
furious.

The story spread from one end of the big cruiser to the
other within ten minutes. To any Navy man that day, there
was a sense of shock, then shame, then anger. To the officers
and men of *Augusta*, there was also a strong sense of personal loss. The little gunboat had been alongside them many
times. *Panay*, with her spunky-looking little 3-inch guns
popped out fore and aft and her two skinny funnels that
hardly reached to *Augusta*'s main deck. The *Augusta* men
remembered her comfortable, beamy, unhurried look, like a
little excursion steamer that had brought alongside a crowd
of ship's visitors for a leisurely Sunday afternoon. But the
sailors on the flagship remembered, too, the vital job she
and the other gunboats did far up the river, where no officious

cruiser or destroyer could go bullying its way. Many of them had friends or acquaintances aboard. A number of former *Augusta* men had transferred to the Patrol over a period of time. And even those aboard the flagship who only knew the men upriver by a name signed to a regular report or a voice over the radio or telephone suddenly felt apprehensive about the safety of men they had never seen who were suddenly missed like close friends. "I wonder what happened to that crazy Dirnhoffer."

"Hell, he'll come out smelling like a rose."

"Two to one he was below sacked out when it happened. It's just like a car wreck, if you're relaxed, you probably won't get hurt."

Or, "What was the name of the *Panay* guy who was down here in sick bay a couple of weeks ago? The kid, you know. Nice guy. Quiet."

"Hods? Hodge? That was it, Hodge. Yeah, Hodge. Hope he got through all right."

All through *Augusta* it was a personal thing by now. And as the news came in of who was dead and who was wounded and who was all right, as the reassurance came in and the anxiety left, anxiety was replaced by anger and a growing desire to get revenge. On *Augusta* the men had first regarded the war with a somewhat neutral attitude. It was just a crazy feud between two sets of slant eyes. In the fall, this casual approach had been replaced by a deep antagonism. On August 20, an antiaircraft shell had hit *Augusta*, killing a man and injuring 18. No one could determine officially whether the shell was Japanese or Chinese. But the sailors had their own ideas. Everything since then had confirmed their suspicions.

12

"You will henceforth exercise greater care"

To some of the Japanese, at least, the news had come with almost as great a shock as to the Americans. Strangely enough a Japanese naval radio and telegraph station at Owada, in the suburbs of Tokyo, may have been the first outside point to know that *Panay* was in trouble. Earlier in the day of Sunday, December 12, the Owada station claimed it had intercepted a short-wave broadcast—apparently from *Augusta*—ordering *Panay* to change her anchorage. The Japanese never heard the message acknowledged and the radio technicians on duty at Owada simply put it down to the fact that the message had never been received. The Japanese Navy had been having trouble with short-wave transmission in China. Topographical conditions would blank off reception in certain areas where there should have been no trouble at all. As a result, the Japanese Navy units were using long-wave transmissions between their headquarters in Shanghai and advance units in Wuhu. Although the *Augusta* message was noted at Owada, there is nothing to indicate that the Owada station made any attempt to pass the information along to Japanese units in

China. There would have been no reason to do so. Owada could assume that *Augusta* would also advise local Japanese headquarters in Shanghai of *Panay*'s position. And in any event, if the gunboat didn't acknowledge the instructions to move, there would be no point in passing on information about a position the ship was ordered to take when she had obviously not heard the instructions. The Owada operators handled a tremendous volume of general traffic. The routine movement of another nation's ship far up a river a thousand miles away was hardly worth worrying about.

Some time later—about 1:40 P.M.—the Owada operators said they heard the rapid start of another message. The sender identified itself as *Panay*. The Japanese radiomen then claim they heard the start of a "distress call," then silence.

But again the interrupted message was activity outside the normal concern of the Owada station. The fragmentary message Owada claimed it heard gave no evidence of the nature of the American gunboat's problem—and certainly no indication that Japanese units were involved in any way. So again, the Owada duty officer saw no reason to take acton; any number of things could happen to make the ship put out such a call. It was another navy's affair. And in all probability, if there were Japanese units in the area, one of them would have picked up the intercept too and given what assistance it could. There had been some friction between the Japanese and the Americans in China, they all knew. But if a ship was in distress, the Owada people had no doubt that the Americans could count on any Japanese assistance that was nearby.

At Japanese headquarters in Shanghai the small hint of trouble that Owada received was not even present. Vice-Admiral Hasegawa, commander in chief of the Japanese fleet in Chinese waters, had been jumpy about "incidents" since the beginning. There were too many bystanders milling around in the middle of the fistfight. Hasegawa had issued a general rule recently against air attacks on shipping in the river. They were no longer necessary. By late fall, he was fairly certain the Japanese had done away with all Chinese naval vessels that could give any support to Chinese military operations ashore. The steamers operating in the upper river now were mostly foreign owned or simply moving civilian refugees out of the battle areas.

In the excitement of an air attack, Hasegawa knew it would be too easy to mistake a target. Added to that, bombing water targets was a less effective use of bombs than a land attack. If bombing wasn't right on the mark in the river, the bomb was probably wasted. That same bomb, going 50 yards wide on shore, would likely still do some damage. Hasegawa's flyers were as well trained as noncombat drill could bring them. But if the Chinese naval forces were as crippled as now seemed likely, there was not much point in having a bunch of enthusiastic but inaccurate pilots throw away their bombs on rusty river scows and junks.

Since the start of the fighting around Nanking, Hasegawa had cautioned his staff to keep particular track of the four British and two American gunboats that were known to be operating in the area. On December 12, Lieutenant Commander Kurio Toibana, Hasegawa's staff officer for air operations, considered one of the best intelligence men in the Japanese naval air forces, had had a long consultation with Commander Toshitane Takata, who had become Hasegawa's senior staff officer for air operations only on December 1. With the fight heating up around Nanking and Japanese air units from the coast—some of them just arrived in the China theater—now entering the combat, Takata was apprehensive. It might be wise, he cautioned Toibana, to give pilots a special briefing on the location and the look of the various gunboats.

Toibana seemed more casual about sending out such information, particularly if it was premature. His reputation and his experience in the China theater weighed heavily with Takata. True, too much information or premature information could lead to confusion. That Sunday both men knew via the Japanese consulate in Shanghai that *Panay* had just been given instructions to move from her last reported position four miles above Nanking. It could lead to confusion among the pilots, Toibana pointed out, to give them the old position when *Panay* had already left it. And it was too soon to give them the new position, because they didn't know yet if the gunboat had arrived there. Commander Takata was not totally convinced. But Toibana assured him that the naval air force could be counted on to identify the gunboat if they saw her and give her a wide berth.

Takata still remembers Toibana's assurances clearly: "I feel quite secure," Toibana told him, "because the other day when the dive bombers of the Japanese Navy bombed Kiangyin near Chinkiang, they only attacked against targets after putting down as low the masthead of a Chinese junk to identify it. Don't worry. No mistake will occur even if there should be foreign men-of-war on the river."

What Toibana didn't say—or didn't know—was that the more experienced pilots of the Kiangyin operation had been rotated back to Japan, and a new and relatively inexperienced group had taken their place.

At 5 P.M., when Lieutenant Commander Toibana finally got the new location of *Panay* from the American consulate in Shanghai, there was only one error in it. She was right at the mileage in the river where Toibana had noted on his chart— but there was 80 feet of muddy water over the top of her. Captain C. H. Carlson of the *Mei An* was already dead. Ensminger and Sandri would not see another sunrise. And a pair of Japanese pursuit planes were making the lazy circles of hungry vultures over the reeds of the marshes where the survivors were hidden, apparently ready to finish them off, too.

In Hasegawa's headquarters, late that Sunday afternoon, the information passed on by the consulate giving *Panay*'s "noon position" came in on top of a request for any information the

Japanese might have about the gunboat. Toibana was told that radio contact with *Panay* had been broken off about 1:30 in the middle of the message. Could they, the Japanese, establish any contact?

Toibana doubted he could help, but he sent through the gunboat's position to air and Army units operating in the Wuhu area and asked for information. They might have something.

It was not until Sunday night when the day's combat reports came in from the squadrons that were operating from the captured Changchow base that the awful suspicion began to dawn on him. He was to describe it years afterwards as the worst mistake he had ever made in his life.

Rear Admiral Mitsunami had been alerted when the first United States request for information came through. Now he was concerned, too. He gave orders for all naval pilots who had been operating in the area to assemble on *Idzumo* the next morning. And he made plans to fly on to the newly captured base at Changchow himself.

At Changchow, the four lieutenants who had led the raid —Murata in the high-level bombers, Okumiya and Komaki in the dive bombers, and Ushioda in the fighters—had gone to bed the night of December 12, tired and somewhat discouraged. Their first attack against the "Chinese" ships had been reasonably successful. But the incident of the late afternoon when they had almost sunk the British gunboats had been a sobering experience. In addition, the new strain of combat flying was harder than they had realized. They had been in the air on three different missions for almost eight hours' flying time, all told. And though there had been no enemy air opposition, they couldn't always count on that. All the time in the air, the aviators stayed tense without really realizing it, constantly casting that glance above, below, and behind them, never knowing when in the periphery of vision they would suddenly pick up the black streak of an enemy plane screaming out of the sky with little sparkles of flame dancing all across it. And by then it would probably be too late. The older pilots said when you finally saw the plane that got you, it was already too late . . .

Safe on the ground at the end of the day, with aircraft snug in the canvas field hangars and the mechanics swarming over them, the youthful Japanese pilots gratefully slumped in their quarters for a cup of hot tea. Suddenly the tiredness hit them at the back of the neck and the base of the spine. All the training in the world still never quite prepared a man for the strain of actual combat. Years later, in World War II, most of the Japanese pilots who had served in the China War would look back on those days as something of a lark, a realistic dress rehearsal for 1941 with the dangers at a minimum. But the first time in combat, the strain of it hit them all much the same way.

Okumiya and the others had finished off a light and early supper, hardly tasting it, had talked briefly, and then fallen into bed. They had no idea what their assignments would be the following day. They were all tired. Their captured quarters were drab, broken up, smelly. Sleep was best. Okumiya had just dropped off after concentrating hard to relax and shake the tensions of the day when he was awakened by an orderly with a radio message. It was signed by Admiral Hasegawa. The message was terse and presented no clue as to why it might have been sent. But the tone was somehow vaguely foreboding. The fact that such a message had been sent meant that something was out of place. Okumiya read it several times, then relayed its contents to his fellow aviators: "Squadron commander of the flying units which attacked vessels on the Yangtze River are ordered to report to flagship *Idzumo* in Shanghai tomorrow morning."

Or did that mean they were getting the unit citation that rumor said would be given for sinking the ships? The word from Lieutenant General Matsui's headquarters that had come by telephone for their morning briefing had ended with the promise that "were this in the Army, a unit citation will be promised for a successful attack." Would there be a ceremony on the flagship with marines and sailors drawn up? Photographers and reporters present? Pictures sent back to Japan? Some of the flyers began to wonder if the uniforms they had with them were presentable enough. But when Okumiya drifted off to sleep again he was still depressed about the close shave of the attack on the British ships.

The next morning the four lieutenants hurried down to Shanghai and were taken aboard the old British-built *Idzumo*, which sat like a dowager empress in the middle of Battleship Row.

Lieutenant Commander Toibana met them and his look was grim enough to dispel all thoughts of unit citations. Toibana was blunt and to the point. The ships they had attacked and sunk on their first flight out of Changchow the day before were three American Standard Oil Company tankers and the gunboat *Panay*.

The four pilots were stunned. Toibana went on quickly. He retraced the chain of events that had resulted in the attack. He reported the confusion over *Panay*'s position. His own conference with Commander Takata. Their decision not to notify air units of the fact that *Panay* was changing her anchorage until a new position had been received. Toibana acknowledged his mistake manfully, but the four flying officers knew the magnitude to which they were involved when Toibana finished his briefing to them with a deep bow. In Japanese etiquette it was roughly comparable to the last respects you pay to a condemned man.

Although Toibana had clearly made a wrong decision, he had made it largely on the basis of having great confidence in naval pilots and their ability to properly identify a target— even one they didn't expect to find there. Toibana had failed to pass on valid information about *Panay*'s move, but that was where his responsibilities ended.

Regardless of the validity of the information on which the attack had been based and the critical absence of the information about *Panay*'s true position, the final responsibility came down to the four squadron leaders. They had been the last men who had a chance to put all the wrongs to right by recognizing their targets as neutral ships and not pressing home the attack. Now Admiral Hasegawa wanted to know why they had failed to do this.

The admiral's area on *Idzumo* was heavy with gold braid— and dour expressions. The four lieutenants stood stiff and uncomfortable, ready to be raked over the carpet. Commander Toibana and Commander Takata, having made a clean breast of some of their own responsibility, now felt a bit better. Rear Admiral Rokuzo Sugiyama, Hasegawa's chief of staff, ran the show and asked most of the questions. Hasegawa himself sat back not saying much, a deep frown on his face. The other members of the staff looked even more grave—if that were possible—in deference to their admiral and in true realization of the magnitude of the situation.

Okumiya later wrote an American friend, explaining about the meeting:

We told them that we had not had the previous knowledge concerning the presence of the third powers' ships in the vicinity of Nanking. We went so far to ignore the Fleet's restriction of the ship bombing in the temporary excitement after having believed too much the Army information. We approached the targets in the high altitude having believed too much the Army information and having little doubt that they were Chinese ships trying to flee. The number and location of the ships were generally as same as reported by the ground forces. We also explained that gunboats of various navies, having similar appearances, were very hard to identify from the air, and the Murata group supposed to have given a hit on *Panay* made the level bombing upon her from the altitude of 2,500 meters: approximately 4,000 meters apart in distance from the target. It was absolutely anything but an intentional and premeditated attack that was carried out on *Panay*, and the tragedy was solely the result of a terrible mistake.

Rear Admiral Mitsunami, who would eventually have to

take the brunt of the blame, was not present. He had flown to Changchow for a personal investigation. It was there he heard the news. "My delight at the capture of Nanking utterly faded away," Mitsunami wrote later in a private memorandum that has never been published (see Appendix for full text of this memorandum). "We started then preparing every necessary measure of sending planes and destroyers with medical materials for the relief of the crew of *Panay*."

Nobody aboard *Idzumo* was happy. But the explanation was really all that could be said. The lieutenants were dismissed. Their orders were to report back to their units immediately. As they left *Idzumo*, they glimpsed Admiral Sugiyama hurrying ashore, still with the same grave expression on his face. Sugiyama was on his way to meet with Admiral Yarnell to express the apologies of the Japanese Navy and to report that two naval flying boats with medical officers and supplies aboard had just been dispatched to the scene of the sinking. The four lieutenants had heard of Yarnell's reputation for toughness and a quick temper. They didn't envy Sugiyama. And they regretted that they had been the ones to cause all the trouble.

It was a relief to get back to Changchow and find the planes ready and new targets picked out. At least when they were flying they could keep their minds off what had happened out on the river and what must be boiling along now in Shanghai and Tokyo and Washington. They would hear little more about it until the following Sunday, when Nanking had finally fallen. On that day, December 19, Okumiya, Murata, Komaki, and Ushioda were ordered to fly into Tachiochang Airfield, immediately outside the Nanking walls. It was a target they had often attacked. And when they landed on the hastily repaired runways, they could see the marks of bomb damage everywhere. Okumiya was first and his plane had the honor of being the first Japanese aircraft to land in the captured capital. The honor was followed shortly by another and

more questionable distinction. Waiting for him and his three
fellow squadron leaders were four stiffly formal reprimands
that had been flown to Nanking from Tokyo by courier plane!
The brass at home were clearly not taking it gracefully. Okumiya's reprimand, signed by the Navy Minister, Mitsumasa
Yonai, was typical of the four of them:

As commander of a dive-bomber squadron of the 13th Air Group,
your action in attacking American and British warships on the
Yangtze River 12 December 1937 without definitely identifying
your target is deemed a failure in the performance of your duties.
You will henceforth exercise greater care.

/s/ Mitsumasa Yonai
Navy Minister
17 December 1937

It was not the phrasing that disturbed the four lieutenants
so much—although its departure from the cautiously polite
Oriental phrasing had its effect on the men—but rather the
extraordinary way in which the reprimands had been rushed
through and the high level from which they had originated.
Normally, a division commander such as Okumiya would
have been reprimanded by his own senior officer, Captain
Sadatoshi. The fact that the reprimands had come directly
from Admiral Yonai made the lieutenants fairly certain that
Yonai had personally chewed out each officer in the chain of
command from Admiral Hasegawa right on down to the four
of them.

It was a dismal experience for flyers who thought they were
only doing their duty. As they had watched the ships flare up
and sink lower in the water, they thought they had done
their duty extremely well.

"The jungle will overcome us all"

The cables and radiograms filed noon Monday, Shanghai
time, by the excited Shanghai press corps hit United States

newsrooms in the quiet of a Sunday evening. It wasn't quiet long. Monday morning papers of December 13 spread the news all across their front pages:

U.S. GUNBOAT SUNK BY JAPANESE BOMBS;
54 REPORTED SAVED; 1 KILLED, 2 INJURED

The Japanese were starting to react, too. Their shock and regret seemed to exceed even that of the United States. *The New York Times* reported that "the Japanese Navy quickly accepted responsibility for the grave incident. A Japanese communique pledged immediate steps to place the blame on the military units responsible and it regretted the bombing 'most deeply.' "

Japanese papers of Tuesday, December 14, carried big, black, alarming headlines:

U.S. MAN-OF-WAR BOMBED AND SUNK.

MISCONCEPTION DURING BATTLE NEAR NANKING

Shanghai Special December 13. Announcement of the Third Fleet Press Section at 1300: — Upon receiving information that Chinese forces were fleeing from Nanking and going upriver on board the Chinese ships, our Navy air forces took off to attack them. Unfortunately, the Navy flyers mistook and bombed two ships belonging to the Standard Oil Company. This disgraceful incident resulted in sinking them and one American man-of-war located in the vicinity of them. This incident is very regrettable in our relations with the U.S. Navy, and Admiral Hasegawa, Commander-in-Chief of the Third Fleet, bears the whole responsibility for this incident and is undertaking the necessary measures.

An "extra" by Tokyo's *Asahi Shimbun* carried a further story:

"MAKE THE BEST OF
THE DISGRACEFUL INCIDENT
INVOLVING U.S. MAN-OF-WAR,"
ANNOUNCES NAVY
VICE-MINISTER'S STATEMENT

The Navy Department announced the following statement of the Vice-Minister of Navy at 5:00 P.M., December 13, concerning the U.S. man-of-war incident that occurred on the Yangtze River on December 12:

"The detailed report has not yet been received. But according to the reports up to this time, Navy air forces having information that the Chinese troops were fleeing from Nanking and escaping upriver on board ships, took off to attack and bombed the ships on the river. This attack resulted in the sinking of one U.S. gunboat located in the vicinity of the ships. This incident was due completely to a mistake. And the Imperial Navy expresses high regret for the occurrence of such a very grave incident. Our Navy intends to pursue the investigation with sincerity and wants to take every possible measure to discover why it occurred."

The punctilious routine of diplomatic protest and apology had begun. In Shanghai, Admiral Hasegawa followed Admiral Sugiyama with a call on Admiral Yarnell to express his regrets. The meeting must have been icy, even though Hasegawa was rumored to have promised Yarnell he would "accept the fullest personal responsibility." In the Japanese military code, that could mean resignation or even hara-kiri.

Japanese ambassador to China Shigeru Kawogoe telegraphed his regrets to his American counterpart, Ambassador Johnson in Hankow. Japanese consular officials in Shanghai expressed similar regrets to U.S. Consul General Clarence E. Gauss.

The tempo of the calls of apology, the accusation of guilt, and the ultimatums demanding satisfaction increased with each hour—and with each fuller account of the sinking. With the increasing tempo of accusation, apology, and ultimatum came double-talk and confusion. The Japanese went on record immediately that the sinking was a terrible case of mistaken identity. But in Western eyes, it was all the more difficult to explain because of the familiar Japanese boast that they had already sunk every Chinese naval vessel on the river; if the opposition's naval force was known to have been wiped out, how could the pilots mistake the floating *Panay* for the sunken enemy?

In Washington, on Monday, December 13, at half past noon, Franklin D. Roosevelt delivered to Japanese Ambassador Hirosi Saito, through Secretary of State Cordell Hull, a memo of protest to the Japanese government. It demanded full apology and compensations for the sinking. Rumor was that an even stronger note was on the way. Then, with action begun on the diplomatic front, Roosevelt moved to make sure his political flanks were well supported, too; White House press secretary Stephen T. Early appealed for newspaper and public support for the administration, emphasizing that there were no political motives involved, only pure patriotism.

In Congress, the debate was already underway. Congress favored being tough but cautious, while taking steps to see that it didn't happen again. One of these steps might mean getting out of China completely. Senator Robert R. Reynolds of North Carolina, an extreme pacifist, adopted an I-told-you-so attitude and took the opportunity to remind press, public, and fellow legislators that he had previously advised withdrawing from China. Senator Hiram Johnson of California called for adequate protection of Americans everywhere and counseled his fellow congressmen to go on record that the United States would refuse to be bluffed by the terrorist tactics of *any* government *any*where.

Between the formal round of apologies, the Japanese diplomatic corps in Washington couldn't decide whether to lie low or go on as if nothing serious had happened. Japanese Ambassador Saito had been invited, along with his Chinese counterpart, to attend FDR's first state reception of the season to be held later in the week, and he saw no reason to cancel his plans to attend. But Japanese naval attaché Captain Kengo

Kobayashi, who had planned a tea for Monday, December 13, decided to call it off. Apparently nobody mourned but the caterers.

Newspapers around the country endeavored to finger local pulses and came up with varying reactions. The San Francisco *Chronicle* wanted no war, but saw trouble ahead for United States prestige far outside the borders of China if we did not take "a firm position." In Texas, where hotheads and quick triggers were a familiar historical heritage, the Dallas *News* thought it saw through all the diplomatic double-talk to the real cause of the incident: "The very probable truth in the situation is that military jingoism in the Japanese Army, feeding on a blood-whetted appetite, has reached the stage of truculence to which conquering armies are invariably prone." The editorial writer of the *Arkansas Gazette* in Little Rock wrote as if he already knew Munich was ahead: "Italy and Germany, Japan's fellows in a world fascist bloc, may find in it [the sinking] further evidence to support the belief in which they have been proceeding—that the 'fat-bellied democracies' are afraid to stand up for their rights against fascist affronts and aggression."

Even if full apologies were forthcoming, the Kansas City *Star* was suspicious of them: "Time after time in the last few years the military authorities have shown only contempt for the more peaceful and conciliatory statements of the civil officials in Tokyo." In Omaha, Nebraska, the *World Herald* longed for a United States hands-off, stay-out policy yet seemed to know that wasn't really the solution: "Never again must we let ourselves be drawn into the wars of other lands. Yet somehow, sometime, there must come an end to the rule and law of the jungle, else the jungle will overcome us all." In Boise, the *Idaho Statesman* already seemed to foresee—and accept—the brinkmanship of the 1950s and 1960s: "In this case our State Department is all excited, of course, and an apology is demanded from Japan. It may be forthcoming in a veiled and ambiguous form. Then everyone will sit back sans excitement—until Japan sinks another of our warships."

Though the nation was not looking for trouble, it was obviously ready to tighten up in anticipation of some. Americans had little intention of backing down. On the West Coast the mood was tough; so much so that shops in Seattle and San Francisco were putting up signs: "This store owned by *Chinese*." In Shanghai, USS *Augusta*, with steam up to return to Manila, had her orders canceled. She would stay and would be supported by USS *Marblehead*, a strangely graceful vintage cruiser whose four stacks gave her the appearance of high speed even while anchored.

Peppery Harry Yarnell, aboard *Augusta*, would be asked by the Japanese to move these two ships, his destroyers, and his gunboats out of the danger zone. The suggestion was made "informally." And it was not repeated. Wire services, with stories aimed at publication in family newspapers, let it go that Yarnell simply "declined."

In fact, if there had been water enough, Yarnell would very likely have been storming up the river with *Augusta*, right into the middle of things. He wanted those survivors back! And now.

13

"The Canal Street Ragpickers"

WITH THE ARRIVAL of daylight Monday morning in Hohsien, things looked much better. The wounded were growing more tender as injured bones and tissues that had been numbed with the first smash of injury began to yield up scores of secondary complaints. Secondary complaints, but annoying ones. And a night of cold, hard beds, or no beds at all, began to bring out stiffness and soreness even in the uninjured. Men had made their bodies perform some fantastic feats of strength and endurance the day before, sparked by the pressure of emergency. Men had lifted tremendous weights, crashed down heavy doors, hauled around wounded comrades who were twice their weight as easily as if they were children. But now, with the shooting stopped, they didn't have the strength to do it again. At least not in the cold light of that December morning in Hohsien.

Though it was better than the swamp, even in daylight the little town of Hohsien didn't have too much to recommend it. But the men who had dragged themselves through the town gate the night before and collapsed where they stood now had a chance to look around and get some reassurance from their surroundings. Most of the reassurance came from the fact that they were obviously among friends. The hospital offered some shelter for the wounded. Everyone else had a place to sleep under cover. There was hot water for washing off the mud of the swamp. Good strong tea and passable food were on hand. The villagers were annoying to some extent because of their curiosity. But they were also friendly enough— and strangely sympathetic too, considering that an Oriental tradition had taught them to take the tragedies of their fellow man with indifference.

But if the Chinese were curious, they were also willing and seemed ready to do anything they were asked. The local magistrate, with his Syracuse University background, provided a reassuring link with the normalcy of the States. Finding him there was almost like finding some foreigner who has been to your home town and remembers an old familiar landmark or two. It was trifling, but heartening. Working with the magistrate, the Chinese representative of Standard Oil based at Hohsien, and the local Chinese Army commander in the town, the Americans seemed to be able to get things done. The men who had no assignments could see that plans were being formed. They all knew contact had been made with the outside. And even though they suspected that the Japanese would still be looking for them, they had the satisfaction of knowing the news was out.

Captain Frank Roberts spent most of Monday morning making a complete check of the condition of all the men, wounded, walking wounded, and fit. They would have to move soon. How far and how fast they moved depended on how well the wounded would travel. There were two who wouldn't be going any farther. Ensminger and Sandri had died. The Italian had lapsed into a coma soon after their arrival in Hohsien. He had never waked and had died sometime after dawn. Roberts had been by Ensminger's pallet repeatedly during the night and the early morning. The store-keeper had only managed a word or two and a weak smile. Occasionally he asked for a sip of water, which Roberts had given him. Ensminger's thanks came in a voice that could hardly be heard. When Roberts came around sometime shortly before four o'clock, Ensminger was dead.

Rough wooden coffins were ordered for each man. The two bodies would have to be left at Hohsien, to be retrieved as soon as a proper expedition could be sent back upstream. Traveling with the wounded was slow enough. Traveling with two heavy coffins in the line of march would be almost impossible work. And it would be constantly depressing to the survivors.

Most of the wounded seemed to be reasonably well. A few more would have to be on litters than the night before. But that was to be expected, too. Many of the ones who could walk had wounds that were not serious now but would become serious soon without proper treatment. It seemed wise to use the intervening days to get everyone moving in the direction of that treatment. To stay in Hohsien might seem at the moment an appealing alternative to weary men. But it probably meant raising the odds against all of them getting out. As long as they were mobile, the party had more options for safety, a better chance all around. Added to that, inactivity would sap the morale of all of them.

During the morning Roberts received a message from Ambassador Johnson that seemed to argue against moving on. Johnson had sent word that warships were on the way and that the survivors should remain in Hohsien until the ships arrived. But the next report from downriver made Roberts sure he had to disregard the ambassador's advice; the Japanese had landed in some strength a few miles below Hohsien, Roberts heard. Whether or not they were looking for *Panay* survivors was not clear. But it wasn't worth the chance. Also word had filtered into Hohsien from several directions telling of Japanese patrols attacking villages in a wide area around them. Roberts decided to move. "At one o'clock George Atcheson and the doctor and I had a final conference in which we decided we would have to go on that night. I set four o'clock as the time for assembly."

Roberts' survey of the group showed that many of the men had brought ashore whatever cash they had at the time of the sinking. By pooling it, the group had enough money to buy enough clothes and quilts to improvise a jury rig of cold-weather uniforms. They collected emergency bedding to take on the road with them, and some simple food supplies were purchased. To keep the load light, they would have to buy most of what they needed to eat at villages along the way. But Roberts figured the money they had would get them to Hanshan, 20 miles to the northwest. By tradition, the Navy urged most men to leave their pay "on the books," drawing it only for leaves and Stateside allotments; as the nest egg carried on the books grew, it made small pay seem more hand-some and made liberty less violent. But this was one time all the officers were glad that several hundred dollars in enlisted men's pay had been squirreled away in lockers and ditty bags. This was not the sort of shore expedition the money was being saved for. But even the hell-raisers figured their pay was never better spent. Tex Anders, clad in a Chinese suit that Swede Mahlmann had bought for him to replace his tattered Navy uniform, started a series of entries in a small pocket notebook, recording who had advanced the expedition how much.

Roberts and Atcheson began planning to get the group on its way. Roberts remembers the discouraging stops and starts:

At two, George and I went to see the magistrate to make final arrangements for junks to transport us up the small canal 20 miles to Hanshan, the next town. Mr. Wang also promised us plenty of bearers and stretchers for the move. When this was done, we went with Chen [the local Standard Oil representative] to get some food at a restaurant, the first real meal we had had in 24 hours.

Roberts would never get a chance to eat it.

We had no sooner started to eat than an alarm signal was given. And though I managed to swallow a little, George simply couldn't choke it down. Paxton's dog, Happy, had attached herself to me, and when she heard the planes, she tried to climb in our laps, and trembled violently—she was badly shell shocked.

Secretly, they all knew, the dog had lots of company.

Atcheson tossed enough money on the table to cover the uneaten meal, and the two men headed for the street. Two Chinese policemen pushed them back under cover, warning that the planes were low. Very low. Roberts caught sight of one of them swooping in. It couldn't have been more than 500 feet up. Bastards!

Inside the hospital, the wounded—some of them feverish and confused—thought they were back on the ship with the attackers coming in again. Dr. Grazier and the men helping him moved quickly among the figures laid out on pallets and straw, explaining, calming the men down. Everyone was nervous. Roberts was angry and disappointed:

I knew then that I had been wrong in ordering an assembly so early. After what seemed an eternity, the clear signal sounded and we made for the center of town, only to see the sailors and others of the party moving up toward the park. There was nothing for it but to park them in an old temple building and wait for dusk. Everybody was on edge to go, but they all took it quietly enough.

The men were sure now that the planes overhead meant the Japanese still intended to hunt them all down and kill them. Later, Tokyo would claim that these were only search planes with Japanese Navy doctors and corpsmen aboard, trying to find where the survivors were so they could land and help. But if the Japanese story was indeed founded in truth, it would have been a hard one to sell to anyone on the ground that day. The whine of the engines sounded too menacing and the dives were too steep and swift. Somehow it didn't have the look of a rescue party.

Three times within a short period that afternoon the planes came back. The men stayed pretty well under cover. But the officers were certain some inquisitive sailor would stick out a head—and a white hat—at some point. And the strafing would start again.

The Chinese were terrified. Hohsien was a small enough town not to attract any attention from enemy aircraft under other conditions. In the ordinary course of the war, it would eventually be taken over by Japanese troops after token resistance. Most of the villagers would simply be exchanging one brand of governmental oppression for another. But now the villagers had heard rumors of the rape of Nanking. And with the Americans present, their village seemed about to get the same treatment. The Americans were responsible. Get the Americans out!

Waiting for dark was the hardest part of all for the survivors. Tex Anders spent the time making some notes about the attack and the events that followed. He knew there would be a court of inquiry. And a tough one. Even though they had gone down fighting, they had lost their ship. There would be a lot of hard questions asked and a lot of angry brass who would want some very thorough answers. The answers were clear enough to Anders but hard to write. The wounds in both of his hands were spreading the pain. His fingers were so stiff it was hard to hold the pencil. The tighter he tried to grip it, the more his hand hurt.

Andy Wisler spent the time trying to get his twisted ankle in shape. Between raids he scrounged some hot water from an old Chinese woman and soaked his foot. Then he washed out his socks. "I was kind to my feet. It looked right then like I was going to use them a lot."

Chief Mahlmann showed the sailors how to lash up their blankets and extra gear so it made a small bundle that was easy to carry. But nothing would fit and nothing would tie up right and it was all strange. The sailors with their lumpy

kits looked to Mahlmann like "a bunch of Canal Street rag-
pickers!" Feather merchants! Old salt Mahlmann was dis-
gusted.

Colin McDonald spent the time being hungry. But he was
having a hard time getting down anything but hot tea. The
London *Times* correspondent was not frightened. He had
been under fire a number of times before. But the previous
day, after Sunday dinner on *Panay*, he had taken out a bridge
that replaced some of the critical teeth he needed to attack
his "meat and two veg." And the bridge had gone down with
the ship. It was a hell of a way to start foraging through the
Chinese countryside.

"Where the hell did you guys come from?"

As dusk approached, they all breathed a little easier. The
Japanese planes had not come back, and there were no fresh
reports of Japanese patrols in the vicinity. But there was one
unpleasant task still to be attended to. Burial of the dead.
The coffins of Ensminger and Sandri were laid out behind
the hospital. Raw, unpainted oblong wood boxes that looked
like two crates of machine parts, consigned for some rural
factory that was struggling to get started. Roberts was able
to scrounge up two American flags and laid them over the
boxes that held the bodies. They thought about improvising
the Italian colors, but there was no time. Roberts made arrangements for the temporary burial of the bodies until the
Americans could get back upriver to claim them. The little
burial party saluted. Roberts, Atcheson, Chief Mahlmann
stood by as witnesses. That was all the ceremony they could
manage.

By 5:30 it seemed dark enough to move the men out from

under cover again and about a mile down to the canal bank, where a group of rented junks were assembling. It was a scene of typical Chinese confusion. Getting darker all the time. Too early for any moon. There were only a few weak, hooded lanterns to work by, and the men were hampered by the strangeness of the place and the difficulty of moving the wounded. The embarkation should have taken about an hour to accomplish. It wasn't completed until nearly eight o'clock. Two and a half hours spent. Mostly in "walla walla." The Chinese helpers—as willing as they were—didn't know the men they were working for. They had no clue as to who should be listened to and who ignored. And all the Americans shouted, muttered. And cussed. The Chinese could tell *that* was beautiful, even if they didn't know the language. When things bogged down particularly, everyone tended to start giving orders. They were all still a little jumpy. And a barking dog, or a piece of falling equipment, or even a sudden and surprising silence, when everyone happened to stop talking at once, was enough to cause them all to stop what they were doing and wheel. It was as if they were expecting to see a Japanese patrol with fixed bayonets dogtrotting down the canal bank at any moment. As a matter of fact, they were. Roberts cursed, shoved, cajoled, threatened. It was bound to help. But to an Army man, used to a quick snap-to when an order was given, whatever happened never happened fast enough. Roberts was discouraged at the delay and the confusion.

It takes time to move a bunch of Chinese. I found, too, I had erred in not making a personal reconnaissance of the riverbank where we loaded. The approach to the junks was very difficult and the loading was slow and exasperating business. Finally we got our wounded and ourselves properly stowed. Then the six junks moved off in column, towed from the bank.

It was a far cry from the warm comfortable quarters on

Panay they had enjoyed 48 hours earlier. Each of the 40-foot boats carried about 10 or 12 men, in addition to its own crew. In the junks where there were wounded, the stretchers were laid under a matting canopy about level with the bulwarks. Two or three stretchers to a junk were all that could be accommodated. The other men were crowded fore and aft. Maybe the crowding would keep them warm; it seemed much colder than the night before. The tow men, or trackers, trudged ahead on a path along the shore. One man stayed in the boat to steer. It was slow progress for the Americans. But it was better than walking—as they had been the night before, stumbling in the potholes of the dinky little road leading into Hohsien.

Most of the Americans were so tired they soon dropped off to sleep, slumped against the sides of the junks or squatting down in cramped positions along the thwarts in an effort to get out of the chilly night air. It was uneasy sleep. To Roberts, who had the responsibility of command and who had been awake for almost 36 hours, sleep was particularly uneasy. "I remember once rousing from a doze to see what looked like the surface of the Yangtze and a boat with a light in its bow coming straight at us. I broke into a cold sweat and got stiffly to my feet, only to discover that what I thought was water was sky. And the light was a low star."

Occasionally Tex Anders would awake to feel no motion at all. The tow men would have stopped to kindle up a fire and make some tea. It was near freezing by midnight. They all knew the exertion the Chinese were putting into the job. And the need for a break, from time to time. But the Americans feared the delays, too. The stops seemed intolerable. A few minutes after each stop was made, the lack of movement would wake up men all along the little convoy. Soon they would be shouting and cursing to get the tea drinkers to hurry, douse the fires, and start on again.

The trip took almost ten hours. At six in the morning the

six junks, with their tow men plodding ahead, pulled into the canal landing nearest the little village of Hanshan. It position, about 20 miles inland almost due west of Hohsien, seemed relatively secure. And though the Americans were still close enough to the river to have seen it from a substantial rise in the land, the long journey of the night before and the low flat landscape that was broken by nothing but an occasional tree or farm building made the Yangtze and the dangers of the day before seem removed now to a much safer distance.

It was not yet daylight when they arrived. And it would be another hour before the sky began to lighten in the east, back down the canal on which they had traveled. The Hanshan gates were still locked at that hour. Roberts and Atcheson were uncertain whether or not word of their arrival had gotten through ahead of them. Paxton might have come through this way on the road to Hofei. But they couldn't be sure. He would have been making this part of the journey in the early morning, too. If he had arrived at Hahshan at the same hour they did—which was probable—the gates would also have been locked for him. Knowing that Hanshan's communications facilities were probably poor, Paxton could very well have pushed on without stopping. In that case, the local troops or constabulary in Hanshan would have no idea who they were. The survivors were all eager to get on into the town for a little more warmth and shelter than the junks provided. But there was something to be said for not barraging up to the village gates in a long, dark column before daylight without the proper introductions. The whole countryside was so trigger happy that one nervous gun could set off a deadly fusillade before they could identify themselves.

They finally decided the best tactic might be to approach full of noise and lights. The Chinese inside the walls might not know who they were but at least they wouldn't be fired on as a Japanese surprise attack. Atcheson, McDonald, and

Roberts went on ahead, loud and visible, beat down all arguments at the gate, and roused the Chinese magistrate. Once the situation was clear, the magistrate, a Mr. Ch'iu, was, in Roberts' words, "hospitality itself." Ch'iu ordered bearers started on the two-mile trip back to the landing on the canal, to bring in the litters. Then the magistrate and Roberts began to get ready for their arrival. "We arranged for the use of a school as quarters, ordered food for the whole party, got through again on the telephone to Hofei with regard to transportation for the next laps, and provided hot water for washing and boiled water for drinking for the weary lot who presently began straggling into the compound of the school."

Dawn was coming up when the most welcome bulletin of all got through to Atcheson, who was trying to call Hankow. A call came into the Hanshan magistrate's office from Hohsien. It was Rear Admiral Holt, R.N. He had arrived the night before off Hohsien with HMS *Bee* and *Ladybird*. Holt had been told by the U.S. Navy that USS *Oahu* was on the way downriver at top speed from Kiukiang. Holt had already taken aboard most of the stragglers from the *Mei Ping* party. And what Holt had to say about the Japanese reaction on the outside was particularly reassuring. The Japanese were, said Holt, "in a dither" about the bombing and were obviously trying to make amends in every way they could. A Japanese naval escort was on the way upriver to meet Holt at Hohsien. This escort would see the survivors down to Shanghai. Japanese naval planes were also being dispatched to the scene with doctors and supplies. Holt wanted the *Panay* men to start back to Hohsien immediately. The gunboats would be ready to receive them no matter what hour they got into Hohsien.

Things were looking better all around. It was a bright, clear morning. As the sun rose higher, it burned off an early mist and seemed to invite the more able-bodied to stretch out. With a good breakfast inside them, most of the men felt relatively secure for the first time since they left the gunboat. Swede Malhmann remembers:

This place was much better and cleaner. Also there was a better hospital. The party all got a good wash and good Chinese hot chow and water that was fit to drink. The Chinese doctor and first-aid men assisted our doctor in changing dressings and treating the men. There was a large room at the school with tables and wooden horses for benches. Here they set up a good hot meal for all hands.

The little courtyard of the school was filled with men sitting or squatting in little groups. Anders, with a wool Navy watch cap perched on the back of his head, looked more like a fisherman just in from the Grand Banks than the executive officer of a man-of-war. He conferred with Hughes about the news just in from Hohsien. Instinctively, from time to time, Tex Anders brought up his hands to make a point—then dropped them self-consciously to his side. The heavy bandages seemed as awkward as boxing gloves. Gunner Geist snoozed on a mat stretched out in the sun, his head pillowed by his white uniform hat. Dr. Grazier made the rounds of his patients and was relieved to see that they seemed to be holding up amazingly well, in spite of the better part of two nights spent in freezing night air. The meager medical supplies Doc Grazier had salvaged from the ship and added to in Hohsien were almost gone by the time he reached Hanshan. But during the morning, an American medical missionary arrived on the scene in a battered Buick loaded with blankets, medicine, and bandages. The missionary, Dr. Burch, had driven down from his hospital in Hofei intending to take the most seriously wounded back with him. When he heard the news that they were headed back for the river, he and Grazier, after a quick consultation, decided that the trip back by canal boat to the Yangtze would be far easier on even the badly wounded than bouncing all the way into Hofei in Burch's Buick. So the missionary turned around and retraced his path until he caught up with Paxton, who was 25 miles farther inland at Chaohsien. After a wild ride that had the crippled Paxton longing for his swaybacked horse of two days before, Burch was able to get the embassy man back into Hanshan by the time the main party was ready to leave for the river. If there had been times when the Navy men came to odds with the missionaries, this was not one of them. Burch was the first American they had seen since the sinking. The sudden arrival of this ecclesiastical Barney Oldfields, boiling up the road in a cloud of dust with his foot to the floorboard, bringing medicine, clean blankets, and a cheery word, became symbolic of a country that knew their plights and was moving to the rescue.

The news of Holt's call spread quickly through the survivors. Roberts, Atcheson, Anders, and Hughes had a brief conference. Roberts was somewhat uneasy. "We were still under such tension from our recent experience that we were hardly reassured. And we wondered if the admiral had really ensured our safe conduct. Still, we knew we should go back. And after giving everybody a chance for a rest and some food, we turned back to the landing." It was early afternoon.

The relative peace of Hanshan, the warm sun, some passable food seemed tempting after two days of being on the move. Most of the men felt more like staying. Andy Wisler remembers a very good Chinese meal during the morning at Hanshan, then the order to head back. "Someone—I don't recall who—told me to stay at a place outside town and direct members of the party down a pathway to get back to the landing. I stayed at this spot until I felt no one else was coming along. I believe that Norman Alley was the last one."

Most of the men had come into Hanshan from the canal that morning in the dark. Going back to the junks, it would be easy to straggle off on one of the innumerable country paths that led to the dozens of little farms in the vicinity of the village. The countryside in almost every direction looked the same. It had a Midwestern flatness. And it was easy to lose your bearings unless you constantly turned to check on the village behind you. Wisler, "the guide," almost had the trouble he was trying to prevent.

After about 15 minutes of waiting after Alley passed, I left also. About two miles farther on I had a problem. There was a fork in the road. Which one? Both looked logical. Since I had never been a Boy Scout, I made a blind guess. Along the first choice, about a hundred yards farther on, I found a cigarette butt. Its length was too long to have been discarded by any Chinese, and it was long enough to see the brand name, indicating an American cigarette. A little farther along, heel marks in the soft dirt verified that our party was ahead. I felt sort of proud of myself. Regular Indian scout.

It was sundown before Wisler, much relieved, caught up with his shipmates at the canal landing and got into the junk he had been assigned to. It was the last one to leave.

Roberts was about two hours out ahead. The Army man had picked out a small, light junk from the six that had brought them inland, loaded Hughes, Atcheson, Paxton, and several of the Chinese boys aboard it, and started for Hohsien as fast as he could push the towline handlers. He covered the distance in about six hours.

A little after eight o'clock we got to the landing at Hohsien. George and I tramped into town to the yamen, where we found Admiral Holt and others. They immediately went back with us to the canal landing, where the first of the larger junks was just coming in, and took charge of the transportation of the wounded, which we turned over with a good deal of thankfulness. Then there was the long walk to the landing on the Yangtze, where the ship's boats took us off to the gunboats. And at last we were back in safe hands.

There are many details of the bombing, the abandon ship,

and the time spent ashore junketing over the Chinese countryside that have grown vague to the survivors with the passage
of time. But no man who went back aboard the gunboats
that night will ever forget the sight and the wave of emotion
that came as they climbed up over the side and into American
hands. Colin McDonald wrote later that

nothing can efface the glow of pleasure with which we heard Admiral Holt welcome us out of the darkness. Soon we were all
bound for British and American gunboats waiting for us off
Hohsien. It was not long before we were back among the de-
cencies and humanities of life after a series of experiences—the
shelling and bombing and machine-gunning and hiding in swamps
like hunted animals—which few of us are likely to forget.

Norman Alley was almost too numb after the journey back
down the canal to appreciate the "homecoming": "It was a
nerve-racking trip, not much better than the trek on foot.
And some of us who were not wounded or dying were suffering badly from mental shock."

Alley, Wisler, and half a dozen others were in a small rice
junk that brought up the tail of the procession. In another
freezing night—the third they had been traveling—it was a
dreamlike, spooky trip.

The only means of illumination, a sickly oil lamp, cast a weird
movie-serialish glow on everyone's face. We were unable to sleep
on the hard boards of the junk, although the captain and the
members of his family did all they could to make our loads
lighter. They divided their scant supply of fish and poor man's
rice with us.

The survivors who had come in just ahead of Alley's group
had one last unnerving experience as they moved down the
final mile toward the canal landing at Hohsien. As Admiral
Holt had reported over the telephone to Roberts in Hanshan,
the Japanese had promised to escort the survivors all the way

back down the Yangtze to Shanghai with a naval convoy. About 10 P.M., just as the *Panay* men were coming down the last mile of canal, a Japanese destroyer boiled upstream and dropped anchor off Hohsien near the *Bee*. Etiquette demanded a 13-gun salute by the destroyer to the British admiral. And etiquette demanded an equal number of guns in reply from the reluctant British. The residents of Hohsien, meanwhile, were expecting a Japanese attack at any minute. Most of the Chinese were holed up in their houses ready for a last-ditch defense—and, seeing naval vessels gathering out on the river, wondering when it was going to happen. Lights were blazing on all the ships and the signal lamps flickered across the water with a mysterious sense of urgency. The Chinese had never seen anything like it and had no idea what all these anxiously flashing lights meant. Undoubtedly trouble. It always was in China.

It was too dark for the Chinese to see any flags or to tell anything about whether the new ships were friends or enemies. When the Japanese destroyer eased up to its anchorage, splashed over its anchor, and cut loose with its 13 guns, the cannonade was enough to "let off every nervous rifle for miles around." None of the Hohsien villagers knew what he was firing at. But just shooting into the darkness probably made them all feel better. Far into the night there would be long periods of quiet, then the sharp report of a single rifle, then a barrage of answering fire. Then quiet. And 30 minutes or an hour later, it would start all over again.

The clear, cold darkness of the night before, when the stars were so vivid that Roberts had mistaken one of them for a river boat, had been replaced shortly after dusk on Tuesday night with a light mist that became a dense fog before midnight. The fog made the work of getting all the men off from shore proceed slowly. But the joyful recognition that was repeated over and over again made it worth it.

Each junk in turn would come ghosting down the canal

into Hohsien. Lights loomed ahead on the landing. Small hand flashlights obviously skittered around nervously to show the way. In the junks, the Americans looked out ahead—and knew those couldn't be Chinese up there. The Chinese didn't operate like that.

Hallos boomed out across the shortening ribbon of water up ahead. Often the first response from shore wasn't clear. But it had enough of a friendly sound to it to raise the half-slumbering men from the bottom of the junk.

"Boat ahoy!" "Panay" the answer came back. And then, more often than not, there was more of a silence than there should have been. On shore and on the junks there were a few throats that choked up and an eye or two that would have looked a little glassy if there had been light enough to see. Fortunately there was darkness. Then the hail came back from shore, "Come on! We're waiting for you!"

The shouts were suddenly confused. Happy. Everything all at once. Good Devon accents answered by Yankee twangs.

"Is Puckett there?"

"Where the hell did you guys come from?"

"Any wounded aboard?"

"Where's the beer?"

"Beer, hell, where's the broads?"

"Easy mate, wait till we get you tied up."

Most of the men were over the side of the junks and onto the rickety canal landing stage even before the boats had touched. Men who had been so stiff from walking and wounds and two nights in the cold that they could hardly trudge back to the boats at Hanshan suddenly felt as spry as if their liberty party had just been called away; they scrambled ashore with the best of them. Men who had never laid eyes on each other before, and might never again, greeted each other like long-lost shipmates.

Slowly in the dark of the landing area, each party in turn was sorted out. The seriously wounded were gently helped out of the junks. Rough, tender hands wrapped them in fresh blankets and helped them through the town and down to Hohsien's Yangtze landing. Out on the river, even as the mist closed in, the survivors could see a bright, warm cluster of lights where the two British gunboats waited. As fast as one launch filled, it started out toward the lights. Now the tiredness in the *Panay* men was all gone. Now they knew they were out of it. There was some laughing. Some poor jokes. The British sailors didn't know much about what was going on on the outside either. They did know they had been bombed and shelled themselves two days before, and they reported they had already picked up some *Panay* survivors who had been on the Standard Oil boats.

How many? They weren't sure. The names? They weren't sure of that either. Any dead? One. Oh, God! Yes, one dead. One of the Standard Oil captains. Secretly the *Panay* men felt a relief. At least it wasn't one of their own. And a lot of Chinese killed, too. Poor bastards.

As the shore boats circled to come alongside the gunboats' gangways, the hollow-eyed survivors could see other British sailors in heavy duffel coats and white hats waiting to help them aboard. It seemed as if every light on each ship was lit. Spotlights were rigged to beam down on the gangways. All along the decks the lights illuminated working parties moving about and little groups of off-duty men who watched quietly as the ragged, dirty *Panay* men were helped aboard. The rescued were happier than they had been in days. But to the rescuers, they were a strange, Oriental-looking lot. Docile. Lumpy. Strangely bulky and awkward. Hobbled by their blankets. Bulky in the padded Chinese suits they had bought for extra warmth since they had been ashore. After their 48 hours of cold, uncertainty, and flight, they found the ships dazzling. A cheery glow beamed from almost every port and window. As the launches pulled alongside, the men could pick up the delicious smells of hot soup, fresh bread, hot coffee. Strong hands reached down to help them up out of the boats. Other hands guided them, dazed and blinking and happy, down the brightly lit decks into the warm sanctuary of the quarters. About midnight, USS *Oahu* steamed up to join the two Britishers. Stubby. Ugly. Not very military. Brave as hell. Beautiful! Some Americans remember that *Oahu*'s arrival was enough to make you cry.

Andy Wisler remembers his first hot drink.

I think it was on the HMS *Ladybird* that I first set foot on deck. A British sailor handed me a mug of English tea. Strong. With milk and sugar. It was delicious. Filled a need. Somewhere we ate. I think this was on USS *Oahu*. I know that in a crew's compartment on *Oahu*, a couple of shipmates from the USS *Palos* and I sat on the deck in a corner. A cup of coffee royal had been concocted—black coffee laced with a wee bit of pure ethyl alcohol —a well-known Navy medicinal specific. Great stuff. Joe Garrighty gave me a pair of dungarees to replace my coolie pants. I slept on a cot on the HMS *Ladybird* that night. It was foreign "soil" but it sure felt like home.

Swede Mahlmann remembers "big, thick sandwiches and real drinking water. This was a godsend." They got their first clue, too, of the fate of the liberty party.

One of the men to meet us was Coleman, chief pharmacist mate from *Panay*. He told us that most of the missing men were aboard HMS *Bee* and that Hodge with Marshall from *Collier's* had started for Shanghai aboard a Japanese plane. Then we were sent to bed for a good night's sleep.

To Frank Roberts, the return to the gunboats was a relief indeed. For almost 60 hours he had shepherded some 70 men, a dozen of them badly wounded, through strange, alien territory. He hadn't lost a man through enemy action or straying. He had succeeded in getting word to the outside world when all the survivors were certain the Japanese were intent on seeing that, above all, the Americans would not be able to accomplish this. And he had avoided inflaming an incident that already seemed capable of starting a first-class war.

Standing anxiously aboard *Bee*, peering out into the night toward the few flickering lights that marked Hohsien and the river landing, Roberts saw the last boat come out from shore with the last of the survivors. As far as he was concerned, they were home. That was it.

Because of the darkness and the fog the gunboats would have to remain off Hohsien until morning, at least. A shore party would go in in the morning to make sure there were no more stragglers; several men from the *Mei Ping* "liberty party" were still unaccounted for. But for all that, Roberts knew the worst of his responsibility was over. "In the admiral's cabin aboard *Bee*, George Atcheson and I had hot rum toddies." For once they were both grateful to the wisdom of the British Navy in seeing that prohibition had not crept aboard the King's ships. "Then we went off to bed on cots on the upper deck. We were cold all night, sleeping in our clothes. But we were much easier in our minds."

Aboard *Oahu*, Lieutenant Commander J. W. Sheehan was checking off the names of the survivors who were reported to be aboard one of the English gunboats. Soon he began to get some unwanted assistance. A boat had come over from one of the Japanese destroyers also standing by. It carried two Japanese naval surgeons, accompanied by a Japanese hospital corpsman. They requested Sheehan's permission to board, saying that they had been sent to assist with the wounded. The American officer at first declined their aid. But they were very insistent. "And rather than cause unpleasantness," Sheehan reported, "I let them stay and sent them to the sick bay to await the arrival of the wounded." A short time after the first survivors started coming aboard, Sheehan looked in to see his own doctor at work, with the Japanese close at the American's side, "ostensibly to assist, but actually they were taking notes of injuries and conditions of men."

Their condition was surprisingly good. And morale began to improve the minute they came aboard. It was around radio sets in the United States that morale was low at that point.

14

"It won't happen again"

By WEDNESDAY, December 15, the day the survivors were getting ready to start back downstream from Hohsien aboard *Oahu*, almost all the Western capitals felt themselves involved in one way or another. All eyes were on Japan.

What Tokyo feared most, outside of an immediate snap-reaction war with the United States, was that the *Panay* incident might push England and the United States into joint animosity or joint retaliation against Japan. Tokyo papers in midweek after the sinking seemed relieved that apparently this was not taking place. "A study of editorial views throughout the United States," one Japanese paper reported, "was said to reveal the general opinion that the *Panay* incident would not justify war." Although as yet there was no official answer to FDR's brief protest memo of Monday, December 13, or to Hull's formal note two days later, the official Japanese diplomatic posture of "genuine apology and resolution to make amends" was helping to keep diplomatic water smoothly oiled. There were heavy ground swells but no breaking whitecaps.

A government official in Tokyo would soon be authorized to say that Japan was "prepared to meet every American demand . . . We are studying yesterday's American note with a view of making all possible amends."

It seemed to be a sincere national reaction that was mirrored all through the Japanese islands. The Japanese paper *Nichi Nichi* deplored the incident but acknowledged that it was the sort of thing bound to happen during a war. The Japanese editors warned the United States against becoming inflamed by British antagonism to Japan and hoped that America, "with the generosity of a great nation," would accept the sincerity of the Japanese apology that was obviously forthcoming.

Other Japanese papers were equally concerned, but were also looking for calming influences. There were reports that a national salute to the United States flag should be considered throughout the islands, along with a program of full military honors for the Americans who were killed. In Tokyo, a delegation of high school girls, representing 500 students at the White Lily School, left a donation at the Navy Ministry for *Panay* survivors. At the Foreign Office, two Japanese boys, 11 and 15, arrived, quietly laid down a donation of $2 for the Americans, and bowed out. Seven other Tokyo students and their teacher called on Ambassador Joseph Grew to express their regrets in person.

Grew was deluged with expressions of regret and sympathy from everyone from high officials to delegations of school children. His wife, Alice, received several "private" calls by wives of highly placed Japanese who could not show a public regret. The conduct of the people was moving. But Grew feared that the United States was in a remember-the-*Maine* situation. He was already planning the details of a hurried embassy evacuation.

More drastic action was taking place at higher levels. The Emperor was reported to have had his naval ministers on the carpet. The Japanese government reported that since the out-break of hostilities in China in July it had faithfully tried to prevent what had just happened. In that time, the government said, a series of fliers had been punished and some sent back from China in disgrace for "reckless flying." More immediately to the point, the government announced that Rear Admiral Teizo Mitsunami, commander of the Japanese naval air group that was operating in China, had been dismissed and ordered to return to Japan immediately. Mitsunami, 48 and a rear admiral for only 12 days at the time of the *Panay* sinking, was something of a fair-haired boy. He had recently been skipper of the big carrier *Kaga*, which was to take part four years later in the Pearl Harbor attack. Virtually his whole career had been with the naval air forces. Now it was pre-sumably over.

The heads were beginning to roll. In a face-saving country, such public rebuke was a drastic measure. "This action," a Shanghai story reported of Mitsunami's removal, "betokens a policy of restraint against the whole air force in the future."

With many apologies and such conspicuous head-rollings, the lid was slowly and correctly going on to cover up the whole unpleasant pot full of trouble. Then word of the first survivors' reports began to seep out from under Navy Department and White House doors.

The leak from Washington said that

deliberate, premeditated action by Japanese aviators, surface ves-sels and troops, have presented a much more serious picture of the incident than was given in first reports. They have brought home a realization here that unless Japan meets the demand of the United States for full satisfaction, an exceedingly grave diplomatic crisis will confront the two countries.

On December 17, five days after the sinking, Friday morn-ing papers throughout the United States would carry head-lines that verified the earlier Washington rumors:

PANAY ATTACK DELIBERATE,
YARNELL REPORT INDICATES;
OUR PROTEST BROADENED

The story went on to say that Secretary Hull had announced at a press conference the day before that the first formal reports of the sinking were confirming what the survivors' accounts in the papers had been hinting at: that the incident was clearly a deliberate act. After the bombings, Hull reported, *Panay* had been machine-gunned by Japanese Army motorboats and planes had strafed the survivors. Then Japanese soldiers had been seen to board the sinking gunboat—while its flag was still flying—and had remained aboard about five minutes, rummaging through the ship. But, Hull cautioned, the final official version of the sinking, though beginning to take shape, was far from complete. There were all sorts of speculations about the delay. The most plausible of these was that the United States was waiting for some official Japanese indication of whether, if deliberate, the bombing had been ordered from high up in the military establishment. Or was it simply the act of hot-headed individual pilots or irresponsible local air commanders?

And with nothing more authoritative than that to go on, the speculation grew. The second theory was the one most people would have preferred to believe—that fire-brand Japanese officers, on or close to the scene, simply decided on their own to let fly in blood lust. The first theory was more sinister and more improbable. But as the days went by, it began to gain considerable strength as people applied logic and circumstantial evidence. Its proponents suggested that Japanese field commanders—men relatively high up and possibly of general-officers rank—had decided to humiliate the Americans with the unauthorized attack. If such an attack didn't bring retaliation, then this would show the Chinese that there was no strength in these Western allies—and there would be no help forthcoming from them. Because four

British gunboats—*Ladybird, Bee, Cricket,* and *Scarab*—had also been involved in bombings or artillery attacks, it appeared that this sort of local humiliation and harassment was indeed being carried out against both powers.

If this was what the Japanese were up to, it had been a fairly successful policy to that date. The tactics had been annoying and humiliating, but not to the point of driving the British and Americans into each other's arms. After all, Secretary Hull had just said that no joint United States–British naval show was planned as a result of the attacks. The British had gotten an it-won't-happen-again note of apology about the incidents involving the gunboats. Apologies seemed to keep things cooled down. For the time being.

"So sorry. So sorry"

It was noon Wednesday, December 15, before the fog at Hohsien began to lift and 1 P.M. before the somber procession started back down the river for Shanghai. A Japanese destroyer, *Kaseage,* was in the lead. Then came USS *Oahu,* with most of the survivors. HMS *Ladybird* and another Japanese vessel, *Kotori,* brought up the rear. *Bee,* with Admiral Holt aboard, had gone on ahead. Colors on all ships were at half mast. The sun had burned off the fog across most of the river. Deep patches of mist lay at points along the banks, hiding some of the territory most of the *Panay* men hoped they would not see again soon. And where the fog still lay on the water ahead, blotting out a horizon line, it gave a strange, out-of-focus quality to the scene, as if the little convoy were steaming through some vague, fictitious land of twisting channels and muddy water toward a destination that could never be picked out ahead. The brightness of the sun reflecting off the remaining haze caused a coppery glare that made the look-outs and the officers on the bridge squint, shade their eyes, and pull the beaks of their caps down a little lower in an attempt to shut out some of the glare. It was good to be moving, but there was an uncomfortable feeling about it all. Along the east bank the two Standard Oil tankers were still smoldering.

Up ahead on *Kaseage*, Gunner's Mate Second Class Spike Hennessy and Quartermaster Second Class James Peck stood stiff and uneasy on the bridge, relaying back to *Oahu* and *Ladybird* instructions from the Chinese river pilot who was taking them downstream. The two sailors would have felt ill at ease at best in the strange surroundings. Some of the conversation—they judged from the tone of it, although they could not understand—was concerned with working the ship. But there were comments passed between the officers and glances in their own direction that the two American sailors felt certain were surely nonbusiness and must concern the sinking and their own presence aboard. The Americans had that uncomfortable, we're-being-talked-about-behind-our-backs feeling that comes when your ears are barraged by a foreign language whose tone and inflection are hopeless to understand. Peck took a distinct dislike to the Japanese. When they bombed him on the destroyer *Pope* at Pearl Harbor, he was sure he had been right.

Everyone on the Japanese ship was scrupulously polite. It was almost as if they were trying to apologize by their kindness. But the two men still felt uneasy and not quite safe being there. It was reassuring to look back and see *Oahu*'s stubby little snout bulling through the Yangtze astern of them, with *Ladybird*, squat and saucy, pushing along after the American gunboat. The Stars and Stripes and the Union Jack stood out stiff in the wind whipped up by the convoy as it boiled along at close to flank speed. But with the English and American ships bracketed fore and aft by Japanese destroyers and with

Japanese planes roaring low overhead from time to time, the Americans up and down the convoy had, at times, an uneasy feeling that they were surrounded by guards rather than guards of honor.

After the first elation of being rescued, there was a strange feeling of let-down for many of the survivors. For three days they had been pushing, hurrying on toward some safety they hoped to find but were never sure of. The uncertainty, the need to keep on the alert, helped them forget their tiredness, their aches, their wounds. Now suddenly they were just "passengers." Someone else had the responsibility. For the first time most of the men had a chance to think back over their escape. It had been a near thing. As a constant reminder, on the stern of *Oahu* were three wooden coffins. Two of them, covered with American flags, contained the bodies of Ensminger and Captain Carlson of *Mei An*. The third, now covered properly with Italian colors that had been found in the flag locker of one of the gunboats, held the body of Sandro Sandri.

Most of the wounded seemed to be responding well enough, considering the ordeal they had been through. The one exception was Coxswain Hulsebus. The machine-gun bullet that had struck his back had severed the spinal cord. The paralysis in his lower body remained. He still did not appear to be in great pain and kept up a cheerful banter with the doctors and shipmates who had a chance to see him. But as soon as they went away, his face lapsed again into the glazed look of a man who knew that death, at best, was only a few days away. It might not have cheered him, but it should have made him proud to see the Navy Cross citation that would come to him posthumously a few months later:

For having distinguished himself by display of heroism on the occasion of the bombing and loss of the USS PANAY on 12 December 1937. Hulsebus was a member of the crew which courageously operated the machine gun battery against the attacking planes, even though these guns could not bear forward from which direction most of the attacks were made. He remained at his post of duty until he was fatally wounded and carried from the ship. His performance of duty on this occasion was in keeping with the highest traditions of the Naval Service.

/s/ Claude A. Swanson

With the shortage of doctors, the Americans reluctantly took advantage of the Japanese naval surgeons who had been flown up the river by seaplane or brought in by the Japanese destroyers. Quartermaster John Lang had his wounds dressed by one of them. The doctor kept saying, "So sorry. So sorry." Lang didn't feel much like answering one way or another. Even the apology was annoying. He felt it would have been more suitable if the Jap croaker had just gone about his business and said nothing. When the last "So sorry" was uttered, Lang had had enough. He was tempted to snap back, "Holy mackerel, forget it! Just get me finished." But he bit his lip against the pain of the dressing and said nothing. One of his wounds had come when a bomb fragment opened a scar on his chin caused by World War I shrapnel 20 years earlier. There was something uncomfortably repetitive about the whole thing. Lang hoped it wasn't an omen that meant the start of another war.

Fireman First Class Newton Davis got back that day the only piece of his property that had been salvaged from *Panay*. Andy Wisler visited Davis in *Oahu*'s sick bay and returned the knife he had picked up from Davis' locker just before he had abandoned ship. Davis kept trying to run over in his mind the really valuable stuff that had gone down in that locker.

Ships Cook Third Class Peres Dix Ziegler of Delaware, Ohio, got his bandages checked by a Japanese doctor, too. The fellow probably meant well enough but he was even more clumsy, to Ziegler's way of thinking, than the Chinese doctor who had dressed his wounds two mornings before in Hohsien.

On that occasion Ziegler had busted loose with a string of cussing that had unnerved the little Chinese sawbones even though he couldn't understand exactly what was being said. This time Zeigler just muttered to himself. The Navy was the Navy, and he wasn't sure just how much trouble he could get himself into if he sounded off at the Japanese Navy doctor. For all he knew, *all* these damn navies had some crazy international system that could slap him on report and get him hauled up to captain's mast on an insubordination charge as soon as he got back to Shanghai.

Quartermaster Tom Spindle and Chief Klumpers also got the apology treatment from the Japanese doctors. Spindle thought that maybe the Japanese were really quite human after all—or thought that for another couple of hours at least, until he saw them open fire on Chinese civilians crossing the river near Nanking.

Seaman Stan McEowen would have preferred to have his wounds tended to by an American doctor. But the Japanese insisted on looking him over. He got the apologies mixed with a certain amount of rough handling of his punctured groin and jaw. The only thing McEowen could remember having said during the attack was, "I guess these Japs don't know it's Sunday." McEowen didn't think of himself as a religious man and he didn't know why he had said it or why that remark had stuck with him. But he was tempted to repeat the question to the Japanese doctors. Then he decided they wouldn't know what the devil he was talking about. On December 7, 1941, the question would come back to him.

Some of the other wounded, Bill McCabe, Marcus Williamson, Speed Adams, didn't get a word from the Japanese. And that was all right with them, too. McCabe figured if they wanted to apologize they could handle that with the officers. Adams heard about the Japanese doctors planning to examine the men and was afraid there would be problems. Somebody might take a poke at somebody. But there were no incidents.

"I don't think we were very friendly," Adams remembers, "but there was no commotion."

John Geist almost made some. He can still remember the rough way in which the Japanese doctor working on *Ladybird* probed and dressed his leg wounds. "If he had been one of our fellows, I might have asked him to take it easy. But then I decided I wasn't going to give any Japanese that satisfaction." Geist simply set his teeth.

For a few of the men, the trip downriver still seemed to hold some dangers. The convoy could move only cautiously and during the day. The Chinese had turned off or destroyed all navigation lights on that part of the river, cut down beacons and ranges, and set spar markers and buoys adrift. As the ships passed Nanking, the sight of the burning city was sobering. Greasy, black smoke came from dozens of fires. The water-front was a wreck. Roberts stood on deck of *Oahu* late Wednesday afternoon, moving his binoculars over the shoreline, trying to see what had happened to several familiar land-marks. A flourish of cannonading on the Pukow side caused them all to start. One badly shell-shocked survivor moved close to Roberts and gripped him arm with fingers that pressed into the Army man's flesh like stevedore hooks. "You don't think the Japs have just got us down here to finish us up, do you, Captain?" Roberts tried to reassure the man. But the Army officer and many of the others were no easier in their minds. By nightfall, they had only gotten about 20 miles below Nanking. The whole convoy anchored after a ridiculous amount of signaling back and forth; the Japanese were trying to establish themselves as commanders of the convoy by giving instructions as to who was to do what, when. So the American and British captains were going out of their way to be inde-pendent about the whole show—even when the Japanese instructions were something they had wanted to do in the first place.

The day had ended with a depressing incident. To Norman

Alley, who had come to China with a pleasant conception of the Japanese as a neat, orderly, and polite people, the incident was almost the last straw. Alley had begun to question his own feeling about Japan when he first saw the Japanese Army in operation in Shanghai. The bombing of the Pukow railway yards had sickened him. The events of the evening of December 15 finished him off: Just before dusk, Alley had watched a group of Chinese refugees on several rafts trying to cross the river. Japanese patrol boats saw them, too. Even Alley's strong stomach, acquired in Chicago police reporting, turned at what came next. "We saw one of the patrol boats deliberately cut widely out of its way, with full speed ahead, to cut the raft in two, tossing the man and his servants headlong into the river."

Luigi Barzini was on deck, too, watching in disgust as the Japanese patrol boat headed for the Chinese raft: "The poor men were on their knees, begging for mercy. The Japanese hit them, sank them, and shot at the bobbing heads in the water. We rescued some of the drowning and wounded people, in spite of stern warnings by the Japanese gunboats not to interfere." A British launch with a Chinese crew also went to the rescue. Barzini watched in some dismay as the Chinese sailors pulled some of the swimmers into their boats, lifted others with a hook, looked at them, and threw them back in the water. "We asked why," Barzini remembers. "They said: 'They were wounded. No good.' The mysterious East. Nobody bothers to help the wounded and the sick because tradition compels the rescuers to take charge of the rescued for life." The Italian correspondent couldn't get the incident out of his mind.

It was an uneasy anchorage that night. The Japanese artillery on one side of the river kept up a desultory fire at Chinese —real or imaginary—on the other side of the river. Most of the shells seemed to pass right over the anchored ships. Japanese artillery was not all that accurate and a short round, landing in the midst of the anchored vessels, could have caused deadly damage. Earlier in the evening, when the British and the Americans had rescued the Chinese from the water, the Japanese lead destroyer had warned *Oahu* by blinker light:

B-E-C-A-U-S-E Y-O-U-R R-E-S-C-U-E T-W-O

E-N-E-M-I-E-S A-D-M-I-R-A-L R-E-G-R-E-T-S

C-A-N N-O L-O-N-G-E-R G-U-A-R-A-N-T-E-E

S-A-F-E J-O-U-R-N-E-Y T-O S-H-A-N-G-H-A-I

As the shells kept coming over, it seemed as if the message had been a prophecy. It was a long night.

The next day, Thursday, was less eventful and their suspicions were quieted a bit. They passed many Japanese launches shuttling troops to the north shore, but there was no more real firing. During the morning, a fast boat up from Shanghai brought Navy Lieutenant M. C. Whiting aboard. A court of inquiry was already in session aboard *Augusta* and Whiting had been sent ahead to receive depositions from some of the survivors. Washington was eager for the most complete story possible, at the earliest possible moment. Because it would be late Friday at the earliest before they reached Shanghai, Whiting's head start on the testimony would put the court at least 24 hours ahead.

Thursday night they anchored off the famous Kiangyin Forts, some 50 miles above Shanghai and at the point where China Sea tides begin to be felt in the river. The next morning they were underway early, passing a grim sight: below the forts the Chinese had sunk a barricade of ships across the river in hopes of stopping the invaders. The Japanese had blasted their way through. But now, on each side of the channel the masts and funnels of the sunken ships were visible like ruined fence posts. The riverbanks now no longer showed the smoke and ruin of war that was so obvious around Nanking. But even as the survivors looked at the apparently peaceful countryside, they had a strange feeling that the war was really only hiding somewhere along the shore. Below Kiangyin, the Yangtze opens up to about eight miles wide, narrows to half that distance abreast of the town of Nantung, then suddenly the bank on the south side of the river falls away at right angles to the channel until there is a 15-mile expanse of water from shore to shore. The land is low on each side and shore can hardly be seen at times. After the winding confines of the river they had just snaked down, it was almost like being in the Fleet again when they passed Nantung. A fresh salt wind came in off the China Sea. Ahead the outline of Isungming Ido Island began to show out of the winter haze. The breeze picked up. Some of the men felt fresh and clean again for the first time in days.

Downtown Shanghai seemed to be bustling and oblivious when the little convoy swung slowly right off Woosung, turned south, and headed up the crowded Whangpoo Road toward the anchorage along Battleship Row. But to those on the ships and to those waiting aboard *Augusta*, the arrival of the convoy seemed to still everything else. Even Japanese transports and hospital ships had their flags at half mast.

Aboard the United States flagship a tense group waited. Among them was Hallett Abend, a *New York Times* stringer in the Far East who would write the most outspoken indictment of all about Japan's intentions during the few days just past. Abend said later that the arrival of the little convoy was one of the most memorable scenes he had encountered in all his years in the Far East:

I was on the bridge of *Augusta*, Admiral Yarnell's flagship, standing not far from the Admiral and Mr. Gauss. A strange hush had come over Shanghai's busy waterfront, and the steamer and launch traffic of the great river was temporarily suspended. All eyes were focused down the Whangpoo, and a hushed expectancy seemed to hold the busy river and the great war-ruined city.

The sunset paled and dulled. The light began to fade, and

newsreel and cameramen muttered despairing curses in tense undertones.

Ladybird came first around the bend. Then *Oahu*. Abend described the scene in a long, moving wireless that was front-paged on the December 18 *New York Times*:

When the Oahu was first sighted a curious murmur of suppressed excitement was felt the whole length of the 10,000-ton cruiser, whose decks were crowded with officers, sailors, marines and a few civilians. It was not a manifestation of relief or enthusiasm when the Oahu was made fast alongside the Augusta. Instead, those aboard the flagship stood in oppressed silence when they saw the survivors on the Oahu decks, whose faces in most cases were drawn and lined, many suffering obviously from shell-shock; others had their arms in slings, while others wore conspicuous bandages. A few hands were raised in salutes and greetings, and a few almost hushed salutations were exchanged across the narrowing waters as the ships drew together while daylight faded rapidly. A hastily improvised gangway, of unplaned and unpainted lumber, was shoved from the Augusta's deck onto the Oahu's top deck, and a few of the Augusta's officers boarded the rescue ship.

Then came a long wait, after which Augusta sailors carried empty stretchers aboard the Oahu, while blue-uniformed marines guarded the gangway and a majority of the Augusta officers stood silent, waiting, in a semicircle. Admiral Harry E. Yarnell, Commander-in-Chief of the United States Asiatic Fleet, sat grim-faced in his quarters awaiting oral reports of surviving officers of the Panay, many of whom were grievously wounded.

Dusk deepened into darkness during the silent period of waiting. Then the Augusta's floodlights illuminated the cruiser's great well deck and the crude gangway to the Oahu's topdeck.

The first survivors to come aboard the Augusta were George Atcheson Jr., second secretary of the United States Embassy in China, supporting J. Hall Paxton, also a second secretary of the Embassy. Mr. Paxton was wounded in the shoulder and injured in a knee; he was limping badly. These two men were escorted to Admiral Yarnell's quarters and the doors were closed.

Next came nearly half a hundred members of the Panay crew, many showing obvious evidence of shell-shock. Then came the wounded who were able to walk. They were taken immediately to the Augusta's sick bay. The more seriously wounded were later taken ashore in navy launches, which were met at the custom jetty by ambulances and conveyed to the county hospital.

By this time a full moon rising over the war-shattered and burned Pootung made a broad path of silver across the sluggish, muddy Whangpoo.

The Japanese saved one last mistake of poor judgment or poor timing until the end. As the survivors were making their way across the rough wood gangway in the glare of *Augusta's* floodlights, a flight of Japanese naval aircraft roared low over the cruiser. It was "a salute," the Japanese said later. Everyone flinched instinctively as the planes came out of nowhere, full throttle and only about 300 feet up. Gunner Geist still remembers a flare of anger:

My leg still hurt from the work a Japanese Army doctor had done on it while we were coming downstream on *Ladybird*. He may have been a fair doctor, but he was rough as hell. I was just making it up the gangway onto the ship when the planes buzzed us. They came in so low and fast you couldn't hear them until they were right on top of you. I almost went into the river. We felt like letting loose at them.

Then the "saluting" aircraft headed inland. The *Panay* men watched them go. And wondered who they were going to make a "mistake" on now.

15

"Heaven help us . . ."

The court of inquiry aboard *Augusta* had been sitting for almost two days by the time survivors got down to the flagship. The four-man court was headed by a Navy captain, Harold V. McKittrick, who had a reputation for being demanding but fair. The word had gotten around quickly that the court would be "tough and thorough." Nothing quite like the sinking had ever happened before, and Washington wanted information quickly and accurately.

Because of the location and condition of the survivors in various hospitals and sick bays, it would necessarily hold a sort of "traveling court." This had gotten underway even while Lieutenant Whiting was riding down the river with the survivors. The first testimony was supplied by the various radio logs kept in Shanghai, by testimony that could be supplied by State Department people in liaison with the Japanese, and by documents submitted by Rear Admiral Sugiyama for the Japanese Third Fleet.

The Japanese offered a statement that purported to be a combat report filed by the pilots. It seemed rather sensational at the time because of its bare-bones admissions. Later it would sound evasive and woefully incomplete. The Japanese claimed the four ships were moving at about five knots at the time of the attack. "No flags were seen although one plane flew as low as 300 meters [about 800 feet] to try to identify the vessels." The pilots said they were convinced the four ships were Chinese. They listed one ship as sinking by 1:30 P.M., another vessel bombed and listing badly at 1:40, and two remaining ships, moored together, as being in sinking condition by 1:50. The times and chronologies did not jibe with United States reports, but there was no doubt in anyone's mind that what was described was the *Panay* attack.

When the survivors began to appear before the court in its third day of sessions, the tempo increased. Lieutenant Whiting, who had joined them on *Oahu* halfway down the river to take advance testimony, was a trained lawyer and represented the office of the judge advocate in the court. The other two remaining members, Commander Morton L. Deyo and Lieutenant Commander Abel C. J. Sabalot, were line officers.

Most of the sessions were held in the *Augusta*'s wardroom, with testimony being taken from time to time in *Augusta*'s sick bay, in Shanghai's U.S. Marine Hospital, and in the hospitals where some of the civilian wounded had been taken. Much of the testimony was repetitious, but the repetition served to confirm certain vital details that would nail down the true facts of the incident: the position of the ships, the time of the attack, the height of the planes, the exact areas of damage aboard *Panay* and the tankers.

But if it was repetitious, it was also at times quite stirring, even in the dry language of the hearing room. Dozens of tales of heroism and sacrifice began to emerge: Jim Marshall crediting Fireman Hodge with saving his life by giving him first aid from *Mei Ping*'s medical chest, forcing a Japanese doctor to treat the wounds, and then half-carrying, half-dragging Marshall to the hospital in Wuhu; Frank Roberts, Stan McEowen, and Maurice Rider working all night in the hospital at Hoh-sien, after Rider had practically carried one man all the way along the six miles from the landing spot; Johnny Geist, wounded in the leg, carrying in another man more seriously wounded than himself; Marcus Williamson, who had started the long adventure soaked to the skin after starting to swim ashore, piggybacking the paralyzed, uncomplaining Hulsebus through much of the night; Homer Truax, another boatswain-turned-nurse, heaving overboard all *Panay*'s gasoline drums in the middle of the strafing attack to lessen the threat of fire and explosion; Thomas Coleman, bringing in the *Mei Ping* stragglers safely to *Oahu*, then heading back to Hohsien to bring out the bodies of Sandri and Ensminger at a time when Chinese sentries all over the countryside were nervously firing on each other and anything else that moved; Yuan Te Erh, scouting through the darkness to find the first little hamlet of safety; Gerry Weimers, taking over the pulling sampan with its cranky outboard motor and nursing it back and forth to shore under fire; little Antonio Rinaldi moving cheerfully through the ship and shore party, making himself useful everywhere at once, and giving them all a good laugh or two in the tight times . . .

The bare facts of the incident were lined out in strict Navy reporting. A 37-point *Finding of Facts* would be circulated through all the departments and bureaus back in Washing-ton. It underplayed "the action" just as Navy reports have done since Oliver Hazard Perry wrote back to Washington, "We have met the enemy and they are ours." The first ten points in the *Findings* establish the situation before the at-tack. Then the court went on to tell the story in dry, official language:

11. That at about 1338 three large Japanese twin motored planes in a "V" formation were observed at a considerable

height passing overhead downriver. At this time no other craft were in the vicinity of the U.S.S. PANAY and convoy, and there was no reason to believe the ships were in a dangerous area.

12. That without warning these three planes released several bombs, one or two of which struck on or very near, close to the bow of the U.S.S. PANAY and another which struck on or very close to the S.S. MEI PING.

13. That the bombs of the first attack did considerable damage to the U.S.S. PANAY, disabling the forward three inch gun, seriously injuring the Captain and others, wrecking the pilot house and sick bay, disabling the radio equipment and the steaming fireroom so that all power was lost, and causing leaks in the hull which resulted in the ship settling down by the head and listing to starboard thereby contributing fundamentally to the sinking of the ship.

14. That immediately thereafter a group of six single engined biplanes attacked from ahead, diving singly and appearing to concentrate on the U.S.S. PANAY. A total of about twenty bombs were dropped, many striking close aboard and creating, by fragments and concussion, great damage to ship and personnel. These attacks lasted about twenty minutes during which time at least two of the planes attacked also with machine guns; one machine-gun attack was directed against a ship's boat bearing wounded ashore, causing several further wounds and piercing the boat with bullets.

15. That during the entire attack the weather was clear and high visibility and little if any wind.

16. That the planes participating in the attacks on the U.S.S. PANAY and its convoy were unmistakably identified by their markings as being Japanese.

. . .

21. That after the PANAY had been abandoned, Mahlmann, chief boatswain's mate, and Weimers, machinist's mate

first class, returned to the PANAY to obtain stores and medical supplies. While they were returning to the beach a Japanese power boat filled with armed Japanese soldiers approached close to the PANAY, opened fire with a machine-gun, went alongside, boarded, and left within five minutes.

22. That at 1554 the U.S.S. PANAY, shortly after the Japanese boarding party had left, rolled over to starboard and sank in from seven to ten fathoms of water, approximately latitude 30-44-3-North, Longitude 117-27 East. Practically no valuable government property was salvaged.

23. That after the PANAY survivors had reached the left bank of the river, the captain, in view of his own injuries and the injuries and shock sustained by his remaining line officers, and the general feeling that attempts would be made to exterminate the survivors, requested Captain F. N. Roberts, U.S. Army, who was not injured, and who was familiar with land operations and the Chinese language to act under his direction as his immediate representative. Captain Roberts functioned in the capacity until the return of the party on board the U.S.S. OAHU on December 15, 1937, performing outstanding service.

. . .

26. That from the beginning of the unprecedented and unlooked for attack at great violence until their final return, the ship's company and passengers of the U.S.S. PANAY were subjected to grave and continuous hardship. Their conduct under these conditions was in keeping with the best traditions of the Naval Service.

. . .

37. That the log book, commanding officer's night order book, the last chart by which the ship was navigated, pay accounts, service records, muster roll, public moneys, and

public vouchers were not salvaged. All the health records were preserved and turned over to proper authority by the medical officer, U.S.S. PANAY.

The court delivered its official Opinion in eight brief points.

1. That the U.S.S. PANAY was engaged in carrying out the well established policy of the United States of protecting American lives and property.

2. That the Japanese aviators should have been familiar with the characteristics and distinguishing markings of the PANAY, as this ship was present at Nanking during the Japanese aerial attacks on that city.

3. That while the first bombers might not have been able, on account of their altitude, to identify the U.S.S. PANAY, there was no excuse for attacking without properly identifying the target especially as it was well known that neutral vessels were present in the Yangtze.

4. That it is utterly inconceivable that the six light bombing planes coming within about six hundred feet of the ships and attacking for over a period of twenty minutes could not be aware of the identity of the ships they were attacking.

5. That the Japanese are solely and wholly responsible for all losses which have occurred as the result of this attack.

6. That the deaths of Ensminger, C. L., SKlc, and Hulsebus, E. W. G., Coxswain, occurred in line of duty and were not the result of their own misconduct.

7. That the injured and wounded members of the crew of the U.S.S. PANAY received their wounds and injuries in the line of duty not the result of their own misconduct.

8. In considering the case and attending incidents as a whole, the court is of the opinion that no offenses have been committed nor blame incurred by any member of the naval service involved.

The court found in summary that everything possible had been done first to defend the ship and then to try to save her, and there were several recommendations:

The first asked that a board be convened to look into the exceptional conduct of certain officers and members of the crew and suggest decorations and awards as appropriate.

The second recommendation dealt with the ship itself. Though a sounding party from *Oahu* had been able to find only a swirl of water where *Panay* went down, there was a chance that someone else might be more successful. And because some of the ship's confidential publications had gone down with her, their security must be considered "compromised" until salvage could be accomplished or ruled out.

The third recommendation looked more to the future. It urged that "the inadequacy of the anti-aircraft defense for naval ships be given immediate consideration by the Navy Department." Two months later, reviewing the findings of the court, the Navy's Bureau of Ordnance replied stonily that "with reference to the Court's third recommendation, the subject of anti-aircraft defense of naval ships is under continual study consideration and study by this bureau." The Ordnance experts maintained that it was "practical to deliver a fairly effective anti-aircraft fire [with *Panay*'s armament] using a barrage system of control, and without anti-aircraft directors, altimeters, remote control or automatic fuse setters, which cannot be furnished to such small vessels on account of limitations of space and cost." The theory was good enough. The barrage system would come into its own on the picket line off Okinawa in World War II. But the guns on *Panay* were woefully inadequate to deliver it.

The investigation report and recommendations were sent to all other bureaus of the Navy also, to be reviewed and noted. Most of their endorsements were perfunctory. One was more prophetic. The voluminous records of the investigation still contain a quickly penned memo on note paper from the office of the judge advocate general. The memo compliments the officers and men on their heroism and notes the fact that the Japanese boarding party that went on the ship before she sank had probably set explosive charges to hurry the job. There is only one more comment scrawled on that piece of paper: "Heaven help us."

There were several bills to be rendered, too. Standard Oil had put its losses at $1,594,435.99. The Navy figured damages to its property, ships, and men at $1,211,355.01. Of this amount, a total of $607,000 represented claims for the death of two sailors and for personal injuries to the 57 officers and men who suffered from wounds, shock, or exposure. When submitting the Navy bill to the State Department for transmission to the Japanese, Secretary of the Navy Claude A. Swanson cautioned that even this substantial amount did not include damages to civilians or to State Department or War Department personnel on board.

The Japanese diplomats in Tokyo and Washington were left to pick up the pieces that the commanders in the field had scattered.

The Japanese at Nanking, after their brief apologies, were proceeding with the business at hand. Japanese General Iwane Matsui issued a brief statement saying that the great victory at Nanking had been dimmed by "a most unhappy incident" affecting United States and British naval vessels. And so having doffed his helmet briefly out of respect for the dead and wounded Americans, he popped it back on his head, spread his army out along the north bank of the Yangtze, and launched three new drives against the retreating enemy.

In Tokyo and Washington the diplomatic apologies and the denials were having a hard time keeping up with the accusations. By the end of the first week following the sinking, Tokyo was busy denying the new claims that Panay had been machine-gunned by Japanese craft. There were no Army launches in the immediate vicinity at the time, the Japanese said. The only ones near had arrived later "for the purpose of bringing medical supplies to relieve the wounded and of aiding in the rescue work."

No villain had yet appeared. But the cry was going up in Tokyo and Washington to produce one. Though the Japanese had admitted officially only that airmen were involved, an Associated Press story from Tokyo on Friday stated that "the conviction is growing that the dismissal of the Japanese air admiral [Mitsunami] is insufficient and that higher army ranks must also be purged."

Scapegoats, however, are often hard to find. One Colonel Kingoro Hashimoto, the officer who had reportedly given orders to fire on any and all ships on the river, a long-time Army firebrand, seemed to be the only man who could shed some light on the incident. And he was the one man no one could get a statement from. In fact, Hashimoto apparently couldn't even be located in the field by his Japanese superiors.

In the meantime, reported the Foreign Office in Tokyo, the reply to the United States note had to be delayed further in order to investigate thoroughly the United States charge that *Panay* had been machine-gunned by a Japanese Army motorboat. This latest accusation had been successfully kept out of Japanese papers. The tone of Tokyo stories by Saturday, almost a week after the sinking, was that United States indignation was subsiding as a result of Japanese investigations, actions, and apologies.

On the contrary, indignation was growing. Back in the United States, atrocity stories of the Japanese Army advance were not helping the official climate in Washington—nor the unofficial climate out and around the country. A dispatch to *The New York Times* by F. Tillman Durdin, from aboard *Oahu* at Shanghai, reported in shocking detail the rape of Nanking by the Japanese. Chinese civilians, Durdin wrote, had been ready to welcome the Japanese occupation forces. It was expected that the Japanese would be tough but would restore law and order. Instead there had been killing, looting, murder, and harassment of civilians. Chinese police and firemen, Durdin reported, had been "special objects of attack." The Japanese Army had quickly lost the confidence of the Chinese inhabitants and was fast losing any support from foreign opinion.

The Japanese reaction to the sudden wide circulation of atrocity stories was immediate, stiff, and largely too late. Orders went out to the armies to crack down severely on the discipline of the advancing troops. But the damage had been done. Suspicions and rumors of atrocity and treachery multiplied almost as rapidly as in the opening days of World War II.

New Jersey's J. Parnell Thomas rose to address Congress on "the whole dastardly subject." And, while in rhetorical flight, he managed to accuse the Japanese of spying on the Panama Canal with intent to destroy it, too. Fishing boats manned by Japanese naval officers were busy off Panama and Costa Rica, Thomas claimed. Their crews had been openly received and feted by the Japanese colony in Panama. Thomas also struck a blow against the erection of some proposed Japanese canning factories in Panama and Costa Rica as potential spy bases. There is no record of a voice raised to request proof or to register dissent.

But not yet being ready to declare war on the Japanese tuna industry, official Washington concentrated on the next step. On Monday, December 20, the Japanese admitted for the first time that there had been, from close range where identification was presumably feasible, a machine-gun attack by Japanese Army launches against the sinking gunboat.

New York Times correspondent Hallett Abend, in a special cable from Shanghai, broke the Japanese admission. While the Japanese still claimed the air attack was unintentional, Abend reported that the machine-gunning "was done on the personal command of Colonel Kingoro Hashimoto, and the situation has now arisen where Japanese officers are beginning to wonder whether General Iwane Matsui, commander-in-chief of the armies in the Yangtze area, dares punish this colonel."

Hashimoto's background revealed some reasons why the general might well have been hesitating. Hashimoto had been one of the prime movers in the February 1936 Tokyo coup, when a clique of about 1,000 young Army officers had seized the government building and communications centers and killed three cabinet members. The plotters had placed the capital under martial law and had staged a reign of terror for several days until subdued by loyal government troops. Hashimoto's punishment then had been mild. He had simply been relieved of duty, whereupon he formed the Greater Japan Youth Party, a general trouble-making organization of young turks. Apparently he had guided the party in its trouble making until he had been recalled to duty and sent to China in the fall of 1937 with Japan's 500,000-man invading army.

Hashimoto had had an early introduction to the art of being a disrupting influence and creating them. In 1917 he had been a young officer attached to the Japanese embassy in Moscow. There he had had an opportunity to observe the fine techniques of mob action, revolutionary violence, and street fighting. As a result, he was reputed to be an expert in street-fighting tactics. Fellow officers speculated that, also as a result, he had become overly impressed with revolutionary ideas. After the 1936 coup he had obviously been able to take advantage of political power to evade punishment. Now he seemed to have sufficient political protection again to enable himself to be "unavailable" somewhere in China. Some fellow officers felt that this lack of discipline far up the Army command was primarily responsible for the lack of discipline in the field that allowed the advancing armies to rape and pillage.

Hashimoto—even though not on the scene——was succeeding once again in splitting the armed services into several factions. General Matsui was reported to be keenly aware of the need to restore discipline at all levels. At the same time, Japanese Navy leaders under Admiral Hasegawa were taking credit for having made every effort to atone for the *Panay* bombing while claiming that the Japanese Army had "done nothing except evade responsibility and attempt to obscure the issue."

In the American press the machine-gunning of the sinking ship was now receiving the major attention, rather than the bombing itself. To Americans, the machine-gunning seemed to indicate clearly that the whole incident, from the first bomb on, had been most carefully planned.

Still there was no Japanese reply to the official United States note of protest delivered the day after the sinking. And with United States antagonism hardening to each new accusation of Japanese aggression, the Japanese press was obviously becoming uneasy. Tokyo editors tried to reassure their readers by noting that United States public opinion would never allow the administration in Washington to act rashly or forcibly against Japan. But their professional uneasiness showed through their professional calm; an experienced Japanese observer warned that "there is a certain unexpectedness in the American character which makes delay dangerous."

Obviously the Japanese diplomats were not taking lightly the drafting of their official reply. On December 21, nine days after the sinking, they were still wrestling with their answer. It was rumored that the delay was being caused by the difficulty of working out some formula with Japanese Army and Navy commanders guaranteeing that such incidents would not happen again—while still not hindering the prosecution of the war. A few days later the Japanese clarified the reason for their delay: it was the "precise and exceedingly comprehensive phraseology of the American demand" that was causing the trouble. The United States had asked for "definite and specific guarantees that hereafter American nationals, interest, and property in China shall not be subject to attack or unlawful interference by Japanese armed forces." It was the part about "interest," Far Eastern experts speculated, that was giving the Japanese trouble.

To the diplomats, "interests" was a loaded word. "People" and "property" were tangibles that could, with proper concern, be protected. Or if protection failed, indemnities could be paid to compensate for damage, loss, or death. But the term "interests" covered that whole issue of United States presence in China, a presence even the most contrite Japanese wished they didn't have to contend with. The militants were already apparently openly trying to wipe out that presence by the most sinister and violent means. If the diplomats acknowledged that Japan would protect United States "interests," they were, in effect, acknowledging the United States' right to be there. While the diplomats pondered, the world got ready to remember its holidays and forget its problems.

In Shanghai, where *Panay*'s wounded were recovering, the Red Cross distributed Christmas packages that contained cards, a sewing kit, a pocket diary, and stationery.

In Tokyo, representatives of 20 organizations that were backing a *Panay* relief fund called at the Foreign Office with their Christmas donations. They included the year's accumulation of petty fines from a girl's school and eight yen tucked discreetly into a bamboo tube. In San Diego, California, Mrs. Lucille Ensminger, wife of the first *Panay* man to die, had received a large bouquet of flowers from the Japanese colony of that city. A delegation of local Japanese had called to express their "deepest regrets." In Savannah, Georgia, a Japanese freighter heading out to sea took special pains to dip her colors to the Coast Guard cutter *Tallapoosa*. It wasn't hard to figure what was behind the gesture. In Los Angeles, federal officials worked off some of *their* antagonism by seizing a 100-foot tuna clipper in the harbor, charging that although it was registered as being owned by an American-born Japanese, it was really the property of a Japanese citizen and carried a Japanese crew. The episode may have been a Christmas present for Parnell Thomas. In Washington, the two daughters of Japanese Ambassador Saito broadcast a

Christmas peace message to the children of the world from the annual international children's party arranged by the Washington Board of Trade and NBC. Everyone thought they were particularly charming. And there were plenty of Americans that week who agreed that it was the only pleasant word they had heard from Japan in some time.

It was almost Christmas Eve in the Capital when the Japanese reply to the United States note finally arrived. And with it came a strange feeling of anticlimax. The reply was, as expected, a complete apology. All the particulars of the United States note had been met. It was, the Japanese maintained, a colossal mistake. But an understandable one. Although *Panay*'s plan of movement had been properly filed with military authorities, the erratic field communications between Japanese units had held up a proper passing of the word. The commander of the air squadron that sank the gunboat had not been notified of the *Panay*'s presence in that part of the river until 5:30 P.M.—an hour and a half after she had gone to the bottom. In addition, said the Japanese, dense smoke had created such poor visibility around the area that Japanese troops had also been bombed.

Nevertheless, punishments had been meted out. The Japanese reply testified that "the commander of the flying force concerned was immediately removed from his post and recalled, on the grounds of a failure to take the fullest measure of precaution. Moreover, the staff members of the fleet and the commander of the flying squadron and all others responsible have been dealt with according to the law." This was strong action for a nation that had been involved in at least ten major incidents since midsummer and had established a precedent of responding with nothing more than apologetic diplomatic verbiage. Colonel Hashimoto was not named or alluded to. Presumably he was still safe on duty at the front.

By January 1, 1938, other news had crowded the *Panay* stories far back into the inside pages of the nation's papers.

Far up the Yangtze at mile 221, divers recovered *Panay*'s safe from the muddy bottom. More than $40,000 in cash and the vouchers and pay accounts that were in the safe were still intact. Not much else was brought up. USS *Oahu* had anchored over the site shortly after the first of the year. With her was the Shanghai salvage tug *Saucy* and eight White Russian divers. The current was swift at the spot and the high content of silt in the water made working below difficult. For some of the time a Japanese patrol boat stood by, not helping, just looking. Each day as they worked, the salvage crews could see the Japanese officers on the bridge, silently watching everything through their binoculars. But there were no signals. No communication. Just a menacing presence. On the west bank the *Mei An* still sat with her bridge blown off. Across the river the burned bulks of *Mei Ping* and *Mei Hsia* were already beginning to turn from black to brown with rust.

After the first few dives it was clear that *Panay* could not be salvaged. She was lying on her side in about 80 feet of water, half-covered with silt. A massive crack ran the length of her bottom. And one bomb had apparently gone all the way through her and out the bottom of the hull without ever exploding.

The divers brought up a number of locked boxes and the personal gear of some of the officers and men. Most of it was already too damaged by water to be usable. But in addition to the naval records, the divers also found 700 feet of newsreel film that Arthur Menken had taken of the Nanking raids and sent aboard *Panay* for safekeeping. Fortunately, most of it was in waterproof cartridges.

Oahu and *Saucy* terminated operations as soon as they could. Before they went up the river, there were rumors that *Oahu* might just stumble into an "incident" too. She had orders to vacate the area as soon as possible. *Saucy* headed downstream for Shanghai. *Oahu* pointed her bow inland toward Hankow. Both ships dipped their colors as they steamed away, just as American warships would dip them at that spot for the next four years. Now the Japanese could search all they wanted to. Perhaps they did. One part of her cargo they would have been interested to see was *not* recovered: a collection of new types of Japanese aircraft equipment, recovered from crashed planes and hidden aboard *Panay*. If the Japanese had known of it, it was almost fair grounds for "an incident."

Unless the Chinese communists have a high regard for old scrap or the resurrected relics of history, *Panay* is still at the bottom of the river off Mananshau Wharf. And until it rotted away, the United States flag on her sunken mast would probably still float out gently, from time to time, when the Yangtze current ran particularly strong.

16

"Supper tonight at the Cathay?"

Ask two automobile drivers involved in a minor accident to describe just how it occurred, and frequently you will come up with two accounts that might well have taken place 50 miles apart. Each man sees events with different eyes, emphasis, and coloration. Finding out what actually happened —if by some happy chance the whole thing has not been recorded by an auspiciously placed photographer—is the hard hunt that has to be undertaken by a trained investigator who will sift out, from the conflicting accounts, the most likely truths.

Regarding an event charged with as much excitement, action, and emotion as the sinking of *Panay* (witnessed on one side or the other by perhaps a hundred different men), you have wild diversity. Some facts of the incident could eventually be decided by a dozen or so confirming reports from those likely to be the most qualified observers. Other things were matters of reasonable opinion. Some relatively simple events were reported so divergently that you might think they were actually the figment of each man's imagination. But fortunately, there *was* an auspiciously placed cameraman on the scene. In fact, several of them.

Norman Soong of *The New York Times* had shot nearly 75 still photographs of the attack, the sinking, and the adventure ashore. Eric Mayell of Fox Movietone had filmed much of it with his newsreel camera. Norman Alley had shot 53 hundred-foot rolls of movie film, beginning in the very first phase of the attack. At one point, on shore in the tall reeds, Alley had wrapped both film and camera in a piece of canvas and buried them in the mud of the riverbank when he thought the Japanese were coming ashore to kill them. The pictures would be an incriminating piece of evidence. Alley doubted the Japanese had any idea the film existed. But if they had, they would make every attempt to get it.

All the way inland to Hanshan, back to *Oahu*, and on the trip down the river to Shanghai, Alley and Mayell had quietly guarded their little stock of critical evidence. The two and a half days steaming downstream with a glowering Japanese destroyer fore and aft seemed to Alley to take as much time as a round-the-world cruise. He kept his camera under cover and his film hidden. But he was jumpy as hell. *Everyone* in the American party knew he and Mayell had shot the whole thing. He was certain someone would let the news slip to the Japanese. The American and British gunboats were still neutral territory. But the Japanese were clearly unpredictable. It would be easy enough to halt the whole convoy and demand a search. Alley couldn't very well ask Commander Sheehan to jeopardize the lives of all of them by his own refusal to give up the film.

It wasn't until the two cameramen walked aboard *Augusta* under the suddenly protective glare of the floodlights and finally placed their precious rolls of exposed film in the paymaster's safe that they breathed the first sighs of relief. The next step was to report to Admiral Yarnell what the film might contain.

Harry Yarnell must have been tempted to see for himself immediately. If the cameramen had gotten all they claimed, the pictures would prove how low the Japanese planes had come, the extent of the visibility at the spot, and the validity of the charges that the Japanese had strafed the gunboat and the survivors. But the commander must also have known the high risk he took during all the time the film was in his possession. If it were ruined in developing—or stolen—Washington, and the world, would never have the answers America needed to prove its case.

Alley and the others arrived back in Shanghai on December 17, Friday. There was a *Clipper* leaving Hong Kong on Sunday, December 19—but that meant almost 900 miles of travel down the China coast from Shanghai to Hong Kong, just to reach the plane. A destroyer could make it in about 30 hours. Nevertheless there were certain risks in the trip that neither man spoke of, yet both of them must have been thinking about them. If the Japanese knew about the film, just how badly would they want to get it? A destroyer hugging the Chinese coast would be an easy target—and in time of war, an easy one for the Japanese to "mistake" again.

Yarnell had a better plan. Four destroyers, headed by the USS *Stewart*, were leaving for Manila the next morning, Saturday, December 18. Alley would be aboard with his film. His testimony had already been taken. It would be most important of all to get that film back to the people in Washington.

With the arrangements made, Alley had one last job to do ashore. The CBS radio stringer in Shanghai knew Alley was back and had arranged for an overseas broadcast that would be the first in-person radio report of the bombing. The enterprising CBS man had been working from a transmitter in the kitchen of a house in the Jessfield area, right outside the International Settlement. It was a bit risky. The Japanese were looking for the transmitter. But Alley, with a newsman's addiction to the principle of the scoop wherever it can be gotten, was tempted to try it.

As he was arranging to go ashore, a Japanese naval attaché came aboard *Augusta* on an official errand. Before leaving, he had asked for a chance to speak to some of the survivors, to express his personal apologies. When Alley was introduced and identified, the officer's interest picked up.

"Did you by any chance take any film?" Alley acknowledged that he had. There was a stage wait, then the conversation turned to other parts of the incident. As he was leaving, the Japanese extended a most cordial invitation. "Could we not have supper tonight at the Cathay?"

The chops of the fox appeared to Alley to curl a bit too hungrily. Alley declined. With profuse thanks. Half an hour later he slipped ashore and took a taxi to the Jessfield address. The broadcast went off smoothly enough, though they were all a bit jumpy. Alley spoke for about ten minutes. And though he knew that it might be better to stay on the cautious side, he found that sort of moderation almost impossible as he told again the events of the last few days.

He finished, wishing there was more time. There was so much he wanted to say. The others were nervous. The CBS man pushed him out the door and into a car. Within an hour he was back aboard *Augusta*. The next morning the USS *Stewart* was on the way on her 1,100-mile dash to Manila. And Norman Alley, with 5,000 feet of incriminating film insured for $350,000, was aboard.

As if to cooperate on the race back home, the *Clipper* arrived in Manila early. Alley signed his films out of the *Stewart*'s safe and climbed aboard the big four-engined Martin flying boat. It seemed only a short time earlier that he and Jim Marshall had been racing westward on the same plane, sharing a pint of Scotch to their new affiliation.

"At each subsequent setting-down point—Guam, Wake, Midway and Honolulu—a naval guard met me and took my films for safekeeping until we were ready to take off again."

The Navy was taking no chances. A Japanese bomber had trailed the *Stewart* suspiciously 400 miles out. Then disappeared. At Alameda Bay when Alley's *Clipper* landed the security was doubled. Waiting for the cameraman were the members of his family, the head of his San Francisco office, two uniformed members of the California Highway Patrol, and two burly strangers: inspectors from the California State Police. They would stick with Alley on the flight to New York. Alley wrote in his book *I Witness:*

At 6 o'clock in the evening of December 29, we taxied to earth at Newark Airport, only ten days and eighteen hours since I had left Shanghai, including three days aboard a destroyer that took me to Manila!

At the Newark Airport, I was greeted by more cops—this time, members of the New Jersey State Police. I never had felt so completely in custody in my life.

And there was an armored car to whisk the negatives to the lab at Fort Lee.

Inspectors Steinmeyer and Ford [of the California State Police] exchanged courtesies with the New Jersey State Police, and we had an escort all the way to the State line. As we rode along, I felt like a fellow who has left his wrist watch on the washstand. This was the first time the films were completely out my hands since they were born on the bomb-racked decks of the ill-fated gunboat.

And so—on to New York and its Hotel Warwick.

At the hotel, we were ushered into a private elevator and the Alley clan, en masse, soared upward to the hostelry's penthouse.

I had thought I was going to be able to relax the next day, but I was wrong. I was never so busy since those teeming twenty minutes on the decks of the "Panay" as I was on the first day in New York. A bunch of metropolitan news scribes arrived, each wanting an exclusive interview; and the daughters wanted to go to Grant's tomb; the wife wanted to go shopping on Fifth Avenue; son Dexter wanted to take in the Statue of Liberty, and I wanted to go to pieces!

It wasn't until late that afternoon at a screening in a

private projection room at Universal Newsreel headquarters in Manhattan that Alley got the first chance to see what he had really taken.

Most news photographers have experienced bringing back with pride the films of some notable scoop only to discover that what is finally developed may not show, or even convey, what they really thought they were photographing. Alley waited nervously as the white, numbered film "leader" flickered through the projector. The first footage was the "staged" stuff he had taken aboard *Panay* at Nanking. In the excitement he had forgotten what was on most of those early reels. He had made notes at the time of some of the names and faces, thinking he would have to identify them briefly later for some brief newsreel filler. And suddenly here were the faces of the men with whom he had been plunged into perhaps the biggest adventure of all. They weren't strange young boys now but old friends: Quartermaster Jimmy Peck, signaling out across the water toward *Ladybird*; Rider, standing in the stern sheets of the captain's gig, *Panay* white and gleaming behind him; Hughes, immaculate in dress blues, headed for a last meeting on shore; Weldon James, incredibly young and handsome, talking animatedly on the wharf at Nanking; Sandri, cheerful and voluble even though no one could understand him—and dead . . .

Then without warning, just as it happened, "it" happened again. Onto a dead white screen *Panay*'s foremast flashed into view, seeming to swing across the screen, wildly. The tiny black cross of an airplane's silhouette zoomed across the picture high above the mast. The mast circled dizzily. Alley groaned to himself. Panning too fast. Bad. More planes diving down diagonally across the *Panay*'s gently curling Union Jack. Men running. The gunners in silent animation, slapping on the ammunition drums now. Tracing their target. Jarring to the recoil of the heavy Lewis guns. Weird. There was not a sound in the projection room. Just the whirr of the film. But to Alley, the noise of the attack was roaring all around. The high whine of aircraft engines. Some magnificent cussing. The steady pound-pound-pound-pound-pound of the machine guns. A silence. A moan . . . And cold sweat on the photographer's forehead.

At midnight that night he boarded the Washington express with a print of the film under his arm. The negatives were safe in the vault in New York now. And duplicates would be made soon. He felt easier.

At Washington, I had to have the films run off at two different sittings in order to bring them before the official eyes of the Secretary of the Navy Claude A. Swanson, Secretary of War Harry H. Woodring, and the Chairman of the powerful and all-important Foreign Relations Committee, Senator Key Pittman of Nevada, who was also president pro tem of the United States Senate.

As I sat in those darkened rooms looking at the pictures with the Federal fathers, I saw again the unpremeditated and wanton attack of the Japanese; the fallen Commander Hughes, the heroic Lieutenant Anders, the dying Sandri, strafed lifeboats loaded with wounded, and the three-day trek through hell.

Official onlookers watched the screen, motionless, spellbound. All during the screening, they said nothing; but, new dollars to the same old doughnuts, they were thinking plenty!

Alley left the screening, feeling for the first time as if his mission were finally accomplished. He was free, for a while at least. He wandered though Washington like a tourist, looking, trying to recollect all that had happened to him with such rapidity in the last few days. Two weeks before he had been climbing aboard *Augusta*. At one point he found himself along the tidal basin. The trees all around him were bare and stark. But they were, he knew, cherry trees—3,000 of them—a token of friendship and good will from the people of Japan. He didn't know whether to laugh or cry.

"I answered everything as thoroughly as I could," Alley remembers of the Washington trip, "and there were plenty of questions—many of them too technical for me." But he also remembers that in his answers he must have been trying unconsciously to lead his questioners to a question they wouldn't ask: Was the attack on purpose? He was sure they were convinced it had been on purpose. And he wanted to express his conviction, too. But no one asked.

When it was all over, Alley remembers, the President had one request. Before the films were shown, Roosevelt asked that about 30 feet of film showing several Japanese bombers down nearly at deck level be removed before the prints were released to theaters. Alley promised this would be done. There was no discussion about why this was taken out. But if the Japanese were to stick to their story of "mistaken identity"—and if an angry American people were to be asked to believe the story—it would hardly do to see planes going by only 100 feet in the air. In that 30 feet of film, a 12-year-old kid munching pop corn at the Saturday matinee could have picked out the features of the Japanese pilots, read the lettering on the fuselage, and counted the bombs left in the half-empty racks. If the kids in the mezzanine could do that, why couldn't a trained combat pilot at the other end of the camera lens spot a 26-by-32-foot American flag when there were three flags to pick from?

Alley relayed the President's request to the film lab in New York. The cutter snipped out the necessary footage. The splice was made. "Let's don't quibble. The stuff is great even without it. And prints are due all over the country chop-chop. Theaters are already advertising it."

To some people the story was finished.

17

"In reward for your audacity"

On April 22, 1938, the *Panay* incident was officially marked closed when the Japanese government presented the United States with a check for $2,214,007.36. It was tendered as "settlement in full" for destroying three large Standard Oil craft, for the loss of *Panay*, for the deaths of one civilian captain and two Navy men, and for injuries suffered by 74 men on all the vessels. The cost was nominal. It was a far better buy than a war.

The Japanese made two last requests—both certainly practical ones, but ill-timed enough to have stirred public opinion again had they not been carefully buried in the official files. Having paid the bill, the Japanese wanted to know if they could salvage *Panay* and the tankers. And secondly, if a new gunboat was to be built to replace her could the contract be let to a Japanese shipyard? Secretary Hull fired off a sharp "No" on both requests.

The men who had been bombed and machine-gunned afloat and harassed ashore didn't close the books so quickly or forget so easily just because a check was passed from one diplomat to another. Fortunately, neither did their country. Of the survivors, 23 would be recommended for Navy Crosses.

Special letters of commendation from the Secretary of the Navy went to Lieutenant Commander Hughes and two other crewmen; one of them was Yuan Te Erh, the Chinese-born mess attendant. Another messman of Chinese origin, King Fong Sung, would later get the Bronze Star for his part that day. Executive Officer Anders, who took over for his disabled skipper, would receive the Navy's Distinguished Service Medal, which in 1937 was the highest decoration the Navy could give, short of the Congressional Medal of Honor. Captain Frank Roberts would win a D.S.M., too. The Navy would further honor Army man Roberts with its Navy Cross for his "fortitude and heroism."

A few of the *Panay* veterans had one more rude surprise coming from Japanese naval aviators. Four years later, 12 former crew members of the gunboat were aboard ships or at shore stations at Pearl Harbor when the sneak attack came. Lieutenant Geist on *Raleigh* joined in the successful day-long battle to keep that torpedoed cruiser afloat with borrowed pontoons and construction barges lashed alongside her like giant waterwings. Denny Biwerse was aboard *Phoenix*, one of only three cruisers and a dozen destroyers that were able to sortie out of Pearl that day in a futile search for the attackers. Coxswain E. E. Cowden, Navy Cross recipient from the Yangtze attack, was stationed on *Maryland*, which was moored alongside *Oklahoma* when that battleship turned turtle and sank. Another *Panay* Navy Cross wearer, Gunner's Mate Hennessy, who had come down the Yangtze on the Japanese destroyer, was attached to *Pennsylvania*; his ship, trapped in drydock, miraculously escaped major damage when two destroyers drydocked just ahead of her were wrecked by bombs. A third Navy Cross winner, Coxswain Rider, who had worked so hard with Roberts in the hospital at Hohsien, was aboard *Arizona*, which burned and sank with 1,100 men entombed in her; ship and men still remain on the bottom of the harbor off Ford Island as a permanent memorial to that day. Rider survived, but in the next four years of war eight of the old *Panay* crew would be killed or missing in action or would die of wounds.

Many of the principal characters on both sides would serve with distinction and pop up in the news again during the fighting. And after the war, one of them would shoulder major blame for helping to bring the whole conflict about.

Commander Hughes, never quite recovering from his crippling *Panay* wounds, was retired for medical reasons late in World War II. He became the president of a large Washington corporation. Often pressed to say the bombing was accidental, Hughes was convinced it was not. Most of the old *Panay* men would still agree with him.

Captain Roberts elected to stay in the Far East, serving in Burma at the beginning of the war as intellingence officer for General Joseph Stilwell and then returning to Washington, eventually to become chief of the Strategy and Policy Group in the War Department's Operation Division and Army representative on the Joint Staff Planners. When President Roosevelt attended Allied conferences in Quebec, Cairo, and Yalta, Roberts was present. Toward the end of the war, he was sent to Moscow as chief of staff of the United States military mission there. Before retiring as a major general in 1957 to join the CIA's Board of National Estimates, Roberts had also served as chief of staff of NATO's Southern European Headquarters.

Embassy Secretary Atcheson saw the Far East as an area of decision and as the sphere for his career. He appeared headed for a brilliant one. During most of World War II he served as chargé d'affaires in the United States embassy in Chungking. After the defeat of Japan, he was tapped by General Douglas MacArthur to become the general's acting political officer in Tokyo and then shortly afterward was made chairman of the Allied Council for Japan. In this role he emerged as a resolute and consistent fighter against the Russians and the Japanese leftists. (The latter group particularly annoyed him; he found its members disturbingly reminiscent of the old Japanese militarists who had plagued him in *Panay* days.) Early in 1947, Atcheson was named Foreign Service Minister for Japan. Called back to the United States for conferences in the summer of that year, he was lost at sea when the Army plane in which he was flying crashed off Honolulu.

Peppery Admiral Yarnell retired in 1939. But if out of harness, Yarnell was hardly out of voice. In the summer of 1940, he spoke out as a strong backer for intervention, recommending immediate United States entry into the war in Europe and support for Roosevelt's plan to send 50 overage destroyers to England. His reputation commanded a hearing then when many Americans were tempted to turn a deaf ear. Early in 1941, Yarnell was recalled to duty and served as a trouble-shooter on production throughout most of the war.

Only one of the four crack flight leaders who led the 24 Japanese planes on their attack against *Panay* survived World War II. Lieutenant Ushioda, who led the fighters, lost his life before the Chinese fighting was over; he disappeared on a mission over central China. Murata, whose high-level bombers launched the *Panay* attack, commanded a torpedo bomber flight of 40 planes from the carrier *Akagi* in the Pearl Harbor raid but died ten months later in the battle of Santa Cruz. Komaki, who led the third flight over *Panay*, was killed in 1944 when his plane crashed at sea during the Japanese evacuation of the Palau Islands. Only Masatake Okumiya lived through four years of combat to see peace come again to Japan. In an article in an American naval journal in 1953, Okumiya wrote his account of the *Panay* sinking, still insisting that it had been a case of mistaken identity. He claimed that the command structure of the two services made it "impossible" for Army fire-eaters to have duped the Japanese Navy and ordered the attack. But Okumiya did have a few barbs for his sister services. He criticized the Army—and particularly Colonel Hashimoto—because Army spokesmen had repeatedly aggravated the bad feeling that followed the sinking by not showing "common sense in regard to international matters, nor did they display good judgment, or even proper knowledge of military etiquette."

Admiral Hasegawa, who commanded Okumiya and all Japanese naval forces in China, was the officer who some observers thought might have to commit hara-kiri because of the *Panay* sinking. He emerged from the incident with his reputation—and his life—intact. Although an able officer, Hasegawa may not have been militant enough for the war party. In 1940 he was named governor of Formosa, an essential but lackluster post in which he served until 1944, when he was recalled to Japan and appointed to the Supreme War Council. When Japan surrendered, Hasegawa was arrested as a war criminal and remained in prison for about a year and a half until he was cleared and released, a tired old man.

There remained the arch-villain, Colonel Hashimoto. In 1937, many of the militarists had privately applauded his arrogance and his suspect role in the bombing. But at that time the Japanese government had to adopt an official attitude of contriteness that ruled out any other public posture toward Hashimoto except displeasure. (He was recalled to Japan early in 1938 and put on inactive duty but he was never disciplined otherwise.) Though carrying a rank of colonel, he was to make his contribution during the war in the Japanese Diet and as a vigorous leader of the extremists and unofficial inner-circle government leaders who advocated Japanese control of not only east Asia, but also Australia, New Zealand, Madagascar, and India. The second hat he wore as director of the Imperial Rule Assistance Association's Youth Corps gave him a ready public platform to be heard from.

In January 1945 a German news agency reported that the Imperial Rule Assistance Association was demanding a more resolute prosecution of the war and was planning to create a new and all-powerful Japanese political party to carry this out. The German source went on to speculate that Hashimoto's IRAA group would certainly gain influence under such a scheme. Then only a week later it was reported that Hashimoto had resigned as Youth Corps director. The move could only be interpreted by the press as an indication of the overall unrest and indecision in the home islands. Apparently the all-out fighters were now fighting among themselves. Hashimoto was out of power. And it was not until after the surrender, in September 1945, that he appeared again in American news reports, this time as one of seven members of the Black Dragon Society who were wanted for war crimes. Three days after the arrest order was published, Hashimoto gave himself up.

On April 29, 1946, the colonel stood among the 28 top Japanese leaders who were indicted for "plotting to rule the world." A staggering 55 counts of war crimes were arrayed against them. It was made clear in the indictment that the trials would involve charges of aggression even before the Japanese invasion of Manchuria in 1931. The trial had been going about three months when the *Panay* incident was revived in court over the strong protest of the defense lawyers. Hashimoto admitted that his artillery had shelled HMS *Ladybird* on her way to aid *Panay*'s survivors. That was as far as he would go. It was almost a year later before Hashimoto came back into the limelight again. This time he admitted to prosecutors his long-time role as a troublemaker; he conceded that he had been a member of a tightly organized group that had been behind incidents to control the Japanese government since 1931 and that he had long advocated bringing to an end British political control in the Orient—"by force if necessary."

When the trial came to an end on November 12, 1948, convictions were brought in against 25 of the original 28 defendants. Tojo and 6 others were sentenced to hang. Among them was General Iwane Matsui, Hashimoto's old antagonist and Army commander in China during the "rape of Nanking" in which Hashimoto's troops had participated. Some 16 defendants, Hashimoto among them, were sentenced to life imprisonment.

On September 17, 1955, ten years and one day after he had given himself up to Allied authorities, the little colonel walked out of Tokyo's Sugamo Prison a free man—but with incurable cancer. He had been released "by agreement of the United States and seven other Allied powers." He and two other political prisoners emerged impeccably dressed in morning coats and striped trousers. About a hundred persons were on hand to greet them. Wire service stories around the world announced the parole of "the man who sunk *Panay*."

But had he?

18

"Peaceful beneath us lay the rich valley"

LIKE MANY MYSTERIES, the more the facts behind the sinking of *Panay* are dug into, the more unanswered questions turn up from the digging. Whether or not Kingoro Hashimoto was the man really responsible for sinking the little gunboat may never be known. On June 29, 1957, Hashimoto died in Tokyo of cancer of the lung. He was 67. *The New York Times* obituary remarked on his death:

One of Japan's "Class A" war criminals, Hashimoto, was convicted by the eleven-nation Allied Military tribunal of sharing responsibility for Japan's "rape of Nanking," bombardment of the American gunboat Panay and the British gunboat Ladybird in 1937, "joint conspiracy for aggressive wars," and other counts.

At the height of his power, Hashimoto was a stocky, middle-sized man who traveled tirelessly and spoke energetically to win recruits to his way of thinking. He lived modestly, shunning luxury, and pursuing a Spartan simplicity.

One man was primarily responsible for starting the legend that Hashimoto had "sunk" *Panay*. He was Hallett Abend, *The New York Times* stringer who had so movingly covered the return of the survivors to Shanghai. Abend was a freewheeling newspaperman of the old school. He hunted hard for a scoop. Wrote for the top dollar. Loved China. Loved the reporter's life. If Abend's story is true, it is damning evidence. Here is that story excerpted from Abend's book, *My Life in China*, written in 1943:

About ten o'clock on the morning of December 13th, the day that Nanking fell, Rear Admiral T. Honda, the Naval Attaché of the Japanese Embassy, called upon me in what seemed a breathless haste. Would I go with him, he begged, to the Japanese flagship, the *Idzumo?* He said that Vice-Admiral K. Hasegawa, then commander of Japan's Third Fleet, wanted to see me on a matter of really grave importance.

We drove down the Bund in Honda's car, crossed the Garden Bridge over Soochow Creek, and alighted in front of the well-guarded Japanese Consulate-General, where the *Idzumo* was moored. Aboard the flagship, we were taken without delay to Admiral Hasegawa's private sitting room, and found him with Rear Admiral Teizo Mitsunami, chief of the Navy's aerial operations in the China war zone. Hasegawa wasted no time.

"I'm afraid," he blurted, "that we have sunk the *Panay!*"

So much was honest and straightforward, but in spite of about twenty minutes of questioning I could get no other positive statements from the highest commander of the Japanese navy in Chinese waters, except that Japan would apologize and would pay any reasonable indemnity.

When I pressed for details which would fix responsibility, Hasegawa at first said that Admiral Mitsunami, although not personally at fault, would be retired in token of Japan's regret.

"But who," I pressed, "ordered the bombing of the *Panay?*"

"It was the Bad Boy of the army, and not the fault of the navy," was Admiral Mitsunami's incautious admission. At the time, I thought he was trying to shield the navy behind some imaginary or anonymous army commander, and let it go at that.

The full truth about the bombing of the *Panay* was not revealed until about two weeks later [Christmas week 1937], and then it came to me in a curious manner. A highly placed Japanese, whose name cannot be revealed even six years after the event, came to me one Sunday morning and asked:

"Would you like to do a personal favor for your friend General Matsui?"

"What kind of a favor?" I asked cautiously.

"A favor that will permit Matsui to retain his command in China. Things have reached such a tension that either he or another officer must be recalled and retired. The general thinks that if the New York *Times* publishes all the facts, and they are then cabled back to Tokyo from New York, that he may be able to reassert his authority."

I had no intention of permitting the New York *Times* to be used as an unconscious participant in a Japanese military feud, and would make no promises, but readily agreed to go at once to Matsui's headquarters and listen to what he might have to say. . . .

He proved as initially frank as Admiral Hasegawa had been the day I learned of the sinking of the *Panay*, for we had no sooner been seated with cups of hot tea and glasses of excellent French brandy before us than he burst out:

"Things have reached such a pass that either Colonel Hashimoto must be recalled, or I must relinquish my command and go home."

"Do you mean Kingoro Hashimoto of Wuhu?" I asked.

"That's the man. He's arrogant and insubordinate and even mutinous. And he's ignorant and dangerous. He wants Japan to fight the whole world—right now!"

Then, in little more than half an hour, General Matsui told me an incredible tale, which, however, I easily verified next day. . . .

Upon the outbreak of the China war in the summer of 1937 Hashimoto had been recalled to active service, and had commanded an army unit which successfully marched around Nanking and captured the river port of Wuhu, up river from the capital.

As General Matsui explained the situation to me, the navy at that time had not yet reached Nanking, but the army was short of bombing planes, as a result of which various squadrons of naval bombers were sent inland to act under orders of various regional army commanders. One such squadron of the navy bombers had spent the night of December 11th on Lake Tai, and on the morning of December 12th had flown to Wuhu and landed on the Yangtze there to receive Colonel Hashimoto's orders.

Hashimoto, evidently drunk with success, ordered the planes to "bomb everything that moved" on the Yangtze River above Nanking. The navy commander of the squadron demurred, and pointed out to Colonel Hashimoto that there were several American, British, French, and Italian gunboats on the river, as well as neutral passenger and cargo vessels, some of which were carrying civilian refugees from the doomed Chinese capital. Hashimoto thereupon flew into a terrible rage, and threatened the navy air commander with execution on the spot on the charge of insubordination in a combat zone if he did not carry out orders. . . .

Hashimoto played his own even more direct part that December 12th. He deliberately ordered his shore batteries to open fire at point-blank range upon two British river gunboats, the *Ladybird* and the *Bee*, with resultant loss of British lives.

Admiral Hasegawa had known what had happened, but Hashimoto was so powerful that even a vice admiral did not dare to expose this mere army colonel, but permitted the navy to take the blame for the bombing, and even sacrificed Admiral Mitsunami into forced retirement rather than expose the truth to the world.

After his daring success at Wuhu, General Matsui said, Hashimoto became unbearable in his defiant assumptions of untouchability. When Matsui went to Nanking to make his formal triumphant entry into the captured capital, Colonel Hashimoto appeared uninvited from Wuhu, and insolently rode through Nanking's battered gates only a few paces behind Matsui. Moreover, Hashimoto had provided himself with a magnificent white saddle horse, a mount which entirely outclassed that of the commander-in-chief.

Matsui told me that day that Hashimoto was intent upon actions which would embroil Japan immediately in hostilities with the United States and Great Britain.

"Either he must go home, or I go home. I cannot longer be responsible for the actions or policies of such a firebrand."

It was a sensational explanation for the bombing. But it was a neat and tidy one. Too tidy, perhaps?

If true, it took the Navy off the hook—somewhat. The commander of the "Navy seaplane squadron" at Lake Tai would have been guilty of obeying a stupid order if he had obeyed Hashimoto's command, but he would have done it at the threat of being shot. From the Navy point of view, perhaps that would have been better than having to admit its crack dive-bomber pilots had made such an incredible blunder in identification. By going along with the Abend story, the Japanese Navy would, in fact, have done just what the admirals might have liked to do from the beginning: put the entire blame on the Army. But if the story really was true, why hadn't the Navy latched onto it from the first instead of waiting for an Army general to break it two weeks following the sinking when international repercussions had threatened to drive the United States and Japan into full-scale war?

Probably because the Japanese Navy knew the story was an Army plant to get Hashimoto withdrawn from China without the necessity of an Army-originated investigation and trial. Matsui could have concocted the tale. Abend could have relayed it in good faith. And—as a result—Hashimoto *was* eventually recalled to Japan.

But if Matsui's story was a plant, what *really* happened? Did the Abend interview with Admirals Hasegawa and Mitsunami ever really take place? And did Mitsunami claim as early as December 13, the day following the bombing, that Hashimoto, the "Bad Boy" of the Army, ordered it? If so, it's a charge that Admiral Mitsunami failed to repeat in a confidential memo about the incident published for the first time at the close of this book.

What other riddles, rumors, plants, and false leads have survived to cloud the story of the *Panay* incident over 31 years later? An amazing number of them. Here are eight:

1. At one time or another, various Japanese reports have

claimed that there were Chinese troops aboard the three Standard Oil ships, implying that even if the bombing was a mistake, it was a mistake made on ships that would have been legitimate targets for Japanese aircraft.

2. Some *Panay* survivors have always suspected that the Japanese Army boarding party that came aboard the gunboat Sunday morning, December 12, radioed *Panay*'s position to Hashimoto's headquarters so he could order the attack. Could it have happened? Did it?

3. The story leaked to *Times* reporter Abend by General Matsui claimed that float planes from Lake Tai under Hashimoto's temporary command sank *Panay*. Were planes there? Did he have command?

4. An American source, made public for the first time 30 years after the sinking, says proof is in hand that planes from the carrier *Kaga* cruising in the China Sea sank *Panay* and that United States intelligence knew it as early as Christmas 1937.

5. And what about the flight of mysterious "twin-engined heavy bombers" that several survivors saw at the start of the attack and are mentioned in the official U.S. Navy court of inquiry *Findings*? These planes disappeared when the Changchow aircraft began to dive. Where did they come from? Where did they go?

6. The survivors were "heavily" strafed as they headed toward shore. The Japanese Navy contends that only one of its planes fired a dozen rounds. Then who else fired on the ship's boats? And who machine-gunned *Panay* when she was abandoned and sinking?

7. A Japanese station near Tokyo reported hearing "a distress call" from *Panay* the afternoon of the bombing, but none was ever sent from the gunboat. Who was on the air calling for help?

8. And finally, there has always been the suspicion that the Japanese Navy was indeed blameless of anything except carelessness, that Hashimoto duped the Navy into making an attack he never could have convinced his superiors to order.

Each of these rumors has hung on long enough so that they are worth examining one at a time.

1. *There were Chinese troops aboard the three Standard Oil ships.*

The last days before the capture of Nanking were confused and chaotic. Civil authority had broken down. The Chinese Army was too busy—and too disorganized—to establish military law. The last-ditch defense was crumbling, not so much from Japanese pressure but from a collapse of morale within the city. The few remaining civil officials were fading away with the last chance to leave. Army officers charged with the final, suicidal resistance made their last inspection of the various strong points, exorting their men to fight to the finish, and then in many cases hurried back to their command posts, shucked their uniforms, and slipped out through the one remaining unsealed gate toward the north. Chicago *Daily News* correspondent A. T. Steele, who stayed behind to report the Japanese take-over, sent back to the *Daily News* a series of stark and harrowing accounts of these last days of Nanking:

I saw Chinese troops looting shopwindows, but later I saw the Japanese troops outdo them in a campaign of pillage which the Japanese carried out not only in the shops but in homes, hospitals, and refugee camps.

I saw Chinese multitudes beginning their retreat through the city's north gate, the only remaining exit. Then I saw that hurried but orderly withdrawal become a pell-mell rush, and, finally, a milling panic as the last line of escape was cut off.

I saw hundreds of Chinese tear off their uniforms in the street, some donning civilian clothes, others running away in their underwear. Many came to me and to other foreigners, imploring protection and offering guns and money in exchange.

I saw fear-crazed troops attempt to force their entry into the headquarters of the international committee and, when refused, begin to toss guns, revolvers, and machine guns over the walls into the hands of the startled missionaries, who gingerly stowed them away for surrender to the Japanese.

With troops trying to escape any way possible, there is no doubt that many Chinese Army units tried to flee the city by water. And there is the possibility that there *were* some soldiers, either in uniform or in peasant clothes, among the 800 or so Chinese passengers aboard the three Standard Oil vessels.

Even if there were not, it's easy to see how such a rumor could start. Chinese security guards employed by the Standard Oil Company wore a dark blue Army-type uniform. As they crowded aboard *Mei Ping*, *Mei An*, and *Mei Hsia* on the panic-filled Nanking waterfront, the guards would have attracted a certain amount of attention, particularly among the unfortunates being left behind to bear the full brunt of the Japanese occupation. An ugly rumor would have spread quickly in the sort of disaster situation that makes even the most harmless rumor race along, growing and becoming more distorted as it goes: "The Americans are saving all their workers." "Even the families?" "Yes. Families, servants, guards. Everyone." "Can we get on the ships, too?" "No. The guards are using their guns to keep others off." A few streets away, the story would be repeated. "The Americans are saving their lackeys. They're using guns to keep the others off the ship. Foreign bastards!" And repeated again halfway across town. "Soldiers are shooting Chinese who are trying to get aboard the Standard Oil ships." "The American ships are leaving. And they're full of soldiers. They're deserting us."

Informers could have picked up the story and relayed it to the Japanese later when the city was overrun. When the news of the sinking was known, the rumor would be good justification for the attack.

Lieutenant Okumiya first heard the rumor about four or five days after the sinking when he and some other Japanese naval air officers were entertained at the residence of a prominent lobbyist for Japanese interests in China, who lived in Shanghai near the Japanese Club. Before the evening was far along, the talk naturally got around to the *Panay* bombing.

"I saw two Chinese generals at the southern part of Shanghai," the politician told the young lieutenant, "who were on board one of the ships of the *Panay* group at the time of the incident. They said there were many other soldiers on board these ships."

Okumiya thought back to the one vivid impression he had had as his plane pulled out of his dive: he had noticed men in what appeared to be dark blue Chinese Army uniforms scurrying about the decks of the ships. Maybe the story was true. Maybe the pilots had struck a blow for Japan after all.

The thought that vessels carrying Chinese troops might try to escape under the cover of neutral flags had also occurred at the Changchow airbase when Captain Morihiko Miki was briefing the Navy bombing pilots. At the end of the briefing, one of the aviators had asked Miki what should be done if they found American or British vessels among their quarry. "I knew instinctively," Miki remembers even today, "that the question had been raised because of our bitter experience in the past with the Chinese raising American and British flags over certain strong positions as a protection of neutrality—and then opening fire with machine guns as our troops came close." Miki thought for a moment, then advised his pilots: "You should not attack the ships if you know definitely that they are American or British. But if you are suspicious that they are Chinese hiding under neutral flags, attack." The way was open for the incident even if some American identification had been made.

One Japanese pilot, it turns out, almost made it. Unfortunately, he was not one of the flight leaders. And he probably could not have prevented the incident even if he had carried the authority to call off the attack. For one thing,

he arrived on the scene too late. Katsumi Oishi, a petty officer
first class under Lieutenant Komaki, led three dive bombers.
He still remembers the day quite clearly. " 'Put your nerve
into it,' was the last thing they told us before we took off,"
Oishi recalled recently. He had put his nerve into it.

My section of three dive bombers—each loaded with two 60-kg.
bombs—took off from the Changchow base and headed for a point
just downstream of Nanking. From this point I turned the nose to
the left and searched the targets along the river for Wuhu at the
altitude of about 3000 meters [10,000 feet].

On the way, at a point upstream of Nanking—but I do not recall a distance from Nanking—I picked up a group of four ships.
The most upstream ship seemed to me something like a man-of-
war due to her rather white color, and the other three ships looked
like big barges.

As I thought that this group might have *not* been our attacking target given at the briefing, my section passed over the group
and searched for other targets in the river as far as the vicinity of
Wuhu. But there was none. Then I reversed course and headed
downstream again.

When I reached a point over the above mentioned group I ordered the two planes following me to stay there and lowered my
plane's altitude to about 500 meters and made a circle over the
group to confirm the types of the target. Although the national
flag of the white colored ship was not clear, she seemed to me a
foreign man-of-war—I have no vivid recollection of whether or not
I used binoculars.

I thought of two cases: one case—the ship was a third power
man-of-war accompanying three barges carrying materials on them;
the other case—Chinese troops might be fleeing on the barges under the cloak of a privilege of a third power flag. Thereupon I decided to attack against the barges—excepting the white colored
ship. I signaled this to the two planes following.

My section of three planes made a single column and made a
shallow dive against the barges. I found that all the bombs had
near-missed when I looked back.

After that my section immediately started on its way home, but one of three planes was forced to land at an airfield midway between Nanking and Changchow due to a shortage of gasoline resulting from an extra flight to search and confirm the attacking target.

Upon landing at the Changchow base, I reported to Captain Miki that we had attacked barges which might have carried Chinese troops on them. And in the same group there was a strange white colored ship which might have been a man-of-war of a third power.

Captain Miki could not have objected. Those were his orders.

Petty Officer Oishi was playing a hunch. In the light of other incidents of Chinese trickery they had heard of, it was a reasonable hunch. And even from a closer distance than a dive bomber's cockpit, it would have been a logical assumption. When the convoy had been stopped that morning by the Japanese boarding party and Hughes had refused permission for the lieutenant to inspect the ships, the same suspicion would loom large in that Japanese officer's mind too; beyond *Panay* in the river he could see the three tankers, their decks crowded with Chinese. Whatever message he relayed to his headquarters might well have contained the suggestion—or the intimation—that the ships carried troops. If not, it still would have been easy to read that meaning into the message at the other end of the line.

Apologists in the United States would say later that even if the ships carried only gasoline and oil, those supplies were probably destined for the Chinese Army, so the tankers were prime targets for bombing anyway. A liberal group at Stanford claimed we had it coming since we were all stooges for Standard Oil. Whatever went through the mind of the Japanese boarding officer that day, it was probably tinged with both suspicion and resentment. He had been coolly and firmly told to leave the gunboat. He had been denied the intelligence information he was after about the position of Chinese troops ashore. And he had been prevented from making a search of the tankers to make sure there were not Chinese troops aboard. His report on the boarding—both what it said and didn't say—*could* have been enough to give another already angry man the thought of taking advantage of a once-in-a-lifetime chance. And Kingoro Hashimoto had never been one to let an opportunity to make trouble go by.

2. *Could the boarding party's report have come in time to trigger the sinking?*

As far as what had to be accomplished in the time allowed, it was possible. As far as being the logical unit to make the report, it is highly probable.

Panay was stopped for boarding shortly after 10 A.M. on the morning of December 12. The fact that the ship was spotted and stopped was probably by accident rather than by design. The questioning was haphazard. And because of the language difficulty, which would have been anticipated in any decent prearranged plot, the conversation was halting. From the time the ship stopped until the time the Japanese headed for shore was probably not longer than 20 minutes or half an hour at the most. Make it 10:30 when the Japanese left. The officers on *Panay* saw no indication that the boarding launch had a radio. It would have taken the boarding party about five minutes to get back ashore to the artillery unit *Panay's* officers had seen on the bank. The time then would have been about 10:40. Barring radio contact, perhaps another 30-minutes would elapse getting word through to the nearest command post and then by telephone or wireless contact to field headquarters in Wuhu and then on to a higher command. Take 11:15 for a reasonable time when word and location of *Panay's* being stopped might have reached General Matsui. Assuming this was the message responsible for launching the attack, how does this jibe with the chronology on the other end?

Okumiya and his fellow pilots had flown a morning patrol out of Shanghai to bomb positions around Nanking's east gate. The distance to Nanking and back to Changchow is some 250 miles. Allowing for an 8:00 A.M. takeoff, flying speed of about 150 miles an hour and 30 minutes' operating time over the target, the flyers couldn't have gotten back to Changchow and on the ground much before 10:30. By the time Okumiya made his report, got out of his flying gear and into the car headed toward the Army command post at Changchow, another 45 minutes or hour might have elapsed: 11:15.

Okumiya's auto must have been halted by Commander Okamura with the message from General Matsui's headquarters and signaled to return to the base about 11:30. At that hour *Panay* had been underway for some 45 minutes to an hour, headed toward doom.

Okumiya would have been back at the Changchow field by 11:45. The briefing and the rearming of the planes could have taken another hour. By 12:45 all the planes could have been in the air headed for the target area about 100 miles to the west. A 45-minute flight would put them over the target at 1:30. The first bomb fell at 1:38 P.M.

Tracing the relay of information on which the attack was based is easy to do from about 11:15 on—the time when the warning arrived in General Matsui's headquarters from "an advance Army unit." Where the chain of it-might-have-beens wears thin is in the period *before* 11 A.M. Did the report that launched the attack originate with the boarding party? Probably. Certainly it originated with some unit operating *up*river from Nanking. And although there was plenty of opportunity for mistaken identity once the planes were in the air, their search obviously proved there was no large convoy of Chinese troops fleeing that day by water. That afternoon, 24 Japanese aircraft made two sweeps of the river, from Wuhu into Nanking. Only two groups of ships were spotted. Both were bombed. One was American. The other British.

3. *Did float planes from Lake Tai, operating directly under Colonel Hashimoto's command, sink* Panay?

The possibility seems unlikely—even to the Japanese. Although various groups of Japanese naval planes were being used in close support of the Army at the time, several Japanese naval officers who were in a position to know state emphatically today that the command structure of the services precluded any such arrangement of Army-over-Navy as Matsui's apparent report to Abend suggests. The situation of an Army command over a Navy unit would have been so unusual that it would have been widely known about and widely discussed. In fact, it would probably have needed the authorization of the Emperor himself.

Takeshi Aoki, Admiral Hasegawa's naval staff officer handling liaison at the headquarters of General Matsui, heard the story for the first time a few months ago—and still doesn't believe it.

This story is news to me. I never heard various squadrons of naval bombers were sent inland to act under orders of various regional army commanders. If the story had been an actual fact, there is no question that I and Matsui's headquarters should have been fully aware of it. The headquarters would then have made the plan [with the Lake Tai squadron] after consulting with me in advance. I never heard the story and never took part in such a consultation.

And also from the Navy's point of view, it is hardly thinkable that various squadrons of naval bombers were sent inland to act under orders of various regional army commanders. If there was necessity for doing such a thing, the needed air arms would accomplish their operations in cooperation with the Army—*but un-*

der the direction of the navy commanders in the light of our traditions and operational conceptions. In short, Mr. Abend's story is
unthinkable to me, and it seems to be something like just a fiction.

A fiction, perhaps. But a good one. The story would have
been convenient for Matsui to invent later for several reasons.
It put the blame squarely on Hashimoto. It also avoided the
fact that the faulty intelligence that launched the attack
originated in or successfully passed through Matsui's own
headquarters.

4. Did planes from the carrier Kaga sink Panay?

A story published recently in the United States and based
on United States intelligence records and code-breaking activity claims that United States intelligence intercepts picked
up radio dispatches from Admiral Mitsunami that revealed
not only the name of the officer who plotted the raid but also
the names of the pilots in the attacking planes. United States
code breakers claimed to overhear the Japanese boast that
the raid was staged so carrier pilots from *Kaga* could "participate in the fun at Nanking."

The Japanese air officers most closely involved deny this
today. The late Admiral Mitsunami (in his memorandum
delivered to Rear Admiral Chikao Yamamoto, official Japanese naval air force historian, and published for the first
time in this book) makes no mention of the *Kaga* planes.
As a former commander of that carrier at the time of the
Panay sinking, Mitsunami—out of pride—would not likely
have omitted mention of his former shipmates if they had
taken part in the attack, even a misdirected one.

Commander Aoki, who was on duty at his liaison post in
Matsui's headquarters, claims he certainly would have known
of the *Kaga* aircraft. "The story is a thing I hear now for the
first time," Aoki, a retired rear admiral, told an interviewer
a few months ago. "I can't believe that any planes from the

Kaga could have accomplished the bombing. I telephoned the information and conveyed the Army's request *only* to the Changchow base. I knew nothing of the whereabouts of the carrier at the time." Because Aoki's message went only by telephone, there is no possibility that *Kaga* could have eavesdropped on the message and sent aircraft on her own initiative.

Captain Miki, then commander of Air Group 12 at Changchow and now also a retired rear admiral, does not believe the *Kaga* planes could have been in on the attack either.

There were some planes of the carrier *Kaga* Air Group at Kunda base, but these planes were fighters, I think.

My conclusion is that they did not participate in the attack on the *Panay*. Such an attack could not have been ordered by Admiral Mitsunami.

Kaga's fighters were based at Kunda for the purpose of strengthening an air combat patrol over the carrier because she had been attacked at sea by the enemy planes, I heard.

Under the command of Admiral Mitsunami, 2nd Combined Air Group commander, there were two Air Groups—12th Air Group, under my command; 13th Air Group, under Captain Sadatoshi Senda. But not only *Kaga* but also her fighters based at Kunda were not under the command of Admiral Mitsunami. So it is unthinkable that Mitsunami ordered the fighters to carry out their attack.

Heijiro Abe, a former *Kaga* bomber pilot, today says much the same. The carrier itself was operating off Hong Kong at the time. Nanking was well out of range of his bombers.

Kaga would get a chance for a surprise strike at the Americans, but not until a December Sunday four years later.

5. *A flight of mysterious and unaccounted for twin-engined bombers were the first to launch the attack on* Panay—*then they disappeared when the Changchow planes dove in.*

In the confusion of the day, it would easily have been possible for a flight of strange twin-engine aircraft to come onto the scene, although the Changchow flyers had one eye out for other planes, because the rumor was that the Chinese were still holding back some first-line aircraft in the interior. Several *Panay* survivors, testifying before the board of inquiry, stated that the first planes seen were Japanese twin-engine bombers, flying very high. The men who gave this testimony were trained in observation. They had been watching Japanese aircraft in action over Nanking for some weeks. The type looked familiar. And about 30 twin-engined, land-based naval planes *were* operating in China at the time. But if they were Japanese, where did they come from? They clearly weren't from the Changchow base. And they were too big to be off any Japanese carrier. Japanese Army aircraft in the area were limited to a few small observation planes.

There are two other possibilities as to whose aircraft they were and where they came from—assuming they really did exist. Both possibilities are somewhat remote. But then so was the fact that *Panay* would be sent to the bottom that day.

They could have been Chinese, in one of their rare, ill-planned raids, swooping in from one of their hidden, back-country fields, unloading their bombs on the first target in sight—regardless of identification—and then heading for home. The haphazard Chinese tactics had caused several bloody incidents early in the war. A single Chinese 1,100-pound bomb meant for the Japanese flagship *Idzumo* and dropped by accident in Shanghai's Foreign Concession early in August had killed 950 Chinese and wounded 1,150 more. And as early as September Admiral Yarnell had authorized American warships to be ready to open fire on Chinese aircraft if they started to bomb. "Experience has shown that pilots of Chinese planes are very likely to make this mistake," Yarnell warned.

Or maybe the dying Sandri *was* right. Maybe the twin-engine planes were Russian aircraft. With Russian pilots. And Chinese markings. Spoiling to start trouble. Bombing what they thought were *Japanese* naval vessels. After all, what else could be floating down there, for the Japanese had boasted for several weeks they had sunk every Chinese gunboat on the river? The Japanese Navy was known to be operating as far inland as Nanking, with Japanese Army units working back toward that city from Wuhu. If the convoy below was a Japanese convoy pushing through to link up with the Wuhu spearhead, it would be a valuable Russian-Chinese target indeed.

The twin-engined planes the *Panay* survivors had seen clearly proceeded downriver toward Nanking. Yet Murata claimed his three bombers had circled for another run. Had there, in fact, been two flights of high-level bombers? Both on target? From 10,000 feet up that was pretty good bombing. But maybe not too good to expect from a Russian aviator experienced in the combat of the Spanish Civil War.

6. *The survivors were heavily strafed by aircraft, yet to this day Japanese naval officers claim only one plane's gun was fired.*

In the excitement of combat, it is easy to see how a mistake in identification could be made by high-level bombers on a target 10,000 feet below and perhaps 12,000 feet distant. But with *Panay* marked as she was, military men on both sides find it hard to excuse the pilots of the dive bombers for not spotting the American flags as they bore down, eyes presumably riveted on the decks where the flags were painted. And when the planes moved in even lower to strafe, the mistake is incredible. To this day naval air staff officer Toshitane Takata is bewildered that the strafing occurred—and perhaps still not convinced that it did. Admiral Hasegawa, his boss, was first incredulous, and then furious. Takata still remembers what happened when Hasegawa was given the news.

Upon hearing the charge that our planes might have fired their machine guns at the American ship, Admiral Hasegawa ordered the commanding officers of the units involved to conduct a strict investigation. In addition to thorough questioning, this included reckoning the number of bullets in the guns of the planes at the time they took off and also when they returned to the field. The report *we* received first was that there was no change. In other words, our planes had not fired a single round. We gave the report to American authorities, but they took a stiff attitude against us.

The Japanese would later have to retract the denial. But Takata, who put great store by the Japanese officer's code of honor, was hurt at the time at not being believed and bewildered at not being able to disprove the charge to the satisfaction of the Americans.

But if the strafing by the Navy planes was a sore point, the machine-gunning and boarding of the gunboat by the Army after she was abandoned and sinking was an even more sensitive charge. Takata still remembers bitterly the admission by the Army that they'd fired on the sinking ship came at a time when apologies by the Navy for the aerial attack seemed well on the way to soothing over the tragic incident. In this regard, Takata himself recalls a strange incident that illustrates the wide gap in communication and understanding between the two services. At the time Takata's incident related below took place, the Japanese Navy did not know about the machine-gun attack by the Army launch on the sinking *Panay*; had it not been for the chance word Takata received, the Navy probably would not have heard about the launch attack until the revelation was made in United States newspapers. Here, according to Takata, is how the Navy was tipped off.

On Friday, December 17, the day the *Panay* survivors arrived back in Shanghai, the Japanese were celebrating their triumphant entry into Nanking. Admirals Hasegawa and

Sugiyama had flown inland to take part. Commander Takata remained on the flagship *Idzumo* in Shanghai. During the afternoon and shortly before he was to witness the slow procession of *Oahu* up the Whangpoo toward the *Augusta*'s anchorage, Takata had received a visit from Captain Kaoru Arima, a naval officer doing duty for Hasegawa as a liaison officer with the Japanese Army High Command. Arima burst in upon Takata to advise him of "a most grave matter!" Arima reported he had been standing on the Nanking wall several days before, after the capture of the capital, when he heard a group of Japanese war correspondents talking in low, excited tones. Arima moved closer, asked what was up. The newsmen told him they had just heard about a report from an Army scout unit that had been proceeding downriver from Wuhu by boat on Sunday afternoon to join in the attack on Nanking. The unit had come across a wild melee in the river: a gunboat was engaged in heavy fire against Japanese planes and was being bombed in return. The troops in the launches naturally assumed the gunboat was Chinese. Their orders to proceed to Nanking "as fast as possible" meant they had to pass through the area. So, according to the newsmen, the troops had skirted the scene, hugging close to shore and firing on the gunboat as they went. It wasn't until after they had aimed several bursts, according to the story, that they realized their mistake. Then their officers had sworn them to keep the mistake to themselves—and they had proceeded on their way. They were chastened and confused, but too busy to worry unduly.

Arima knew the seriousness of the situation and knew the information was bound to get out. He had come downriver as soon as possible from Army headquarters to confer with Takata. Takata repeated the whole thing to his admiral as soon as the latter returned from Nanking on December 19. Hasegawa thought it serious enough to arrange to send Takata to the Navy Department in Tokyo to report in person.

Takata arrived late on the 22nd and the following day summarized the whole story to the officers of the Naval General staff. They were as alarmed as his superiors in Shanghai had been. United States papers were carrying the story now. But Tokyo newspapers and radio still were not allowed to use it. A call to the Army War Ministry brought only the reply "We don't know what you're talking about." And a brusque hang up. But about an hour later the phone rang for Takata, asking him to come over anyway.

Takata remembers a painful session at the War Ministry the next day, going over the whole thing with the antagonistic, arrogant chief of the Military Affairs section and his staff. "I knew what I was going to say wouldn't appeal to them," Takata remembers. "But I asked them to hear me out to the end of it."

When Takata had finished, Colonel Kenshiro Shibayama, the ranking officer, answered sharply, "All right. We're acquainted with the incident. It has been reported to the War Ministry by Army agencies in the field in China. But the War Ministry has ordered Army sources there and here to carry through a policy of knowing nothing. Once an order like that has been issued, it is impossible to change. That's the stance we're taking."

To Takata, it seemed a dangerous stance and he said so. He particularly reminded Colonel Shibayama that the various refugees on the gunboat had included newspapermen and cameramen. Probably pictures had been taken. "Won't the Army be thrown into confusion," Takata cautioned, "when the United States comes forth with real evidence after developing the films?"

Shibayama shrugged. He was stuck with the War Ministry directive. As it turned out, no good film came from any of the cameramen showing the Army launches actually machine-gunning the ship. But if Shibayama could have seen the reels that Norman Alley was rushing toward Washington that day, he would have known he was in for a hot time.

Before he returned to Shanghai, Takata would have one more high-level audience. This time with Ambassador Grew. The heat was on now. Even the War Ministry was having to back down from its know-nothing stand. And Takata was on the griddle with the rest of them. He accompanied Colonel Shibayama and Admiral Isoroku Yamamato, Navy Vice-Minister, to the ambassador's residence the following night. All would speak frankly. It was tough crow for Shibayama to eat in the sumptuous American embassy drawing room. But the colonel ate it. "He reported all the messages about the machine gunning sent from Army units in China without concealment," Takata remembers. Grew was impressed with the sincerity and frankness of all of them. But he was still quietly furious—particularly when one of the Japanese Army officers attending tried to denigrate the American reports by saying the survivors were in such a state of shock that their statements were not necessarily reliable.

7. *Was there a distress call from* Panay *the afternoon of the bombing? The Japanese claim they heard one.* Panay *claims it was never sent.*

Radioman James Murphy was on duty in *Panay*'s radio shack on the upper deck that afternoon. And even today he remembers the sequence of events with a precision and detail that would still please Commander Hughes, who had a feeling that radiomen were a class apart, a bit superior to the rest of the crew in intellect, training, and performance.

Murphy was in the midst of sending the most normal—if it had been received—and critical—because it was not—message of the day: *Panay*'s "position report." There was a very strict protocol about how these should be handled. *Panay* reported to *Luzon* at Hankow, because she was the flagship for the commander of the Yangtze Patrol. *Luzon* in turn had the job of keeping tabs on all the ships of the Patrol and relaying information as necessary to *Augusta* over a "unit commander's" circuit, which carried similar messages from the flagships of the destroyers, the submarines, and the other units operating as part of the Asiatic Fleet. This unit commander's circuit was a different one than the gunboats would normally use in communicating among themselves on routine business. And it was also different from the one *Augusta* used in connection with high-priority messages for shore stations in China and for transmission and receipt for the outside world. This high-priority circuit was called "five points" by the radiomen because it linked *Augusta* with shore stations at Peking, Shanghai, Guam, and the Navy Yard at Cavite, outlet for all trans-Pacific traffic. The "five points" circuit was constantly in use for coded, classified messages, whereas contact between the gunboats of the Patrol was frequently in plain-language Morse code.

Radioman Murphy claims he will never forget the number of words in that position report: 52. It contained *Panay*'s mileage position above the mouth of the river, the names of the Standard Oil ships in company with *Panay*, and a report of the boarding incident earlier. He was halfway through. It was quiet in the radio shack, although a few moments before he had heard some rather unexpected shouting and running outside. Then *blooie!*

The first bomb so violently wrenched *Panay* that it snapped off the foremast—which was about 18 inches in diameter and made of oak—and dropped all the antenna, which was strung between the foremast and the mainmast. In 1937 we were still using wet-cell DC battery-operated receivers. The explosion threw the whole bank of batteries to the deck. Stopped the ship's main generators. I was out of business. The equipment was secured for good. So I went to my battle station: the Number 1 machine gun, forward on the starboard side.

Luzon would receive nothing else from *Panay*. Ever. Though the next message she got from the crew on shore would eventually break some records for speed of transmission to the United States that had long been held on the China station.

Murphy knows it was impossible for any station in Japan to have received a distress call from *Panay* because none was ever sent. But it would have been possible through an atmospheric trick for the position report to have been picked up in Japan. And—because the report was interrupted and never resumed—the Japanese operators could have assumed that there was trouble. Serious trouble.

Or did certain sources in Japan know the gunboat was going to be attacked? And were they standing by, anticipating a distress signal? Were they ready to jam it the minute it was sent out so that no one else might receive it clearly and ever know the fate of the gunboat?

Murphy won't speculate. But he will marvel at the speed with which *Luzon* flashed the word to the outside world when she received news the next day that *Panay* had gone under.

Luzon drafted an "URGENT" message to the Chief of Naval Operations in Washington and an "information copy" to the Commander in Chief Asiatic Fleet. It was sent manually to *Augusta*, again manually to Cavite, and then on the automatic trans-Pacific circuit via Honolulu and San Francisco to Washington. Tracers sent as a follow-up indicated that from the time of origin to the time of delivery in Washington required just 12 minutes— 30 years ago that was not easy.

Four years later it was not so easy either. The attack warning message from General George Marshall in Washington to General Walter C. Short at Ft. Shafter, Hawaii, on the morning of Pearl Harbor took 10 hours and 38 minutes to get into Short's hands.

Whether or not the Japanese were trying to jam the news, the fat was now in the fire.

8. *And was the fat in the fire because Hashimoto had been able to dupe the Japanese Navy into making an attack it never would have made on order?*

It is obviously possible. It is very likely probable. And it will almost certainly never be proved. A few months ago contact was made in Japan with Shinichi Hashimoto, a nephew of Kingoro Hashimoto and apparently his closest surviving kin in Japan (the colonel had no children). Would the nephew, now 30 years after the event, sit down with an interviewer and try to help clear the record once and for all, making available whatever information he could that the family might have learned in those last, more mellow days after the colonel's release from prison and before his death?

The first contact was through a telephone conversation. Hashimoto thought the proposal reasonable. He might be able to help. But he wanted some time to think it over. He would call back. Several weeks passed. The contact was made again. A flat no. There would be no interview. No clearing of the record. No comment or revelation about the colonel's last conversations or days.

Why the change? Like so many parts of the mystery, the West will never know.

What we *do* know is that along the fantastic chain of "coincidences" that led up to the last fatal mistaken identity of the gunboat, a man of Hashimoto's temper, persuasion, and political agility certainly had favorable ground on which to operate. If so, he obviously felt he was acting for the good of Japan.

By December 11, Nanking was surrounded on three sides and Japanese troops occupied the east bank of the river almost all the way from Nanking upstream to Wuhu. Sometime on December 12 or 13 the first Japanese units crossed the river near Wuhu, moving west, and began to fan out north and south along the far bank. One of these early units was the party that stopped *Panay* on the morning of the 12th. The advance up to then had been rapid. The field organization was somewhat loose at the time because the forward troops were moving ahead at such a pace. Word to and from these units tended to funnel through Wuhu, which had Army telephone communication back to the headquarters of General Matsui. Colonel Hashimoto was the ranking Japanese officer at Wuhu, the communications funnel. He was in a position to filter any orders headed for advance units on the west side of the Yangtze. And more vital, in the case of *Panay*, he was in a position to screen—*or originate, if he chose*—any intelligence from forward units that were working along both sides of the river between Nanking and Wuhu. It was in this area, not at Nanking, that the first report of "Chinese steamers loaded with troops fleeing Nanking" most probably originated.

To Japanese troops taking part in the Nanking siege, *Panay* would have been a familiar sight. The situation around the capital had been static enough for several days so that Japanese commanders in the area were well briefed on the presence of the gunboat, her identity, and the identity of other neutral shipping. It is not likely when she started to move upriver from the capital that there was any reason to confuse her silhouette. There *may* have been room for the suspicion that there were Chinese soldiers on the Standard Oil ships because of the presence aboard of Standard Oil security police. But *Panay*'s position was clear. She was a third-power gunboat. She was free to move as she chose.

When *Panay* weighed anchor to move upriver, Japanese units at Nanking having seen her on station there for a number of days and having been warned not to fire on her—might well have rankled at the thought that she could be escorting some Chinese out of the area. But the Japanese units around Nanking were not likely to give the report that the *Panay* group was a Chinese convoy escaping.

Nor was there any confusion about her identity when she

was stopped by the Japanese boarding party at 10 A.M. at mileage 216, five miles below the spot where she would finally be sunk.

But at *this* point the story begins to get garbled. Official Japanese reports credited several different reasons for the boarding and at least three different lieutenants are named as being the officer who carried out the search. One report says the purpose of the boarding was only "to exchange calling cards," a rather quaint military practice to be followed in the blood and mire of the middle of the China War. But in peacetime China the train of etiquette had been a strict one and the round of calls and cards required of a new officer reporting for duty on the China station was tremendous. Obviously the true purpose of the boarding was to try to get some information on Chinese military movements that *Panay's* officers might have noticed coming upstream. When Hughes properly refused, as a neutral, the boarding officer, in a face-saving attempt, very naturally demanded the right to search the Standard Oil ships. When *this* request was also refused and Hughes somewhat starchily asked the Japanese to leave the gunboat, a situation of anger and hurt pride could have occurred. Even though the Japanese soldiers could not understand the conversation on the deck of the gunboat, it would probably have been clear to them that their lieutenant had come off second best. Second best was a position the Japanese did not care to occupy, general or admiral, seaman or buck private. And "lost face" or the threat of it had already gone to make up some of the testiest incidents of the China War. (Any protest lodged back in Shanghai with Matsui or Hasegawa and finally affected because of joint Allied pressure was never agreed to openly. The face lost would be too great. Instead, a reply such as this was likely to come back: "We do not agree with your claims and your point of view and see no reason to accept them. But for certain convenience to our own plans, we have decided not to send troops into your area at this time. When we do so at a later date and will advise you." The later notice would rarely come. The Japanese would have backed down without backing down.)

When the Japanese boarding officer was back ashore he might well have been smarting a bit about high-handed treatment on the deck of *Panay*. Exactly what he reported is not known. That a "Chinese" convoy was proceeding upriver? That an American convoy was escorting ships that might be loaded with Chinese troops? That the ships were American but he could not ascertain whether or not they were loaded with Chinese troops?

The boarding craft had no radio, a search of Japanese records shows. But the message would probably have been relayed to some field communications post by runner and then back to headquarters in Wuhu by field telephone. If the message came in at all garbled—in content or sentiment— and suggesting a Chinese convoy with fleeing Chinese soldiers, and if Kingoro Hashimoto saw it, then the colonel would have seen his duty clearly. Even if the report came in with a clear picture of all the facts, a man on horseback could probably have seen his golden opportunity to ride.

The conjecture stops there. What *is* known follows. Back at General Matsui's headquarters, located about halfway between Nanking and the captured airdrome at Changchow, Lieutenant Colonel Mitsunari, Matsui's staff officer for air operations, hurried into the billet of the naval air force liaison officer with the Japanese Central China Army, Lieutenant Commander Takeshi Aoki.

Colonel Mitsunari's report to Aoki was verbal. Even today, retired Captain Aoki remembers the phrasing as being terse and apparently uncomplicated: "According to the report of an advance Army unit, many Chinese troops are fleeing up the river from Nanking. They are on six or seven large merchant ships. Our ground forces can't reach them now. So it is requested that the naval air arm make an attack at once."

There was nothing about the report to cause Commander Aoki any suspicion at the time. And he still remembers the attitude in the headquarters as being more "imploring" than commanding. The colonel indicated that the message had come through by telephone to field headquarters, then by wireless to Matsui's headquarters. There was not much more to go on. The location the colonel reported was vague: about 20 miles upstream from Nanking. The description of the ships was equally vague: six or seven, of large size. But Aoki felt he had enough to go on. Colonel Mitsunari was a reliable officer and Aoki's dealings with him during the campaign had been smooth enough.

There was an Army telephone line to Changchow. Commander Aoki asked the colonel to put through a call. It usually took quite a long time to raise Changchow. But Aoki remembers there was a clear line in several minutes on that occasion. Everything was cooperating to make the blowup possible. Mitsunari heard the operator on the other end report, "Navy on the phone." He handed the instrument to Aoki. Aoki still remembers the conversation clearly:

I had no idea that there were any naval vessels such as *Panay* or any merchant ships belonging to a third power in the area. Owing to these circumstances, I did not caution the Navy to be careful on this point. In fact, I never considered it to be a necessary thing at the time.

It's possible that I conveyed the idea that a unit citation might be granted for successful attack. It would have been the Army's way of expressing appreciation. And in light of the "imploring" atmosphere I spoke of earlier in Matsui's headquarters, the promise might have suggested itself.

That was all. I have no vivid memory who received the information on the other end. But it might have been Lieutenant Commander Motoharu Okamura.

It was. Okamura was on duty that morning at the "air to ground" liaison post the Army maintained at the Changchow base on the other side of the airdrome and some distance from the headquarters of Captain Morihiko Miki, commander of the 12th Air Group. There was no telephone between the liaison post and Miki's office. Okumura hung up from talking to Commander Aoki, made a few brief notes, and headed by staff car for Miki's unit. On the way he met Lieutenant Okumiya, just returned from his early-morning bombing run to Nanking. He signaled Okumiya to turn around and both headed back for the Navy hangars at top speed.

In high excitement, Okamura relayed Aoki's conversation, including the promise of a unit citation. Captain Miki remembers the last point clearly. Then the captain prepared to brief his pilots. At this point the message had been through at least eight persons: from the boarding party verbally back to the command post near Wuhu, by field telephone to Wuhu, through the Wuhu Army message center operators, by wireless to General Matsui's headquarters, verbally from a wireless operator on duty there to Colonel Mitsunari, then verbally to Aoki, verbally again over the phone to Okamura, verbally to Miki. Anyone who has ever played the old parlor game of passing a whisper from ear to ear around a circle of eight or ten people knows what is likely to happen to the simplest sentence.

Captain Miki's instructions to his assembled pilots were necessarily vague, as far as the exact location at which they would find the ships and any details of their appearance. His intelligence was vague. "I don't recall anything in Aoki's message that gave such specifics. But I felt intuitively that the ships were not so small in size as a sampan, but would have to be larger in view of the fact that they were loaded to capacity with Chinese troops."

Miki then briefly outlined how the various attack units would be organized and gave what little information he had about the ships. Then added the word of encouragement that several men still remember: "Put your nerve into it."

Now the coast was clear. The visibility was good. There was a light breeze from the southeast. Perfect weather for flying. Perfect weather for bombing.

Everybody wanted to be first in the air. And the planes took off so close together that on several occasions it looked as if there might be a casualty or two before they ever left the ground. Rising as rapidly as full throttle could carry them, the flight leaders formed up the nucleus of each flight as rapidly as they could, then headed hell-for-leather for the Wuhu front about a hundred miles to the west, the stragglers strung out behind them to catch up as best they were able. None of the pilots wanted to be last on the scene when all the good hunting was shot up.

They hit the Yangtze shortly after 1 P.M. about 20 miles upstream from Nanking. "Peaceful beneath us lay the rich river valley," Lieutenant Okumiya wrote later, remembering the scene from the cockpit of his dive bomber.

A few miles to the southwest in Wuhu, Colonel Kingoro Hashimoto's artillery men were swabbing out their field guns after having ripped off a salvo of shells at HMS *Ladybird* as she went to the rescue of an English tug suffering heavy Japanese machine-gun fire. And then they had fired on HMS *Bee* as she boiled up in support. It was all a mistake, the colonel said when British officers, including a rear admiral, swarmed ashore to protest the shellfire that had killed one seaman and wounded several others. "Poor visibility." The British were hardly convinced. To them, Hashimoto "showed no sign of contrition." He frankly boasted that he had orders to fire on every ship on the river. At any event, mistakes, the colonel assured his British visitors, were bound to happen in combat. Considering the magnitude of the fighting, a mistake here and there was a small thing.

But big enough to start a war, perhaps. And certainly big enough to win a medal. Even if it took four years coming.

JAPANESE IS
DECORATED FOR
1937 PANAY
SINKING

Jan. 25, 1942 AP—Back in 1937 Japan was "so sorry, please" because Colonel Kingoro Hashimoto ordered attacks on all foreign ships in China's Yangtze River, sinking the United States gunboat Panay and damaging the British gunboat Ladybird.

But yesterday Colonel Hashimoto, who was cashiered after the attacks on December 13, 1937, received the Kinshi Kinsho Medal for his audacity, the Berlin radio said in a broadcast heard by The Associated Press. Japan swiftly paid indemnity for the Panay and apologized to Britain about the Ladybird.

It was just 49 days after Pearl Harbor.

Epilogue

FROM BEGINNING TO END, the *Panay* incident was a relatively fast-moving story. From 1:38 P.M. on December 12, when the first bomb fell, until sometime in the early morning of December 15, when the last survivor climbed over the rail of USS *Oahu*, only about 58 hours elapsed.

These are the official dispatches that set the stage and first relayed the story that could have started World War II. (Note: Navy time, measured from 0001 hours [one minute after midnight] to 2400 hours [the midnight immediately following], has usually been converted to conventional time in these messages.)

GOVERNMENT STATE PRIORITY: AMERICAN CONSUL SHANGHAI. AMERICAN EMBASSY PEKING. ROUTINE SECSTATE WASHINGTON. AMERICAN EMBASSY HANKOW.

DECEMBER ELEVEN FIVE PM

AT TWO FORTY FIVE PM TODAY SHELLS BEGAN FALLING ON THE NEAR SHORE NOT FAR UP RIVER FROM THE PANAY. RELUCTANT TO LEAVE SAN CHIA HO AND POSSIBILITY OF FURTHER CON-

TACT WITH AMERICANS. PANAY DELAYED MOVING UNTIL SHELLS
WERE FALLING IN THE WATER AHEAD AND ON THE OPPOSITE
BANK. AND THEN PROCEEDED UP RIVER ABOUT TWELVE MILES
FROM NANKING TO MILEAGE TWO HUNDRED EIGHT ABOVE WOO-
SUNG WHERE VESSEL IS NOW ANCHORED. AS FROM THIS EMBASSY
PLEASE COMMUNICATE POSITION TO JAPANESE EMBASSY WITH
REQUEST THAT APPROPRIATE INSTRUCTIONS BE ISSUED TO JAP-
ANESE FORCES INCLUDING AIR FORCE, SINCE JAPANESE BOMBING
PLANES HAVE FLOWN DAILY OVER THE PANAY AT THE SAN CHIA
HO AS WELL AS FORMER HSIAKUAN ANCHORAGE.

BRITISH VESSELS ALSO PROCEEDED UPRIVER.

SENT TO SHANGHAI, REPEATED TO DEPARTMENT HANKOW, PE-
KING.

PEKING PLEASE REPEAT TO TOKYO WITH REQUEST THAT EM-
BASSY TOKYO KINDLY TAKE APPROPRIATE ACTION WITH RESPECT
TO LAST SENTENCE FIRST PARAGRAPH ABOVE.

GEORGE ATCHESON

SECRETARY, NANKING EMBASSY

TO: AMERICAN CONSUL SHANGHAI   DECEMBER TWELVE
                                                ELEVEN AM

SHELL FIRE AT NINE OCLOCK THIS MORNING CAUSED THE PA-
NAY TO MOVE FARTHER UPSTREAM AND VESSEL IS NOW AN-
CHORED TWENTY SEVEN MILES ABOVE NANKING AT MILEAGE TWO
TWENTY ONE ABOVE WOOSUNG. STANDARD OIL COMPANYS STEAM-
ERS MEIPING, MEIAN, AND MEIHSIA ARE ANCHORED NEARBY.

AS FROM THIS EMBASSY PLEASE INFORM JAPANESE EMBASSY
OF PRESENT POSITION OF PANAY AND AMERICAN MERCHANT VES-
SELS NAMED, AND REQUEST THAT APPROPRIATE INSTRUCTIONS BE
ISSUED TO JAPANESE FORCES. PLEASE ADD THAT CIRCUMSTANCES
MAY AGAIN CAUSE PANAY TO MOVE EITHER UP OR DOWN RIVER
AND THAT PANAY EXPECTS TO RETURN DOWN RIVER TO NANKING
AS SOON AS FEASIBLE IN ORDER TO REESTABLISH COMMUNICATION
WITH AMERICANS WHO REMAINED IN NANKING AND IN ORDER

THAT THIS EMBASSY MAY AS SOON AS PRACTICABLE RESUME ITS
FUNCTIONS ASHORE. PLEASE STATE THAT THE AMERICAN EMBASSY
HOPES THAT APPROPRIATE STEPS TO FACILITATE THIS PLAN WILL
BE TAKEN BY ALL AUTHORITIES WHO MAY BE CONCERNED.

SENT TO SHANGHAI, REPEATED TO DEPARTMENT HANKOW, PE-
KING. PEKING PLEASE REPEAT TO TOKYO WITH REQUEST THAT
EMBASSY TOKYO COMMUNICATE TO JAPANESE FOREIGN OFFICE.
ATCHESON

FROM: COMMANDER IN CHIEF ASIATIC FLEET
TO: COMMANDER YANGTZE PATROL　　　12 DECEMBER 4:33 PM
PANAY UNHEARD SINCE 1342. WHAT IS NATURE OF CASUALTY.
ARE YOU IN CONTACT WITH PANAY VIA BRITISH.

FROM: COMMANDER YANGTZE PATROL
TO: COMMANDER IN CHIEF ASIATIC FLEET 12 DECEMBER 5:05 PM
NO COMMUNICATION SINCE 1335 WHEN DURING PANAY TRANS-
MISSION NITE DISPATCH SIGNAL CEASED. BRITISH ENDEAVORING
DETERMINE NATURE CASUALTY. BUT BELIEVE NO BRITISH SHIP
NOW WITHIN SIGHT.

FROM: COMMANDER YANGTZE PATROL
TO: COMMANDER IN CHIEF ASIATIC FLEET

12 DECEMBER 8:10 P.M.
LAST REPORT PANAY ANCHORED MILEAGE TWO TWENTY ONE
ABOVE WOOSUNG. BRITISH HAVE NOTIFIED THEIR GUNBOATS THAT
VICINITY CONTACT VESSEL IF PRACTICABLE.

FROM: COMMANDER YANGTZE PATROL
TO: OPNAV　　　　　　　　　12 DECEMBER 9:10 PM
FOR INFORMATION TO: 2ND MARINE BRIGADE, ALL YANGTZE PA-
TROL SHIPS. COMMANDER SUBMARINE SQUADRON FIVE, COM-
MANDER DESTROYER SQUADRON FIVE, COMMANDER IN CHIEF
ASIATIC FLEET, COMMANDER SOUTH PACIFIC AUXILIARY TRANS-
PORTS, AMERICAN AMBASSADOR CHINA, U.S.S. MARBLEHEAD,
AMERICAN EMBASSY NANKING, ALL U.S. NAVY PEKING.
PANAY ENDANGERED BY ARTILLERY FIRE FORCED MOVE AN-

CHORAGE FARTHER UP RIVER. BRITISH GUNBOATS AND FOREIGN MERCHANT VESSELS BETWEEN WUHU AND NANKING SUBJECTED DIRECT ARTILLERY AND AIR ATTACKS THROUGHOUT DAY. HMS LADYBIRD STRUCK FOUR TIMES BY JAP SHELLS AT WUHU. ONE SEAMAN KILLED, SEVERAL WOUNDED. SITUATION NANKING UNCERTAIN BUT CHINESE APPARENTLY STILL HOLD CITY.

FROM: U.S.S. LUZON
TO:SECSTATE WASHINGTON, AMERICAN EMBASSY PEIKING
                                        12 DECEMBER 10 PM
    COMMANDER YANGTZE PATROL HAS BEEN UNABLE TO CONTACT PANAY SINCE 1335 TODAY. AM INFORMED THAT JAPANESE ARMY FORCES HAVE ORDERS TO FIRE UPON ALL SHIPS ON RIVER. IN VIEW OF WHAT HAPPENED TO BRITISH NAVAL VESSELS NEAR NANKING AND AT WUHU TODAY, PLEASE ASK TOKYO TO MAKE URGENT REPRESENTATIONS TO FOREIGN OFFICE AND TO NOTIFY IT OF WHEREABOUTS OF PANAY AND STANDARD OIL COMPANY SHIPS LOADED WITH AMERICAN REFUGEES, LAST REPORTED ANCHORED AT MILEAGE TWO TWENTY ONE ABOVE WOOSUNG. PEKING REPEAT URGENT TO TOKYO. SENT TO DEPARTMENT PEKING AND INFORMATION COMMANDER IN CHIEF ASIATIC FLEET.
NELSON T. JOHNSON
U.S. AMBASSADOR

FROM: U.S.S. LUZON
TO: SECSTATE WASHINGTON, EMBASSY PEKING
    AMERICAN CONSUL SHANGHAI   12 DECEMBER 10 PM
    BRITISH GUNBOATS SCARAB AND CRICKET WITH JARDINE HULK AND MERCHANT SHIP WHANGPOO LOADED WITH FOREIGN REFUGEES WERE DELIBERATELY BOMBED THIS AFTERNOON. NO CASUALTIES REPORTED BUT AS THERE ARE AMERICAN REFUGEES FROM NANKING ON HULK, I HOPE DEPARTMENT WILL URGENTLY INSTRUCT TOKYO TO PRESS THE JAPANESE GOVERNMENT TO ISSUE INSTRUCTIONS WHICH WILL PREVENT THIS IN FUTURE. JAPANESE INFORMED BRITISH AT WUHU TODAY THAT JAPANESE MILITARY FORCES HAD ORDERS TO FIRE ON ALL SHIPS ON YANGTZE. UNLESS JAPAN CAN BE MADE TO REALIZE THAT THESE SHIPS ARE FRIENDLY

AND ARE ONLY REFUGE AVAILABLE TO AMERICANS AND OTHER FOREIGNERS, A TERRIBLE DISASTER IS LIKELY TO HAPPEN. SENT TO THE DEPARTMENT. REPEATED TO PEKING, SHANGHAI, INFORMATION OF COMMANDER IN CHIEF ASIATIC FLEET.
NELSON T. JOHNSON

FROM: COMMANDER YANGTZE PATROL
TO: COMMANDER IN CHIEF ASIATIC FLEET
12 DECEMBER 10:48 PM
BRITISH REPORT NONE OF THEIR VESSELS WITHIN VISUAL DISTANCE PANAY. LAST REPORT PANAY ANCHORED 221 ABOVE WOOSUNG AT 1100 IN COMPANY WITH THREE STANDARD OIL VESSELS.

U-R-G-E-N-T
FROM: COMMANDER YANGTZE PATROL
TO: COMMANDER IN CHIEF ASIATIC FLEET
INFORMATION: U.S.S. OAHU   13 DECEMBER 10:03 AM
MESSAGE RECEIVED BY TELEPHONE FROM NANKING. PANAY BOMBED AND SUNK AT MILEAGE 221 ABOVE WOOSUNG. FIFTY FOUR SURVIVORS, MANY BADLY WOUNDED, NOW ASHORE AT HOHSIEN ANHWEI. HMS BEE WILL PROCEED THIS POINT TO ASSIST AND BRING SURVIVORS TO WUHU. USS OAHU FUELING KIUKIANG PREPARATORY DEPARTING WUHU. NAMES OF PERSONNEL LOST NOT KNOWN. ATCHESON SAFE. CAPTAIN HAS BROKEN LEG. FURTHER INFORMATION WILL BE FORWARDED WHEN RECEIVED.

FROM: AMBASSADOR CHINA
TO: AMERICAN CONSUL SHANGHAI, SECSTATE
AMERICAN EMBASSY PEKING   13 DECEMBER 11 AM
I HAVE JUST HAD THE FOLLOWING TELEPHONE MESSAGE FROM DOCTOR TAYLOR AT NANKING QUOTE DOCTOR TAYLOR SAID THAT HE HAD HAD A FURTHER COMMUNICATION WITH MISTER ATCHESON. ATCHESON REPORTED THAT THE STAFF OF THE GUNBOAT WERE SAFE. ALTHOUGH ONE SAILOR HAD DIED, AND THE CAPTAIN AND EXECUTIVE OFFICER HAD BEEN WOUNDED.

DOCTOR TAYLOR STATED THAT ATCHESON WAS AFRAID THAT THEY COULD NOT GO TO THE RIVER AS THE JAPANESE WERE MACHINE GUNNING HOHSIEN. HE SAID THAT HE HAD TOLD ATCHESON TO REMAIN IN HOHSIEN FOR THE TIME BEING. HE SAID THAT ATCHESON ASKED THAT THE JAPANESE BE ASKED NOT TO ATTACK HOHSIEN, AS JAPANESE PATROLS WERE ON THE NORTH BANK OF RIVER AND WERE ABOUT TO, OR HAD ALREADY ATTACKED HOHSIEN UNQUOTE.

IMMEDIATELY COMMUNICATE THIS INFORMATION TO THE APPROPRIATE AUTHORITIES. SENT TO SHANGHAI. REPEATED TO DEPARTMENT PEKING.

JOHNSON

FROM: COMMANDER YANGTZE PATROL
TO: COMMANDER IN CHIEF ASIATIC FLEET
INFORMATION: U.S.S. OAHU   13 DECEMBER 11:32 AM

FOLLOWING RECEIVED FROM ATCHESON BY TELEPHONE FROM DR. TAYLOR. NANKING EMBASSY STAFF SAFE. ONE SAILOR DIED. CAPT AND EXECUTIVE OFFICER WOUNDED. SURVIVORS UNABLE TO GO TO RIVER AS JAPANESE NOW MACHINE GUNNING THE TOWN. DR. TAYLOR ADVISED EVERYONE REMAIN HOHSIEN. REQUEST JAPANESE BE ASKED NOT TO ATTACK HOHSIEN. JAPANESE PATROLS NOW ON NORTH BANK OF RIVER AND APPEAR TO BE ABOUT TO ATTACK THE TOWN.

FROM: VICE ADMIRAL BRITISH YANGTZE PATROL
TO: HMS BEE, ALL SHIPS BRITISH YANGTZE PATROL,
      BRITISH COMMANDER IN CHIEF SHANGHAI

                              13 DECEMBER

COMMANDER YANGTZE PATROL INFORMS THE USS PANAY SUNK BY BOMBS PM YESTERDAY 12 DEC. FIFTY FOUR SURVIVORS AMERICAN AND BRITISH. MANY WOUNDED NOW AT HSIA SHAN. EVERYTHING POSSIBLE SHOULD BE DONE TO ASSIST AND YOU SHOULD ATTEMPT TO BRING WOUNDED TO WUHU. ANY INFORMATION YOU CAN GATHER OF THIS OCCURRENCE SENT TO ME AT ONCE FOR INFORMATION OF COMMANDER YANGTZE PATROL.

FROM: COMMANDER YANGTZE PATROL
TO: COMMANDER IN CHIEF ASIATIC FLEET

13 DECEMBER 12:47 P.M.

HAVE URGED HASHIMOTO THROUGH BRITISH AT WUHU NOT ATTACK HOHSIEN UNTIL AMERICAN AND OTHER FOREIGN REFUGEES HAVE BEEN EMBARKED. EXPECT OAHU ARRIVE WUHU EARLY TO-MORROW MORNING AND HAVE REQUESTED BRITISH CONVEY THIS INFORMATION TO LOCAL JAP AUTHORITIES.

FROM: COMMANDER YANGTZE PATROL
TO: COMMANDER IN CHIEF ASIATIC FLEET

13 DECEMBER 11:56 P.M.

FOLLOWING RECEIVED FROM BEE. QUOTE FOLLOWING ARE NOW ON BOARD BEE: SHERWOOD, PICKERING, AND GOLDIE OF SOCONY, JORGENSON OF MEI HSIA, MENDY AND BLASINA OF MEI PING. PUCKETT, HOYLE, COLEMAN, GRANES, BONKOSKI, DIRNHOFF-ER, BROWNING ALL OF PANAY. ALL MOVING INTO STREAM FOR THE NIGHT TO AVOID DANGER FROM BURNING HULKS OF MEI PING AND MIA HSIA. SURVIVORS ACCOUNT OF WHAT HAPPENED FOLLOWS. I AM SIGNALING OVER NORTH BANK WITH SEMAPHORE LIGHT SAYING BEE WILL BE OFF HOHSEIN AGAIN IN THE MORNING. UNQUOTE.

Perhaps one other radio signal should be added that might properly be part of this sequence of events. On another Sunday, almost four years to the day after *Panay* went down, this message would be dispatched to all U.S. Navy ships and stations around the world from the radio room of the commander in chief of the Pacific Fleet at the Naval Submarine Base, Pearl Harbor.

0800 AIR RAID ON PEARL HARBOR. THIS IS NO DRILL.

Appendix

THE TRUTH OF THE PANAY INCIDENT

By Rear Admiral Teizo Mitsunami
Commander Second Combined Air Group, Shanghai

1. The General Situation During the Days of the Incident

Japanese Army and Naval forces were driving in unanimous cooperation upon Nanking: from the eastward Prince Asaka's force advanced from the Shanghai area; from the southward Yanagawa's force landed at Hangchow Bay; Navy ships were advancing upstream on the Yangtze River. The Naval air forces were under the command of Admiral Mitsunami and were based at Shanghai and at an advanced base in Changchow under Captain Miki; they were cooperating with the Army operations. But these air operations were suspended when the Army troops reached the line of the fortified city wall of Nanking, and the Navy fliers were given a rest at their bases.

Meanwhile, with the development of the Nanking operation, our Third Fleet headquarters had requested foreign Naval authorities concerned to give information of movements of their men-of-war located in the vicinity of Nanking; we had asked the foreign Naval ships to evacuate from these areas for the purpose of avoiding the troubles with the third country. The American man-of-war [*Panay*] evacuated also upstream and informed Third

Fleet headquarters of her location, but had not notified our air forces with the same information due to the communication trouble. Thereupon the movements of men-of-war of these third countries were utterly unknown to the air forces.

On the other hand, Mitsunami was making arrangements with the Third Fleet headquarters regarding the matter of our air forces participating in the formal entry into Nanking.

2. Misbombing of the Panay

On the morning of December 12, 1937, during the above-mentioned situation, Lt. Commander Takeshi Aoki, who was dispatched to the headquarters of Prince Asaka's forces as a liaison officer, sent a message to Captain Miki, Commander of the advanced base at Changchow, that Chinese troops were fleeing upstream from Nanking on board seven merchant ships, and asked Miki that the Naval air arm make an attack against them.

Upon learning of these fine targets, Captain Miki, the 12th Air Group Commander, ordered at once the departure of the air arm at Changchow—six dive bombers and six level bombers from the 12th Air Group; six fighters and six dive bombers from the 13th Air Group.

Each squadron searched independently for the targets along the River, found and bombed the ships. The level bomber squadron bombed against one ship (U.S.S. Panay) from the altitude of 3500 meters, scored two hits, and sunk the ship.

It was difficult to make a distinction at the time between the civilians and the Chinese soldiers who were wearing the blue service uniform. And the Panay, though anchored on the river, seemed to be sailing due to the current of the river passing her. Furthermore, there were the difficulties distinguishing the types of ships owing to a high altitude. That, coupled with the intelligence that they were indeed Chinese ships, which had been conveyed by Commander Aaki, made it inevitable that an attack on the ship would occur.

After returning to their base, each squadron was ordered to launch a second attack, and took off again. The dive bomber squadron under command of Lt. Okumiya dived from 4000 meters and bombed ships it sighted. When a British flag on one of the ships caught his eye, Okumiya at once waggled his plane as a signal for the following planes to hold off their attacks, but it was too late.

3. Subsequent Measures

In the late afternoon of December 12, the U.S. Asiatic Fleet headquarters in Shanghai requested the Japanese Third Fleet headquarters to the effect: "As there has been no communication contact with the U.S.S. *Panay* since 2:00 P.M. today, it is desirable to ascertain her condition by Japanese planes."

Since I (Mitsunami) was given the U.S. Navy's proposal, I took off from the Shanghai base by plane the following morning [December 13, Monday] and arrived at the Changchow base. But before my departure from Shanghai, I had been given the order by Admiral Hasegawa that all the squadron leaders who participated in yesterday's attack against the ships on the Yangtze River be hurried to the *Idzumo*. Upon knowing this at the Changchow base, the pilots made a hurried trip to our Fleet headquarters. I returned to Shanghai and went to the *Idzumo*.

I learned of the actual circumstances when I returned to the headquarters: there were American crew who evacuated to the bank of the river from their ship, U.S.S. *Panay*, and they reported that she was sunk by the bombing of Japanese planes the previous day, December 12. My delight at the capture of Nanking utterly faded away when I heard this and we began preparing every necessary measure for sending planes and destroyers which carried medical materials, and so forth to the relief of the crew of the *Panay*.

Thereafter Rear Admiral Denhichi Okochi, Commander of Japanese Special Landing Forces at Shanghai, called on me and advised: "You had better submit an informal resignation." Upon agreement with him, I visited Admiral Hasegawa and submitted my informal resignation: "It is in deep regret for attacking the third power ships, particularly the American warship, under the current grave circumstances. I ask that you will punish me as you think it may well be suitable." Then the Admiral said, "Since we, you and I, must bear the responsibilities concerning the *Panay* incident, I will submit your resignation note to the Navy Minister."

I was convinced I had reached the end of my long Japanese Navy life. I flew to Changchow base on the following morning and made preparations for participating in the Nanking triumphal entry. On December 17, I took part in the entry at the head of the Navy planes, and that brought the last glory to my Navy life.

I met Rear Admiral Sugiyama at Shanghai base when I returned there from the Nanking ceremony, and heard from him that I had been transferred to Japan. On the following day, December 18, my duties was handed over to my successor, Rear Admiral Nishizo Tsukahara. On December 19, I arrived at Sasebo by plane, and in September, 1938, was ordered to serve in the Naval General Staff before retirement from the Navy.

4. Settlement of the Panay Incident

It was reported that the Third Fleet headquarters had not subjected the persons concerned to a severe rebuke, in view of the mistake taking place in the vicinity of a confused battle front, and since it was not expected that the situation would be developed into a serious incident. But thereafter, since public opinion in the United States had stiffened, the headquarters were worried about this. The following factors might well be considered as the causes of this stiffening of United States public opinion:

a. World opinion was raised against the China incident, calling it an aggressive war.

b. When gunboat *Ladybird*, with the Commandant of the British Fleet in China aboard, was approaching Wuhu, she was fired on by an artillery unit under command of Colonel Kingoro Hashimoto. The British Commandant landed at Wuhu and protested against this illegal act to the Colonel. Then Hashimoto answered the protest by saying that he had ordered his men to bombard even against warships if they should enter into our combat area. That hurt the Commandant's feelings very much.

He reported the conversation in detail to the British Admiralty. It was feared that there had been opinion in Great Britain claiming the misbombing of the American gunboat, which occurred on the same day, was the result of the intentional acts of Japanese air officers who had disobeyed their superior officers in the same way Hashimoto had done in the *Ladybird* incident. And the British made a stiff protest to the Japanese government in conjunction with the United States.

c. A cameraman, who was on the *Panay* when she was bombed and sunk, filmed a disastrous scene of injuries and damages of the ship. These films were sent to Hong Kong, and were carried to the United States by a Pan American plane. American movie companies and air transport companies propagandized the films of the *Panay* incident for their own interests at each point when those films arrived at Manila, Hawaii, and the United States.

Consequently, the public opinions in the United States were stimulated, and that made the settlement of the incident more difficult.

It seemed to me that the incident was settled in the end by means of an indemnity for damage done and a dismissal of responsible persons and so forth. A friend of mine in the United States at the time sent me an American newspaper which carried a top four-layer item: "Rear Admiral Mitsunami Ousted" and a letter which sympathized heartily with me, knowing that I had been sacrificed for the country. I knew the domestic situation in the United States by these papers.

Thereafter opportunities of serving in the front line were not given to me. I was treated as just a man behind the scenes and was only a humble member of the party when the admirals, including Hasegawa, returned to Japan from China front as triumphant commanders and were received in audience by His Majesty; all this was reported in papers with large headlines in May, 1938.

INDEX

Index

DATE DUE